THE
HAMLYN
DICTIONARY
of
COMPUTING

THE
HAMLYN
DICTIONARY
of
COMPUTING

S.M.H. Collin

HAMLYN

First published 1989 by
The Hamlyn Publishing Group Limited
Michelin House, 81 Fulham Road
London SW3 6RB

ISBN 0 600 56521 1

Typeset by Systemset, Stotfold, Herts

Printed in Great Britain by
William Collins and Sons

INTRODUCTION

The aim of this dictionary is to give the user a comprehensive coverage of words and expressions used in computing. The vocabulary covers not only programming terms, but also words relating to hardware, including peripherals. The terms are defined in such a way as to make them readily understandable by the layman, with many detailed explanations and cross-references which link or contrast items of terminology.

The dictionary should prove useful to students of computing, but also to computer users, whether at home or at work.

A

A (= ampere) The base SI unit of electrical current; defined as the current flowing through an impedance of one ohm which has a voltage of one volt across it.

A The hexadecimal (base 16) equivalent to the decimal number 10.

A-bus The main internal bus in a microprocessor.

A programming language (APL) A high-level programming language that is used mainly for scientific and mathematical work.

A to D or **A/D (analog to digital)** Changing a signal from an analog form to a digitally coded form. An **A to D converter** converts an analog input to a digital output form (which can be understood by a computer). An A to D converter works by measuring the amplitude of the analog signal, and outputting a binary number relating to this. The opposite is **digital to analog** or **D to A**.

abbreviated addressing or **abb. add.** The use of a smaller computer address word than normal which provides faster address decoding operations.

abend see **abnormal end**

abend recovery program Software that will reload a program (or system software) and restart it at the point where the abend occurred.

abnormal end or **abend** or **abnormal termination** The unexpected stoppage of a program being run, caused by a fault or error or power failure.

abort To end a process either before it has finished or because a malfunction occurs. This can be done either by pressing a break key (usually the Control and C keys pressed together) or a reset key or by switching the computer off manually or by an internal feature. See also **reset.**

absolute address or **actual address** or **machine address 1** An address that can directly, without any modification or additional information, accesses a location or device. An absolute address executes faster than an indexed address because no other information is required — an indexed address uses an offset added to a base address to produce a usable address. **Absolute addressing** is the locating of a data word in memory by the use of its absolute address. **2** A computer storage address that can only access one location. Compare **indexed address.**

absolute assembler An assembler program that is designed to produce code which uses only absolute addresses and values. This usually means that the assembly pass takes longer, but that the code executes faster.

absolute code A binary code which directly operates the central processing unit, using only absolute addresses and values (this is the final form of a program after a compiler or assembler pass). See also **object code.**

absolute instruction An instruction which completely describes the operation to be performed, and no other data is required.

absolute loader A program that loads a section of code into main memory at a specific address. Executable programs are normally stored in one of two formats: an exact image which must be loaded at an absolute address, or in a relocatable form which can be loaded anywhere in memory.

absolute maximum rating The maximum values or limits of a system. A small computer might have an absolute maximum rating specified by the number of users it can support or tasks it execute. A power supply would be rated in Watts of power available.

absolute program A computer program written in absolute code.

absolute value The actual size or value of a number, regardless of its sign. The positive number 12 and the negative number -12 both have the same absolute value of 12.

AC (alternating current) Electric current whose value varies with time in a regular, sinusoidal way. The mains electricity supply uses an alternating current to minimize power transmission losses, with a frequency of 50Hz in the UK and 60Hz in the USA.

ACC (accumulator) The most important internal CPU storage register, containing the data word that is to be processed. When adding two stored numbers, the first would be loaded into the accumulator from its storage address, then the second would be added to it. The result would be contained within the accumulator.

acceleration time 1 The time it takes for a disk drive to spin a disk at the correct speed, starting from rest. **2** The total time between an access instruction being issued (to a peripheral) and the data being transferred.

acceptance sampling The testing of a small random part of a batch of products to see if the whole batch is up to a required standard.

acceptance test or **testing** A method of checking that a piece of equipment will perform as required or will reach required standards.

access 1 Being allowed to use a computer and read or alter files stored in it (this is usually controlled by a security device such as a password). In a multi-user computer system, the access allowed to users is often arranged in layers, with only one person, the system manager, allowed to access every file. **2** To call up (data) which is stored in a computer; to obtain data from a storage device. For example, a personnel department may want to access an employee's personal records which are stored on the company's central computer.

access arm A mechanical device in a disk drive used to position the read/write head over the correct track on a disk.

access charge The cost incurred when logging onto a system or viewing special pages on a bulletin board or on-line information service. This is different from connect charges (which are incurred for the time spent on-line to a system).

access code The series of characters or symbols that must be entered to identify a user before access to a computer is permitted. Often the access code is just one part of a logon, and usually has to be backed up with a password. See also **password.**

access control A security device (such as a password) that only allows selected users to use a computer system or read files. A good access control system should allow valid users to gain access and operate the computer easily with the minimum of checks, whilst barring entry to hackers or other unauthorized users.

access line A permanently connected communications line between a terminal and a computer. This type of line is sometimes called a **land line.**

access method The means used for the internal transfer of data between memory and display or peripheral devices (differences in the methods used is often the cause of compatibility problems).

accessory A useful device which is attached to or used with another. For example, a printer may come with several accessories, such as a soundproof hood and a sheet feed

access point A test point on a circuit board or in software, allowing an engineer to check signals or data.

access time 1 The total time which a storage device takes between the moment the data is requested and the data being returned. Dynamic RAM devices usually have an access time of around 50-200 nanoseconds; hard disks usually have an access time between 10-60 milliseconds. **2** The length of time required to find a file or program, either in main memory or a secondary memory source.

accordion fold or **fanfold** A method of folding continuous paper, one sheet in one direction, the next sheet in the opposite direction, allowing the paper to be fed into a printer continuously with no action required on the part of the user.

accumulator or **ACC (register)** The most important internal CPU storage register, containing the data word that is to be processed.

accumulator shift instruction A command to shift the contents of an accumulator left or right by one bit.

accuracy The total number of bits used to define a number in a computer, the more bits allocated the more accurate the definition. Most high level languages allow numbers to be represented in a more accurate form by using two or more words to store the number. A maths co-processor provides greater numerical accuracy than a normal CPU by using wider words.

ACIA (asynchronous communications interface adapter) A circuit that allows a computer to transmit and receive serial data using asynchronous access.

ACK (ACKNOWLEDGE) A signal that is sent from a receiver to indicate that a transmitted message has been received and that it is ready for the next one to be sent.

Ackerman's function A recursive function used to test the ability of a compiler to cope with recursion.

acknowledge 1 A signal that is sent from a receiver to indicate that a transmitted message has been received and that it is ready for the next one. **2** To tell a sender that a message or letter has been received; to send a signal from a receiver to show that a transmitted message has been received.

acknowledge character A special code sent by a receiver to indicate to the transmitter that the message has been correctly received.

acoustic coupler A device that connects to a telephone handset, converting binary computer data into sound signals to allow data to be transmitted down a telephone line. The acoustic coupler also converts sound signals back to digital signals when receiving messages; it is basically the same as a modem but uses a loudspeaker on which a handset is placed to send the signals rather than a direct connection to the phone line. It is portable, and clips over both ends of a normal telephone handset; it can even be used in a public telephone booth.

acoustic delay line The original data storage method that delays data (in the form of sound pulses) as it travels across a medium.

acoustic hood A soundproofing hood placed over a printer to reduce the noise the printer makes. This are used for impact printers, such as a dot-matrix or daisy-wheel printer — both of which are noisy.

acoustic store or **acoustic memory** An old form of regenerative memory that uses an acoustic delay line as the storage medium.

ACR see **audio cassette recorder**

ACR interface An interface which allows a cassette recorder to be linked to a computer.

acronym An abbreviation, formed from various letters, which makes up a word which can be pronounced. For example: the acronym FORTRAN means Formula Translator; the acronym RAM means Random Access Memory.

action cycle The complete set of actions involved in one operation (including reading data, processing, storing results, etc.).

action message A prompt given to inform the user that an action or input is required.

active device An electronic component that requires electrical power to operate and provides gain or a logical function. For example, an amplifier is an active device, a cable is not. Compare with **passive device.**

active file The file which is currently being worked on.

active star A network consisting of a central point with nodes branching out, in which a central processor controls and routes all messages between devices.

active state The electronic state in which an action occurs.

active window The area of a screen in which the operator is currently working. See also **window.**

activities Separate jobs or tasks which are being performed on a computer. See also **multitasking.**

activity loading A method of organizing the contents of a disk so that the most often accessed files or programs can be loaded quickly. See also **cache.**

activity ratio The ratio of the number of files currently in use compared to the total stored.

actual address or **absolute address** A storage address that directly, without any modification, accesses a location or device. Compare with **indexed address.**

actual code The binary code which directly operates the central processing unit, using only absolute addresses and values (this is the final form of a program after a compiler or assembler pass).

actual instruction The resulting instruction executed after the modification of an original instruction.

actuator A mechanical device that can be controlled by an external signal (such as the read/write head in a disk drive).

ACU (automatic calling unit) A device which allows a computer to call stations or dial telephone numbers automatically.

A/D or **A to D (analog to digital)** Changing a signal from an analog form to a digitally coded form.

ADA A high-level programming language that is used mainly in military, industrial and scientific fields of computing.

adapt To change to fit, as, for example, adapting a computer to take 5.25 inch disks.

adapter or **adaptor** A device that allows two or more incompatible devices to be connected together. Adaptors are most often found between two different shaped connectors of a standard bus. For example, an adaptor is required to connect the 25-pin RS-232 device to a 9-pin serial port.

adapter card An add-on interface board that allows incompatible devices to communicate.

adapter plug A plug which allows devices with different plugs (two-pin, three-pin, etc.) to be fitted into the same socket.

adaptive channel allocation Providing communications channels according to demand rather than a fixed allocation.

adaptive routing The ability of a system to change its communications routes according to various events or situations such as line failure.

adaptive speed control modem An intelligent modem that changes its data transmission speed according to the conditions of the line.

adaptive systems The ability of a system to alter its responses and processes according to inputs or events or situations.

adaptor see **adapter**

ADC (analog to digital converter) A device used to convert analog input to a digital output form, that can be understood by a computer.

add time The period of time taken to perform one addition operation (either of a CPU or adder).

addend The number which is added to the augend in an addition operation.

adder A device or routine that provides the sum of two or more digital or analog inputs.

adder-subtractor A device that can either add or subtract

add-in Something which is added into a system to enhance the performance or abilities.

addition An arithmetic operation that produces the sum of an addend and an augend.

addition record A record which contains changes — used to update a master record or file.

addition time The time an adder takes to carry out an add operation.

addition without carry An addition operation without any carry bits or words. This is the same as **EXOR function.**

add-on A piece of software or hardware that is added to a computer system to improve its performance. For example, an add-on hard disk will boost the computer's storage capabilities or a new add-on board will allow colour graphics to be displayed.

address 1 A unique number allowing a central processing unit to reference a physical location in a storage medium within a computer system. The larger the address word, the greater the number of possible combinations, so the greater the area of memory that can be directly addressed. For example, an eight-bit address word supports 255 different locations, a sixteen-bit address word could support 65,536 different addresses. **2** To place data onto an address bus that will identify which word in memory or a storage device is to be accessed. See also **absolute address** or **actual address** or **direct address.**

addressability The amount of control available over pixels on a screen. The higher the resolution of the graphics available on-screen, the greater their addressability.

addressable Which can be addressed. In some personal computers, the newest operating systems provide a 16Mbyte area of addressable RAM. An **addressable cursor** is one whose position on the screen can be defined — usually from within a program in the form of an instruction with horizontal and vertical coordinates. An **addressable terminal** will only accept data if that data has the correct address and identification number within its message header.

address access time The total time which a storage device takes between the moment the data is requested and the data being returned.

address bus The physical connection that carries the address data (in parallel form) from the central processing unit to main memory, storage devices and external peripherals.

address computation An operation on address data (in an instruction).

address decoder A logical circuit that will produce a signal when a certain address is placed on the address bus.

address field or **operand field** The part of a computer instruction that contains the location of the operand.

address format The rules defining the way the operands, data and addresses are arranged in an instruction.

addressing The process of accessing a location in memory. **Absolute addressing** is using the absolute address of a data word stored in memory to locate it. **Abbreviated addressing** is the use of a smaller address word than normal, which provides faster address decoding operations.

addressing capacity The highest location that a certain program or CPU can directly address, without special features (such as virtual memory or memory banks). This is dependent upon the size of the address word: an eight-bit address word has an addressing capacity of 256, while a 16-bit address word would have a larger addressing range of 65,536 locations.

addressing level The various levels at which data can be addressed are defined as: **zero-level:** The operand is the address part of the instruction; **first-level:** The operand is stored at the address of the instruction; **second-level:** The operand is stored at the address given in the instruction.

addressing method The manner in which a section of memory is located and accessed.

addressing mode The way in which a location is addressed; this could be either sequential, indexed, direct, etc.

address mapping The process of translating a virtual address to an absolute, real address.

address mark A special code on a disk that indicates the start of sector location data.

address modification Changing the address field, so that it can refer to a different location.

address register A register in a computer that is able to store all the bits that make up an address which can then be processed as a single unit (in small micros, the address register is usually made up of two or three data bytes). See also **MAR.**

address space The total number of possible locations that can be directly addressed by the program or CPU.

address strobe A signal or pulse that indicates that a valid address is on the address bus.

address track A track on a magnetic disk containing the addresses of files, etc., stored on other tracks.

address word A computer word in a small micro, usually made up of two or three data words that contain the address data.

administrator The controlling or supervisor or executive software of a system (also a person, such as a systems manager).

ADP (automatic data processing) Data processing done by a computer.

advance To move forward; to make something move forward, as, for example, when paper is advanced by turning a knob or the cursor is advanced two spaces along the line.

advanced version A program with more complex features — for use by an experienced user.

adventure game A game played on a computer, where the user pretends to be a hero in an imaginary land and has to get through various dangerous situations, fight monsters, etc.

affirmative Meaning "yes". **Affirmative acknowledgement** is the acknowledge signal from the receiver that it has accepted the message and is ready for the next message to be transmitted.

AFNOR (in France) Association Française de Normalisation (the French standards organization).

afterglow see **persistence**

AGC (automatic gain control) An electronic device that provides a constant amplitude output signal from a varying input signal by changing its gain.

AI (artificial intelligence) The design and development of computer programs that attempt to imitate human intelligence and decision-making functions, providing basic reasoning and other human characteristics. See also **expert system, IKBS.**

air gap The narrow gap between a recording or playback head and the magnetic medium.

alarm Ringing or other sound which warns of a danger, such as the bell which sounds when the printer has run out of paper.

ALC (automatic level control) see **AGC**

ALGOL (algorithmic language) A high level programming language using algorithmic methods for mathematical and technical applications.

algorithm The rules used to define or perform a specific task or to solve a specific problem.

algorithmic language A computer language specifically designed to process and express algorithms, such as ALGOL.

alien disk A disk formatted on another system or containing data in a format which is in a form that cannot be read or understood by the current system. In order to read alien disks, an **alien disk reader** must be used. This is an add-on device which allows a computer to access data on disks from other computers or systems. If, for example, the operator has an alien disk, he selects a multi-disk option to allow him to turn the disk drive into an alien disk reader.

align 1 To make sure that the characters to be printed are spaced and levelled correctly. **2** To ensure that a read/write head is correctly positioned over the recording medium.

aligner A device used to make sure that the paper is straight in a printer.

aligning edge The edge of an optical character recognition system which is used to position a document.

alignment The correct spacing and levelling of printed characters. If a line of characters are in alignment this means they are correctly spaced and are level; if paper is out of alignment, any text printed on it will be crooked.

alignment pin A peg that fits in a hole to ensure that two devices are correctly aligned. A number of alignment pins are used in a sprocket-feed system to pull paper through a printer.

allocate To divide a period of time or a piece of work in various ways and share it out between users. So, for example, an operating system will allocate most of main memory to a spreadsheet pro-gram.

allocation routine A small program that divides the memory resources of a system between the software and peripherals that use it.

allophone The smallest unit of sound from which speech can be formed. A number of speech synthesizers use allophones to synthesize speech, rather than using digitized speech.

alpha beta technique Free structure technique used in artificial intelligence for solving game and strategy problems.

alphabetical order The arrangement of records (such as files, index cards) in the order of the letters of the alphabet (A,B,C,D, etc.).

alphabetic character (set) The characters (capitals and small letters) that make up the alphabet.

alphabetic string A string that only contains alphabetic characters.

alphabetize To put into alphabetical order, such as alphabetizing names and addresses in a mailing list.

alphageometric codes A set of codes that instruct a teletext terminal to display various graphics patterns or characters.

alphameric see **alphanumeric**

alphamosaic character set The character set used in teletext to provide alphanumeric and graphics characters.

alphanumeric characters or **alphanumerics** Roman letters and Arabic numerals (and other signs such as punctuation marks).

alphanumeric data Data that represents the letters of the alphabet and the Arabic numerals.

alphanumeric display A display device that is capable of showing characters as well as numbers.

alphanumeric keyboard A keyboard containing character keys as well as numerical keys.

alphanumeric operand An operand which can contain alphanumeric characters, such as a string.

alphanumeric string A series of alphanumeric characters that are manipulated and treated as a single unit.

alpha-particle sensitivity A problem experienced by certain (MOS) memory devices exposed to alpha radiation, causing loss of stored charge (which represents data).

alphaphotographic Which represents pictures using predefined graphics characters, used for teletext services.

alphasort To sort data into alphabetical order.

alpha-test version The earliest version of a program or piece of hardware. This is debugged and tested, to produce a beta-test version, which is again tested to lead to the final, full version of the product.

alpha wrap The method used for feeding tape past a helical scan recording head to ensure the alignment is correct.

alterable see **EAPROM, EAROM**

alternate mode An application for multi-user use where two operators can access and share a single file apparently at the same time.

alternate route A backup path or line in a communications system, which is used in case of a fault or breakdown.

alternation A logical function that produces a true output if any input is true.

alternating current or **AC** Electric current whose value varies with time in a regular, sinusoidal way (changing direction of flow each half cycle).

alternative denial A logical function whose output is false if all inputs are true and true if any input is false.

ALU (arithmetic logic unit) The section of the CPU that performs all arithmetical and logical functions.

AM see **amplitude modulation**

ambiguous filename A filename which is not unique to a single file, making it difficult to locate the file.

ambiguity Something which is not clearly defined. An **ambiguity error** is an error due to incorrect selection of ambiguous data.

AMM (analog multimeter) A multimeter that uses a graduated scale and a moving needle as a readout for voltage, current and impedance levels. Compare with **DMM.**

amendment record A record containing new information used to update a master record or file.

American National Standards Institute (ANSI) The organization in the USA which specifies computer and software standards including those of high-level programming languages.

American Standard Code for Information Interchange (ASCII) The code which represents alphanumeric characters as binary codes.

amp or **ampere (A)** The base SI unit of electrical current which can be defined as the current flowing through an impedance of one ohm which has a voltage of one volt across it.

ampersand The printed sign (&) which means "and".

amplifier An electronic circuit that magnifies the power of a signal.

amplification The output-to-input signal strength ratio.

amplitude distortion Distortion of a signal due to uneven non-linear amplification, when high levels are amplified less than low.

amplitude modulation (AM) A modulation system that varies the amplitude of a constant frequency carrier according to an external signal.

amplitude quantization The conversion of an analog signal to a numerical representation.

analog or **analogue** The representation and measurement of numerical data by continuously variable physical quantities, such as the size of electrical voltages. Compare with **digital.**

analog channel A communications line that carries analog signals such as speech.

analog computer A computer which processes data in analog form (that is, data which is represented by a continuously varying signal — as op-posed to digital data).

analog gate A logic gate whose output is proportional to an input signal. Compare this with a digital gate, whose output can only be at one of two levels.

analog input card All the circuitry on one PCB required for amplifying and converting analog input signals to a digital form. If this is an add-in card for a computer, then additional logic will be required to interface with the computer's bus.

analog multimeter A multimeter that uses a graduated scale and a moving needle as a readout for voltage, current and impedance levels. Compare with **DMM.**

analog output card All the circuitry on one PCB required to convert digital output data from a computer to an analog form.

analog recording The storing of signals on a (usually magnetic) medium in their natural form without conversion to digital form.

analog representation A value or variable in analog form.

analog signal A continuously varying signal.

analog to digital (A to D or A/D) converter A device used to convert an analog input to a digital output form which can be understood by a computer. An A to D converter works by measuring the amplitude of the analog signal, and outputting a binary number relating to this. The opposite is a **digital to analog converter (DAC or D to A converter)** which is a circuit that outputs an analog signal that is proportional to the input digital number, and so converts a digital input to an analog form. A DAC allows the computer to work outside the computer's environment, controlling machines, producing sound or speech, etc.; an ADC allows real-world signals to be processed by a computer.

analyser A piece of electronic test equipment that displays various features of a signal. A **frequency analyser** displays the amplitudes of the various frequency components of a signal.

ancestral file A system of backing up files (son to father to grandfather file), where the son is the current working file.

ancillary equipment Equipment which is used to make a task easier, but which is not absolutely necessary.

AND or **coincidence function** A logical function whose output is true if both its inputs are true.

AND or **coincidence gate** or **circuit** or **element** An electronic gate that performs a logical AND function on electrical signals.

AND or **coincidence operation** Processing two or more input signals, outputting their AND function. If both inputs are 1, results of the AND will be 1; if one of the input digits is 0, then AND will produce a 0.

angstrom The unit of measurement equal to one thousand millionth of a metre.

annotation A comment or note in a program which explains how the program is to be used.

annotation symbol A symbol used when drawing flowcharts, to indicate comments.

annunciator A signal that can be heard or seen, used to attract the operator's attention.

anode The positive electrical terminal of a device.

ANSI (American National Standards Institute) Organization which specifies computer and software standards, including those of high-level programming languages.

answer back A signal sent by the receiving end of a communications system to identify itself or to transmit a message.

answer time The time taken for a receiving device to respond to a signal.

anticoincidence circuit or **function** A logical function whose output is true if either of two inputs is true, and false if both inputs are the same.

anti-tinkle suppression (In a modem) a switch which prevents other telephones on a line ringing when a modem dials out.

aperture mask The mask used in colour televisions or monitors to keep the red, green and blue beams separate.

APL (A Programming Language) A high-level programming language used in scientific and mathematical work.

append To add data to an existing file or record.

appliance computer A ready to run computer system that can be bought in a shop, taken home and used immediately for a particular purpose. See also **turnkey.**

application A task which a computer performs or problem which a computer solves (as opposed to an operating system which is the way in which a computer works).

application layer The top layer in an ISO/OSI network, which requests a transmission from a user's program.

application orientated language A programming language that provides functions that allow the user to solve certain application problems.

applications package A set of computer programs and manuals that cover all aspects of a particular task (such as payroll, stock control, tax, etc.).

applications software or **applications program** Programs which are used by a user to make the computer do what is required, designed to allow a particular task to be performed.

applications specific integrated circuits (ASIC) Specially designed ICs for one particular function or to meet particular specifications.

applications terminal A terminal (such as at a sales desk) which is specially configured to carry out certain tasks.

approximation error An error caused by rounding off a real number.

APT (Automatically Programmed Tools) A programming language used to control numerically controlled machines.

Arabic numbers or **figures** Figures such as 1, 2, 3, 4, etc. (as opposed to the Roman numerals I, II, III, IV, etc.).

arbitration or **bus arbitration** The protocol and control of transmission over a bus that ensures fair usage by several users.

architecture The layout and interconnection of a computer's internal hardware and the logical relationships between CPU, memory and input/output devices.

archive 1 The storage of data over a long period. An **archive file** contains data which is out of date, but which is kept for future reference. **2** To put data into storage. An **archived copy** is a copy of a file that is kept in storage.

archival quality The length of time that a copy can be stored before it becomes illegible.

area A section of memory or code that is reserved for a certain purpose.

area search Search for specific data within a certain section of memory or files.

argument A variable acted upon by an operator or function. See also **operand.**

arithmetic Concerned with mathematical functions such as addition, subtraction, division and multiplication. The **arithmetic capability** of a device is its ability to perform mathematical functions. An **arithmetic check** is carried out to ensure that a result is correct.

arithmetic functions Calculations carried out on numbers, such as addition, subtraction, multiplication, division.

arithmetic instruction A program instruction in which the operator defines the arithmetic operation to be carried out. Compare with **logical instruction.**

arithmetic logic unit (ALU) or **arithmetic unit** The hardware section of a CPU that performs all the mathematical and logical functions.

arithmetic operation A mathematical function carried out on data.

arithmetic operators A symbol which indicates an arithmetic function (such as + for addition, x for multiplication).

arithmetic shift A word or data moved one bit to the left or right inside a register, losing the bit shifted off the end. Compare with **logical shift.**

arm 1 To prepare a device or machine or routine for action or inputs. **2** To define which interrupt lines are active. An **armed interrupt** is an interrupt line which has been made active (usually by setting a bit to one within an interrupt mask).

array An ordered structure containing individually accessible elements referenced by numbers, used to store tables or sets of related data. An array whose elements are letters and numbers is an **alphanumeric array.**

array bounds The limits to the number of elements which can be stored in an array.

array dimension Number of elements in an array, given as rows and columns.

array element One individual piece of data within an array.

array processor A computer that can act upon several arrays of data simultaneously, for very fast mathematical applications. For example, an array processor allows the array that contains the screen image to be rotated with one simple command.

artificial intelligence (AI) The design of computer programs that attempt to imitate human intelligence and decision making functions, providing basic reasoning and other human characteristics.

artwork Graphical work or images which are to be printed.

ascender The part of a character that rises above the main line of printed characters (as the 'tail' of a 'b', 'd', etc.). Compare **descender.**

ASCII (American standard code for information interchange) Standard code which represents each alphanumeric character as a unique binary code.

ASCII character A character which is within the ASCII list of codes.

ASCII file A stored file containing only ASCII coded character data.

ASCII keyboard A keyboard through which all the ASCII characters are accessible.

ASIC (application specific integrated circuit) A specially designed IC that carries out one particular function or that is designed to meet special specifications. This is an alternative to using a number of standard ICs to carry out a function.

aspect ratio The ratio of the width to the height of pixel shapes.

aspect system A method of storing and indexing documents in a retrieval system.

ASR (automatic send/receive) A device or terminal that can transmit or receive information. An ASR terminal can input information via a keyboard or via a tape cassette or paper tape. It can receive information and store it in internal memory or on tape. Compare **KSR.**

assemble 1 To put a product together from various smaller parts. The parts for a disk drive may be made in Japan and assembled in France, for example. **2** To translate assembly code into machine code. There is normally a short wait during which time the program is assembled into object code, and syntax errors may be spotted whilst the source program is being assembled. **3** To insert specific library routines or macros or parameters into a program.

assembler (program) An assembly program or program which converts a program written in assembly language into machine code. An **absolute assembler** is a type of assembly language program designed to produce code which uses only absolute addresses and values.

assembler error messages Messages produced by an assembler program that indicate that errors have been found in the source code.

assembly Converting a program into machine code.

assembly code The mnemonics which are used to represent machine code instructions in an assembler program.

assembly language or **assembler language** A low-level programming language using instruction mnemonics that directly represent a single machine code instruction. When an assembly language program is assembled, it is converted into machine code.

assembly listing The display of an assembly language program.

assembly program A number of assembly code instructions ordered in such a way as to perform a task.

assembly routine or **system** see **assembler**

assembly time 1 The time taken by an assembler program to translate a program. 2 period during which an assembler is converting a program from assembly language into machine code.

assertion 1 A program statement of a fact or rule. 2 A fact that is true or defined as being true.

assign 1 To give a device or a computer or someone a specific task or job of work, as, for example, assigning to a programmer the job of writing the screen-handling code. 2 To set a variable equal to a string of characters or numbers. 3 To reserve part of a computer system for use while a program is running.

assignment Setting a variable equal to a string of characters or a value. A basic programming command that sets a variable equal to a value * string or character is an **assignment statement.**

associative addressing or **content-addressable addressing** A location addressed by its contents rather than its address.

associative storage or **memory** or **content-addressable memory** A method of data retrieval that uses part of the data rather than an address to locate the data. A processor that uses associative storage is an **associative processor,** and a register that is located by its contents rather than by a name or address is an **associative storage register.**

astable multivibrator An electronic circuit whose output voltage repeatedly switches between two voltage levels. Prior to the general use of quartz crystals as clock generators, astable multivibrators, constructed from separate logic gates, were used.

asterisk A graphical symbol (*) used as a symbol meaning for multiplication.

async or **asynch** (informal) see **asynchronous.**

asynchronous Serial data or equipment which does not depend on being synchronized with another piece of equipment.

asynchronous access Communications using handshaking to synchronize data transmission rather than a clock or timing pulse.

asynchronous communications Data transmission between devices that is not synchronized to a clock or timing pulse, but is transmitted when ready.

asynchronous communications interface adapter (ACIA) A circuit that allows a computer to transmit and receive serial data using asynchronous access.

asynchronous computer 1 A computer that changes from one operation to the next according to signals received when the process is finished. 2 A computer in which a process starts on the arrival of signals or data, rather than on a clock pulse.

asynchronous mode A terminal linked to another piece of equipment in such a way that data transfer between them need not be synchronized.

asynchronous port A connection to a computer allowing asynchronous data access.

asynchronous transmission Data transmission that uses handshaking signals rather than clock signals to synchronize data pulses. Asynchronous transmission of data is mainly for transferring data between computers and peripheral devices, whilst synchronous communication is usually used for data transfer between computers.

ATC (authorization to copy) The permission of a software publisher to a user, allowing him to make a certain number of copies of a program. See also **site licence.**

ATE (automatic test equipment) Computer controlled testing facilities, that can check a complex circuit or PCB for faults or problems.

ATM see **automated teller machine**

atom A value or string that cannot be reduced to a simpler form.

attached processor A separate processor in a system that performs certain functions under the control of a central processor. See also **coprocessor.**

attachment A device which is attached to a machine for a special purpose, such as a single sheet feed attachment to a printer.

attack envelope The shape of the initial section of a signal.

attended operation A process which has an operator standing by in case of problems.

attention interruption An interrupt signal that requests the attention of the processor.

attention key A key on a terminal that sends an interrupt signal to the processor.

attribute 1 A field entry in a file. 2 Information concerning the display or presentation of information. A single pixel will often have two bytes of data associated with it: the location byte and an attribute byte describing its colour, brightness, etc.

auctioneering device A device that will select the maximum or minimum signal from a number of input signals.

audio cassette A reel of magnetic recording tape in a small protective casing inserted into an **audio cassette recorder** (used in computing for recording data in an audio form — either as a cheap backup medium or as a main backing store for home computers without disk drives).

audio response unit A speech synthesizer that allows a computer to respond (in speech) to requests.

audit Recording the tasks carried out by a computer.

audit trail Recording details of use of a system by noting transactions carried out (used for checking on illegal use or to trace or recover from a malfunction).

augend (In an addition) the number to which another number, the **addend,** is added to produce the sum.

augmented addressing Producing a usable address word from two shorter words.

augmenter A value added to another.

authentication of messages Using special codes or cipher systems to identify the sender of messages, so that the sender and their messages can be recognized as being genuine. This is widely used in high-security computer-to-computer communications such as between computers in a bank to ensure that each computer is receiving authentic data or instructions.

authoring system A computer system that is able to run an author language.

author language A programming language used to write CAL and training programs.

authority file or **list** A list of special terms used by people compiling a database and also by the users of the database.

authorization code A code used to restrict access to a computer system to authorized users only.

authorization to copy (ATC) The permission of a software publisher to a user, allowing him to make a certain number of copies of a program. Some companies have introduced ATC schemes which allow users of certain software to make duplicates of the companies' programs for a fee. See also **site licence.**

authorized user A person who is allowed to access a system or a particular file or area.

auto advance Device which makes the paper in a printer automatically move forward to the next line at the end of a line.

auto-answer (A modem) that will automatically answer a telephone when called.

auto-baud scanning Part of a communications circuit that can automatically sense and select the correct baud rate for a line.

auto boot A computer system that will initiate a boot-up procedure when it is switched on.

auto-dial To dial a number automatically (using a stored number).

auto-login or **auto-logon** A communications program that will automatically dial a phone-number, then send the password and user's number when requested by a remote system to automate the logon procedure. See also **login, logon.**

automated teller machine (ATM) An automatic telling machine or machine linked to a main computer that allows cash to be taken out of a bank account when a special card is inserted and a password or authorization code is entered.

automatic calling unit (ACU) A device which allows a computer to call telephone numbers automatically.

automatic carriage return System in which the cursor automatically returns to the beginning of the next new line when it reaches the end of the previous one.

automatic checking Error detection and validation check carried out automatically on received data.

automatic data capture A system in which data is automatically recorded in a computer system as it is input.

automatic data processing (ADP) Data processing carried out by a computer.

automatic decimal adjustment The process of lining up all the decimal points in a column of figures.

automatic error correction The correction of received data. Firstly the error must be detected, then corrected. (This is usually achieved by using either a Gray code system or a complex algorithm).

automatic error detection The use of an alphanumeric code, such as a gray code, that will allow any errors to be detected.

automatic gain control (AGC) An electronic device that provides a constant amplitude output signal from a varying input signal, by changing its gain.

automatic letter writing Writing form letters (using a wordprocessor in which the main body of the letter remains the same).

automatic loader A small program (usually in ROM) that will boot up a system and load a program when the machine is switched on.

automatic message accounting A system of logging telephone calls automatically so that details of them can be given to the user.

automatic programming The process of producing an optimum operating system for a particular system, environment or task.

automatic repeat A feature of most keyboards, in which a character is automatically repeated if a key is kept pressed down.

automatic sequencing The ability of a computer to execute a number of programs or tasks in a certain order without extra commands. See also **batch file.**

automatic test equipment (ATE) Computer-controlled testing facilities, that can check a complex circuit or PCB for faults or problems.

automation The use of machines to do work with very little supervision by people.

auto-redial A modem that dials a telephone number again if engaged — until it replies.

auto repeat A facility where a character is automatically repeated if the key is kept pressed down.

auto restart A computer that can initialize and reload its operating system if there is a fault or power failure or at switch on.

auto start A facility to load a program automatically when the computer is switched on.

auto verify A verification procedure carried out automatically, as soon as the data has been saved.

auxiliary equipment Backup or secondary equipment in case of a breakdown. In case of a power failure, it is useful to have an **auxiliary power supply.**

auxiliary processor An extra, specialized processor, such as an array or numerical processor that can work with a main CPU to increase throughput by reducing the workload of the main CPU.

auxiliary storage or **memory** or **store** Any data storage medium (such a magnetic tape or floppy disk) that is not the main high speed computer storage (RAM).

available list A list maintained by the operating system of unallocated memory and resources within a system.

available point The smallest single unit or point of a display whose colour and brightness can be individually controlled. See also **pixel.**

available power The maximum electrical or processing power that a system can deliver.

available time Time during which a system may be used.

avalanche One action starting a number of other actions, such as an avalanche of errors after the operator has pressed the wrong key.

average access time The average time taken between a request being sent and data being returned from a memory device.

average delay The average time that a user must wait when trying to access a communications network. The average delay increases at 9.30 in the morning when everyone tries to log-in. See also **mean.**

axis A straight reference line which is the basis for coordinates on a graph. The **X-axis** is the horizontal axis and the **Y-axis** is the vertical.

azerty keyboard Method of arranging the keys on a keyboard where the first line begins AZERTY (used mainly in Europe). Compare with **QWERTY.**

azimuth The angle of a tape head to a reference (such as a tape plane). The correct horizontal angle of a tape head to the magnetic tape is the **azimuth alignment.**

B

B The hexadecimal (base 16) equivalent to decimal number 11.

babble Crosstalk or noise from other sources which interferes with a signal.

BABT (British Approval Board for Telecommunications) BABT approval is required for a device to be connected to the public telephone system.

back-end processor A special purpose auxiliary processor.

background 1 A system in a computer where low-priority work (a **background job**) can be done in the intervals when very important work is not being done. **2** Part of a picture which is behind the main object of interest: a graphics processor chip can handle background, foreground and sprite movement independently.

background colour The colour of a computer screen display (characters and graphics are normally displayed in a different foreground colour). A white background colour with black characters is less stressful for the eyes than the more usual dark screen with light characters.

background noise Unwanted noise which is present along with the required signal. This can be electrical noise (from un-shielded equipment) or audible noise, such as on a telephone line (to which modems are very sensitive).

background printing Printing-out from a computer while it is processing another task. Background printing is often a feature of word-processors, allowing the user to continue editing a document whilst another is being printed.

background processing 1 A low priority job which is executed when there are no higher priority activities for the computer to attend to. **2** A process which does not use the on-line capabilities of a system.

background program A computer program with a very low priority.

background task A process that can be executed at any time by the computer's operating system, not normally noticed by the user. These processes are normally used for carrying out housekeeping or low-level tasks.

backing store or **storage** or **memory** Permanent storage medium onto which data can be recorded before being processed by the computer or after processing for later retrieval. By adding another disk drive to a processor, the backing store capabilities can be increased. Paper tape is one of the slowest access backing stores. Compare with **main memory.**

backlog Work or tasks that have yet to be processed.

backplane The part of the body of a computer which holds the circuit boards, buses and expansion connectors (the backplane does not provide any processing functions). See also **motherboard, rack.**

backspace The movement of a cursor or printhead back by one character.

backspace character A code that causes a backspace action in a display device. (The ASCII code for a backspace character is 8).

backspace key A key on a keyboard which moves the cursor back one space. If a mistake is made in entering data, the backspace key is used to move the cursor back to the incorrect character so that it can be corrected.

backtrack To carry out list processing in reverse, starting with the goal and working towards the proofs.

back up To make a copy of a file or data or disk in case the original is damaged or corrupted in some way. Company accounts, for example, should be backed up on disk as a protection against fire damage or loss. **backups** or **backup files** or **backup copies** should be made for security against errors or corruption in the original or master copy, and kept in a separate place from the master. **Battery backup** is used to provide power to a volatile device such as a RAM chip to retain data after a computer has been switched off.

backup procedure The method used when making backup copies of files.

Backus-Naur-Form (BNF) A system of writing and expressing the syntax of a programming language.

backward channel A channel from the receiver to transmitter allowing the receiver to send control and handshaking signals that will control data transmission to it.

backward error correction The correction of errors which are detected by the receiver and a signal is sent to the transmitter to request a retransmission of the data.

backward mode Negative displacement from an origin.

backward recovery Data retrieval from a system that has crashed. Backward recovery is carried out by passing the semi-processed data from the crashed computer through a routine that reverses the effects of the main program to return the original data.

backwards supervision Data transmission controlled by the receiver's signals rather than being dictated by the sender.

bad break The wrong hyphenation of a word at the end of a line of text.

badge reader A machine that reads data from an identification badge. A badge reader makes sure that only authorized personnel can gain access to a computer room.

bad sector A sector on a magnetic disk which has been wrongly formatted * which contains an error or fault and is unable to be correctly written to or read from. The operator will probably receive error messages when trying to copy files that are stored on bad sectors on a disk.

bag A number of elements in no particular order.

balance 1 The placement of text and graphics on a page in an attractive way. A DTP package will allow the user to see if the overall page balance is correct. **2** To plan something so that two parts are equal. A **balanced**

circuit presents a correct load to a communications line (the correct load is usually equal to the impedance of a line element). Such a circuit must be used at the end of the line to prevent signal reflections. The communications line that is terminated at each end with a balanced circuit is a **balanced line.**

balanced error The probability of any error occurring (from a number of errors) is the same for all errors.

band 1 A range of frequencies between two limits. **2** A group of tracks on a magnetic disk. See also **base band.**

bandlimited (A signal) whose frequency range has been limited to one band.

bandpass filter A circuit that allows a certain band of frequencies to pass while stopping any that are higher or lower.

band printer A printer in which the characters are located along a movable steel belt.

bandwidth The limits of frequencies used. On a normal telephone line the bandwidth is 3100 Hz. **Bus bandwidth** is the rate at which data is transmitted over a computer's data bus — this can often be faster than the speed of the processor, especially if driving a high-speed interface such as a SCSI disk drive.

bank A collection of similar devices, such as a bank of minicomputers used to process raw data. **Bank switching** is the selection of a particular memory bank from a group.

bar A thick line or block of colour. A **bar chart** or **bar graph** shows values as vertical or horizontal bars.

bar code (American English is **bar graphics**) Data represented as a series of printed stripes of varying widths. Bar codes are found on most goods and their packages; the width and position of the stripes is sensed by a light pen or optical wand and provides information about the goods, such as price, stock quantities, etc. The optical device that reads data from a bar code is a **bar-code reader** or **optical scanner.**

bar entry to a file To stop someone accessing a file.

bar printer A printer in which the characters are on arms which strike the paper to print characters. See also **daisy wheel.**

barrel A conducting post in a terminal.

barrel printer A type of printer where characters are located around a rotating barrel.

barrier box A device that electrically isolates equipment from a telephone line to prevent damage.

base 1 The lowest or first position. **2** A collection of files used as a reference. **3** A notation referring to a number system, such as **base 8,** etc.

base address An initial address in a program used as a reference for others.

base band The frequency range of a signal before it is processed or transmitted. For example, the voice base band ranges from 20Hz to 15KHz.

base band modem A communications circuit that transmits an unmodulated base band signal over a short distance.

base 8 The octal number system (using the eight digits 0 - 7).

base language Assembly language.

base line A reference line used when printing to locate characters correctly.

base register A register in a CPU (not usually in small computers) that contains the address of the start of a program.

base 16 The hexadecimal number system (using the ten digits 0 - 9 and six letters A - F).

base 10 The decimal number system (using the ten digits 0 - 9).

base 2 The binary number system (using only the two digits 0 and 1).

BASIC (Beginner's All-purpose Symbolic Instruction Code) A high-level programming language for developing programs in a conversational way, providing an easy introduction to computer programming.

basic code The binary code which directly operates the CPU, using only absolute addresses and values (this is the final form of a program after a compiler or assembler pass).

basic control system satellite (BCS) A system that runs dedicated programs or tasks for a central computer, controlled using interrupt signals.

basic input/output operating system (BIOS) System routines that interface between high-level program instructions and the system peripherals to control the input and output to various standard devices, this often includes controlling the screen, keyboard and disk drives.

basic instruction An unmodified program instruction which is processed to obtain the instruction to be executed.

basic mode link control A standardized control of transmission links using special codes.

basic operating system (BOS) Software that controls the basic, low-level running of the hardware and file management.

basic telecommunications access method (BTAM) A method of providing access (i.e., read or write operations) to a remote device.

batch 1 A group of items which are made at one time, such as a batch of disk drives. **2** A group of documents which are processed at the same time or a group of tasks or amount of data to be processed as a single unit. **3** To put data or tasks together in groups. **Batched communication** is the high-speed transmission of large blocks of data which does not require an acknowledgement from the receiver for each data item.

batch file A stored file containing a sequence of system commands, which the operating system will execute in sequence — used instead of repeatedly typing in the commands. Batch files are used to save time and effort when carrying out a repeated series of tasks.

batch mode (processing data in) see **batch processing**

batch number A reference number attached to a batch.

batch processor A system able to process groups of tasks.

batch processing A system of data processing where information is collected into batches before being processed by the computer in one machine run. Batch processing is the opposite to interactive processing (where the user gives instructions and receives an immediate response).

batch region The memory area where the operating system executes batch programs.

batch system The system that executes batch files.

batch total The sum of a number of batches of data, used for error checking, validation or to provide useful information.

battery-backed A volatile storage device that has a battery backup. For example, a RAM disk card may have the option to be battery-backed.

battery backup The use of a battery to provide power to volatile storage devices (RAM chips) to retain data after a computer has been switched off.

baud or **baud rate** The measure of the number of signal changes transmitted per second. Baud rate is often considered the same as bits per second, but in fact it depends on the protocol used and the error checking (300 baud is roughly equivalent to 30 characters per second using standard error checking). A modem with auto-baud scanner can automatically sense at which baud rate it should operate.

baud rate generator A device that produces various timing signals to synchronize data at different baud rates.

baudot code A five-bit character transmission code, used mainly in tele-typewriters.

B box A register in a CPU (not usually in small computers) that contains the address of the start of a program.

BBS (bulletin board system) An information and message database accessible by modem and computer link.

BCC (block character check) An error detection method for blocks of transmitted data.

BCD (binary coded decimal) The representation of single decimal digits as a pattern of four binary digits. For example, the BCD representation of decimal 8 is 1000. A **BCD adder** is a full adder able to add two four-bit BCD words.

BCH code see **Bose-Chandhuri-Hocquenghem code**

BCPL A high level programming language — this was the early predessor of C.

BCS see **British Computer Society, basic control system (satellite).**

bead A small section of a program that is used for a single task.

beam A narrow radiated stream of waves or particles such as the thin beam of light produced by a laser.

beam deflection A change in beam direction. A magnetic field is used for beam deflection in a CRT.

beep 1 An audible warning noise: a printer will make a beep when it runs out of paper. **2** To make a beep. See also **bleep.**

beginning of file (bof) A character or symbol that shows the start of a valid section of data.

beginning of information mark (bim) A symbol indicating the start of a data stream stored on a disk drive or tape.

beginning of tape marker or **bot marker** A section of material that marks the start of the recording area of a reel of magnetic tape.

Beginner's All-Purpose Symbolic Instruction Code (BASIC) A high-level programming language for developing programs in a conversational way, providing an easy introduction to computer programming.

bell character A control code which causes a machine to produce an audible signal. (The ASCII code for a bell character is 7).

benchmark 1 The point in an index which is important, and can be used to compare with other figures. **2** A program used to test the performance of software or hardware * a system. Testing a system or program with a benchmark is known as **benchmarking.** The same task or program (the **benchmark problem** or **benchmark test**) is given to different systems and their results and speeds of working are compared.

Bernoulli box A high capacity storage system using exchangeable 20MB cartridges.

best fit A function that selects the smallest free space in main memory for a requested virtual page.

bias 1 An electrical reference level. **2** A high frequency signal added to recorded information to minimize noise and distortion (the high frequency is removed on playback). **3** Deviation of statistical results from a reference level.

biased data Data or records which point to one conclusion.

biased exponent The value of the exponent in a floating point number.

bid (Of a computer) to gain control of a network in order to transmit data. For example, a terminal may have to bid several times before there is a gap in transmissions on a network.

bi-directional An operation or process that can occur in forward or reverse directions, such as bi-directional file transfer.

bi-directional bus Data or control lines that can carry signals travelling in two directions.

bi-directional printer A printer which is able to print characters from left to right and from right to left as the head moves forwards or backwards across the paper (this speeds up the printing operation). Compare **omnidirectional**.

bifurcation A system in which there are only two possible results.

Big Blue An informal name for **IBM**

billion A number equal to one thousand million or one million million. Note that in the US it means one thousand million, but in the UK it usually means one million million. With figures it is usually written **bn**.

BIM (beginning of information mark) A symbol indicating the start of a data stream stored on a disk drive or tape.

binary Base 2, the number notation system which uses only the digits 0 and 1.

binary adder A device that provides the sum of two or more binary digits.

binary arithmetic The rules and functions governing arithmetic operations in base 2.

binary bit Smallest single unit in base 2 binary notation, either a 0 or a 1.

binary cell A storage element for one bit.

binary chop see **binary search**

binary code Using different patterns of binary digits to represent various symbols, elements, etc.

binary coded characters Alphanumeric characters represented as patterns of binary digits.

binary coded decimal (BCD) The representation of single decimal digits as a pattern of four binary digits. In BCD, decimal zero is 0000, decimal one is 0001, etc.

binary counter A circuit that will divide a binary input signal by two (producing one output pulse for two input pulses).

binary digit or **bit** The smallest single unit in base 2 binary notation, either a 0 or a 1.

binary dump The display of a section of memory in binary form.

binary encoding Representing a character or element with a unique combination * pattern of bits in a word.

binary exponent One word that contains the sign and exponent of a binary number (expressed in exponent and mantissa form).

binary fraction The representation of a decimal fraction in binary form. For example, the binary fraction 0.011 is equal to one quarter plus one eighth (i.e. three eighths).

binary half adder A binary adder that can produce the sum of two inputs, producing a carry output if necessary, but cannot accept a carry input.

binary loader A short section of program code that allows programs in binary form (such as object code from a linker or assembler) to be loaded into memory.

binary mantissa The fractional part of a number (in binary form).

binary notation or **representation** Base 2 numerical system using only the digits 0 and 1.

binary number A quantity represented in base 2.

binary operation 1 An operation on two operands **2** An operation on an operand in binary form.

binary point The dot which indicates the division between the whole unit bits and the fractional part of a binary number.

binary scale The power of two associated with each bit position in a word. For example, in a four bit word, the binary scale is 1,2,4,8.

binary search or **chop** A fast search method for use on ordered lists of data (the search key is compared with the data in the middle of the list and one half is discarded, this is repeated with the remaining half until only the required data item is left).

binary sequence A series of binary digits.

binary signalling The transmission using positive and zero voltage levels to represent binary data.

binary synchronous communications (BSC) An old standard for medium/high speed data communication links.

binary system The use of binary numbers or operating with binary numbers.

binary-to-decimal conversion The process to convert a binary number into its equivalent decimal value.

binary tree A tree structure for data, where each item of data can have only two branches.

binary variable A variable that can contain either a one or zero.

bind To link and convert one or more progams in object code form into a form that can be executed. The time taken to produce actual addresses from an object code program is the **binding time.** See also **linker.**

BIOS (basic input/output system) System routines that interface between high-level program instructions and the system peripherals to control the input and output to various standard devices, this often includes controlling the screen, keyboard and disk drives.

bipolar coding A transmission method which uses alternate positive and negative voltage levels to represent a binary one, with binary zero represented by zero level.

bipolar signal The use of positive and negative voltage levels to represent the binary digits.

bipolar transistor A transistor constructed of three layers of alternating types of doped semiconductor (p-n-p or n-p-n). Each layer has a terminal labelled emitter, base and collector, usually the base signal controls the current flow between the emitter and collector.

biquinary code Decimal digits represented as two digits added together (for decimal digits less than 5, represented as 0 + the digit, for decimal digits greater than 4, represented as 5 + the digit minus 5).

bistable device A device that has two possible states: on and off. A **bistable circuit** or **multivibrator** is one which can be switched between two states. Compare with **astable.**

bit (binary digit) 1 The smallest unit in binary number notation, which can have the value 0 or 1. **2** The smallest unit of data that a system can handle.

bit addressing Selecting a register or word and examining one bit of it.

bit density The number of bits that can be recorded per unit of storage medium.

bit handling CPU commands and processes that allow bit manipulation, rotating, changing, etc.

bit manipulation The various instructions that provide functions such as examine a bit, change or set or move a bit within a word.

bit-map To define events or data using an array of single bits; this can be an image or graphics or a table of devices in use, etc. In **bit-mapped graphics** the individual pixels of an image can be controlled by changing the value of its stored bit (one is on, zero is off; in colour displays, more than one bit is used to provide control for the three colours — Red, Green, Blue).

bit pattern A certain arrangement of bits within a word, that represents a certain character or action.

bit position The place where a bit of data is located within a computer word.

bit rate A measure of the number of bits transmitted per second.

bit slice design Construction of a large word size CPU by joining a number of smaller word size blocks. For example, a bit slice design will use four four-bit word processors to construct a sixteen-bit processor.

bits per inch (bpi) The number of bits that can be recorded per inch of recording medium.

bits per second (bps) The measure of the number of binary digits transmitted every second.

bit stream A binary data sequence that does not consist of separate, distinct character codes or groups.

bit stuffing The addition of extra bits to a group of data to make up a certain length required for transmission.

bit track A track on a magnetic disk along which bits can be recorded or read back. Compare **logical track.**

black and white or **b&w** The use of shades of grey to represent colours on a monitor or display.

black level The level of a video signal that produces no luminescence on screen.

blackout or **black out** A complete loss of electrical power. Compare with **brown-out.**

black writer A laser printer where toner sticks to the points hit by the laser beam when the image drum is scanned. A black writer produces sharp edges and graphics, but large areas of black are muddy. Compare **white writer.**

blank character A character code that prints a space. (The ASCII code for a blank or space character is 32).

blanking Preventing a television signal from reaching the scanning beam on its return trace. Also called **horizontal blanking.**

blanking interval The time taken for the scanning beam in a TV to return from the end of a picture at the bottom right of the screen to top left.

blanking pulse An electrical signal used to start the blanking of a TV signal.

blank instruction A program instruction which does nothing. See also **NOP.**

blank string An empty string; a string containing spaces.

blank tape or **blank disk** Magnetic tape or disk that does not have data stored on it.

blast 1 To write data into a programmable ROM device. 2 To free sections of previously allocated memory or resources.

blast-through alphanumerics Characters that can be displayed over graphics on a videotext terminal when it is in graphics mode.

bleed off To make a line of printing or a picture run off the edge of the trimmed page.

bleep 1 An audible warning noise; a printer will make a bleep when it runs out of paper. 2 To make a bleep. See also **beep.**

blind Something which will not respond to certain codes. **Blind dialling** is the ability of a modem to dial out even if the line appears to be dead, used on certain private lines. A **blind keyboard** is one whose output is not displayed but is stored directly on magnetic tape or disk.

B-line counter An address register that is added to a reference address to provide the location to be accessed.

blinking Flashing effect caused by varying the intensity of a displayed character.

block 1 A series of items grouped together 2 A number of stored records treated as a single unit. 3 A wide printed bar. See also **building block, data block, end of block (EOB).**

block character check (BCC) An error detection method for blocks of transmitted data that uses a character word whose value is either the number of blocks transmitted or the result of a parity check.

block code An error detection and correction code for block data transmission.

block copy To duplicate a block of data into another section of memory.

block diagram A graphical representation of a system or program operation.

block error rate A number of blocks of data that contain errors compared with the total number transmitted.

block header Information at the start of a file describing content organization or characteristics.

block ignore character A symbol at the start of a block indicating that it contains corrupt data.

blocking factor The number of records in a block.

block input processing An input system that requires a whole error-free block to be received before it is processed.

block length The number of bytes of data in a block.

block list A list of the blocks and records as they are organized in a file.

block mark A code that indicates the end of a block.

block operation Processing carried out on a block of data.

block parity A parity error check on a block of data.

block synchronization The correct timing of start, stop and message bits according to a predefined protocol.

block transfer Moving large numbers of records around in memory in one go. Many CPU's have block transfer instructions which will move a block of data from area to another — this is often used for updating memory-mapped graphics displays.

bloom A bright spot on the screen of a faulty video display.

bloop To pass a magnet over a tape to erase signals which are not needed.

blow To program a PROM device with data.

blueprint A copy of an original set of specifications or design in graphical form.

blue-ribbon program A perfect program that runs first time, with no errors or bugs.

blur 1 An image in which the edges or colours are not clear. **2** To make the edges or colours of an image fuzzy.

bn see **billion**

BNF (Backus-Naur-form) A system of writing and expressing the syntax of a programming language.

board The flat insulation material on which electronic components are mounted and connected. See also **bulletin board, bus board, printed circuit board.**

BOF (beginning of file) A character or symbol that shows the start of a valid section of data.

boilerplate A final document that has been put together using standard sections of text held in a word processor. The action of putting together a final document out of various standard sections of text is called

boilerplating. Usually, the only piece of text that changes is the name and address of the recipient.

bold or **bold face** A thicker and darker form of a typeface.

bomb (Informal, of software) to fail. A system can bomb if several desk accessories or memory-resident programs are set up at the same time.

Boolean algebra or **logic** The rules set down to define, simplify and manipulate logical functions, based on statements which are true or false. See **AND, NOT, OR**

Boolean connective A symbol or character in a Boolean operation that describes the action to be performed on the operands.

Boolean operation A logical operation on a number of operands, conforming to Boolean algebra rules.

Boolean operation table A table showing two binary words (operands), the operation and the result.

Boolean operator A logical operator such as AND, OR, etc.

Boolean value One of two values, either true or false.

Boolean variable A binary word in which each bit represents true or false, using the digits 1 or 0.

boot To execute a set of instructions automatically in order to reach a required state.

boot up or **booting** The automatic execution of a set of instructions usually held in ROM when a computer is switched on.

bootleg An illegal copy of recorded material.

bootstrap (loader) A set of instructions that are executed by the computer before a program is loaded, usually to load the operating system once the computer is switched on. Compare **loader.**

borrow An operation in certain arithmetic processes, such as subtraction from a smaller number.

BOS (basic operating system) The software that controls the basic, low-level running of the hardware and file management.

Bose-Chandhuri-Hocquenghem code (BCH) An error correcting code.

bot or **BOT** see **beginning of tape**

BOT marker The section of material that marks the start of the recording area of magnetic tape.

bottom up method Combining low-level instructions to form a high-level instruction (which can then be further combined).

bounce An error of multiple key contact caused by a faulty switch. See also **de-bounce.**

boundary protection Preventing any program writing into a reserved area of memory.

boundary punctuation Punctuation which marks the beginning or end of a file.

boundary register A register in a multi-user system that contains the addresses for the limits of one user's memory allocation.

BPI or **bpi (bits per inch)** The number of bits that can be recorded per inch of recording medium.

BPS or **bps (bits per second)** The number of bits that can be transmitted per second.

bracket Printed sign that shows that an instruction or operations is to be separated.

bracket together To print brackets round several items to show that they are treated in the same way and separated from the rest of an equation or text.

branch 1 A possible path or jump from one instruction to another. 2 A line linking one or more devices to the main network. 3 To jump from one section of a program to another.

branch instruction A conditional program instruction that provides a choice of following actions depending on the outcome of a condition. In BASIC, the instruction GOTO makes the system jump to the line indicated; this is an **unconditional branch.** The instruction IF...THEN is a **conditional branch,** because the jump will only take place if the condition is met.

branchpoint The point in a program where a branch can take place.

breadboard A solderless connection board that allows prototypes of electronic circuits to be constructed quickly and easily.

break 1 Action or key pressed to stop a program execution. 2 To decipher a difficult code, such as a cipher system.

breakpoint A symbol inserted into a program which stops its execution at that point to allow registers, variables and memory locations to be examined (used when debugging a program).

breakpoint instruction or **halt** A halt command inserted in a program to stop execution temporarily, allowing the programmer to examine data and registers while debugging a program.

breakpoint symbol A special character used to provide a breakpoint in a program (a debugging program allows breakpoint symbols to be inserted, it then executes the program until it reaches one, then halts).

breezeway A signal used to separate the colour information from the horizontal synchronizing pulse in a video signal.

B register 1 An address register that is added to a reference address to provide the location to be accessed 2 A register used to extend the accumulator in multiplication and division operations.

bridge or **bridging product** 1 Matching communications equipment that makes sure that power losses are kept to a minimum. 2 Hardware or software that allows parts of an old system to be used on a new system.

bridgeware Hardware or software used to make the transfer from one computer system to another easier (by changing file format, translation, etc.).

bridging To use bridgeware to help transfer programs, data files, etc., to another system.

brightness The luminance of an object which can be seen. A control knob can allow the operator to adjust brightness and contrast of a monitor; excessive brightness of a monitor can hurt the eyes.

British Standards Institute (BSI) Organization that monitors design and safety standards in the UK.

broadband A transmission channel whose bandwidth is greater than a voice channel (allowing faster data transmission).

broadband radio A radio communications link using a broadband channel.

brown-out A power failure with low voltage level rather than no voltage at all. See also **black-out.**

browse To search through and access database material without permission.

brute force method A problem-solving method which depends on computer power rather than elegant programming techniques.

BSC (binary synchronous communications) An old standard for medium/high speed data communication links.

BSI (British Standards Institute) The organization that monitors design and safety standards in the UK.

BTAM (basic telecommunications access method) A method used to provide access (read or write operations) to a remote device.

bubble memory A method of storing binary data using the magnetic properties of certain materials, allowing very large amounts of data to be stored in primary memory.

bubble memory cassette A bubble memory device on a removable cartridge that can be inserted into a controller card (like an audio cassette) to provide high capacity, high speed, removable memory.

bubble sort A sorting method which repeatedly exchanges various pairs of data items until they are in order.

bucket A storage area containing data for an application.

buffer 1 A circuit that isolates and protects a system from damaging inputs from circuits or peripherals. **2** Temporary storage area for data waiting to be processed. **3** Using a temporary storage area to hold data until the processor or device is ready to deal with it. Buffers allow two parts of a computer system to work at different speeds (i.e. a high-speed central processing unit and a slower line printer). See also **driver.**

buffered input/output The use of a temporary storage area on input or output ports to allow slow peripherals to operate with a fast CPU.

buffering Using buffers to provide a link between slow and fast devices.

buffer register A temporary storage for data read from or being written to main memory.

buffer size The total number of characters that can be held in a buffer.

bug (Informal) an error in a computer program which makes it run incorrectly. **Bug patches** are temporary corrections made to a program or small corrections made to software by a user on the instructions of the software publisher. See also **debug.**

building block A self-contained unit that can be joined to others to form a system.

built-in A special feature that is already included in a system, such as a built-in adapter card or a built-in hard disk. A **built-in check** is an error detection and validation check which is carried out automatically on received data. The opposite is **add on.**

bulk erase To erase a complete magnetic disk or tape in one action.

bulk storage medium A medium that is able to store large amounts of data in a convenient size and form, such as magnetic tape.

bulk update terminal A device used by an information provider to prepare videotext pages off-line, then transmit them rapidly to the main computer.

bulletin board system (BBS) An information and message database accessible by modem and computer link.

bundle A number of optic fibres gathered together.

bundled software Programs which are included in the price of a computer hardware package.

bureau An office which specializes in keyboarding data or processing batches of data for other small companies.

burner A device which burns in programs onto PROM chips.

burn-in A heat test for electronic components.

burn in 1 To mark a monitor screen after displaying a high brightness image for too long. 2 To write data into a PROM chip.

burn out Excess heat or incorrect use that causes an electronic circuit * device to fail.

burst A short isolated sequence of transmitted signals.

burst mode Data transmission using intermittent bursts of data.

burster A machine used to separate the sheets of continuous fanfold paper.

bus A communication link consisting of a set of leads or wires which connects different parts of a computer hardware system, and over which data is transmitted and received by various circuits in the system.

bus address line A wire which carries one bit of an address word.

bus arbitration The protocol and control of transmission over a bus that ensures fair usage by several users.

bus board PCB containing conducting paths for all the computer signals (for the address, data and control buses).

bus control line A wire which carries one bit of a control word.

bus data line A wire which carries one bit of a data word.

bus driver High-powered transistor or amplifier that can provide enough power to transmit signals to a number of devices.

bus master A data source that controls the bus whilst transmitting (bus master status moves between sending stations).

bus network A network of computers where the machines are connected to a central bus unit which transmits the messages it receives.

bus slave A data sink which receives data from a bus master.

bus structure The way in which buses are organized, whether serial, parallel, bidirectional, etc.

business computer A powerful small computer which is programmed for special business tasks. It will run a **business system** or **business package,** a set of programs adapted for business use (such as payroll, invoicing, customers file, etc.).

busy An electrical signal indicating that a device is not ready to receive data. For example, when a busy line goes low, a printer will accept more data.

bypass An alternative route around a component or device, so that it is not used. There may be an automatic bypass around faulty equipment.

byte A group of bits or binary digits (usually eight) which a computer operates on as a single unit.

byte addresses The location of data bytes in memory.

byte machine A variable word length computer.

byte manipulation Moving, editing and changing the contents of a byte.

byte serial transmission or **mode** The transmission of bytes of data sequentially, the individual bits of which can be sent in a serial or parallel way.

C

C 1 A high level programming language developed mainly for writing structured systems programs. 2 The hexadecimal (base 16) number equivalent to decimal 12.

cache or **cache memory** A section of high-speed memory which stores data that the computer can access quickly. File access time is much quicker if the most frequently used data is stored in cache memory.

CAD (computer aided design or **computer assisted design)** The use of a computer and graphics terminal to help a designer in his work.

CAD/CAM (CAD/computer aided manufacture) The interaction between computers used for designing and those for manufacturing a product.

CAI (computer aided instruction or **computer assisted instruction)** The use of a computer to assist pupils in learning a subject.

CAL (computer aided learning or **computer assisted learning)** Use of a computer to assist pupils in learning a subject.

calibration Comparing the signal from an input with a known scale to provide a standardized reading.

call To transfer control to a separate program or routine from a main program. After an input is received, the first function is called up; the subroutine call instruction should be made at this point. Many programs use a separate routine to see if the user has pressed any keys on the keyboard.

call accepted signal The signal sent by a device to show that it is willing to accept a caller's data.

call control signal The signal necessary to establish and end a call.

call duration The length of time spent between starting and ending a call.

calling A signal to request attention, sent from a terminal or device to the main computer.

calling sequence The series of program commands required to direct execution to or back from a subroutine.

call instruction A programming instruction that directs control to a routine (after saving the program counter contents to show the return instruction where to return to in the main program).

call up To ask for information stored in a backing store to be retrieved and displayed. For example, an operator might want to call up customers' addresses on his monitor.

CAM 1 (computer aided manufacture or **computer assisted manufacturing)** The use of a computer to control machinery or assist in a manufacturing process. **2 (content addressable memory)** Memory that is addressed and accessed by its contents rather than a location.

Cambridge ring A local area networking standard used for connecting several devices and computers together in a ring with simple cable links.

cameo Reversed out characters, that is, white on a black background.

cancel To stop a process or instruction before it has been fully executed.

cancel character A control code used to indicate that the last data transmitted was incorrect. The software will automatically send a cancel character after any error.

canonical schema A model of a database that is independent of the hardware or software available that it will run on.

capability list A list of operations that can be carried out.

capacitance The ability of a component to store electrical charge.

capacitor An electronic component that can store charge. They are usually in the form of **ceramic capacitors,** which are general-purpose, non-polar, small capacitors made from ceramic materials.

capacitor microphone A microphone that uses variations in capacitance due to sound pressure to generate an electrical signal.

capacitor storage A device using capacitative properties of a material to store data.

capacity 1 The amount which can be produced or amount of work which can be done. **Channel capacity** is the maximum rate for data transmission over a channel. **2** (Also **storage capacity**) The amount of storage space available in a system or in RAM or on a disk or tape.

capitals (also informally **caps**) Large form of letters (A,B,C,D, etc.) as opposed to lower case (a,b,c,d, etc.).

caps lock A key on a keyboard or typewriter that allows all characters to be entered as capitals. Often the caps lock key has an LED that lights up when the caps lock is on.

capstan A device in a tape player which ensures that the tape moves at a constant speed.

caption A note or explanation under or next to a picture or diagram

capture 1 (Also **data capture**) The action of obtaining data (either by keyboarding or by scanning or often automatically from a recording device or peripheral). **2** To take data into a computer system. Software allows captured images to be edited; scanners usually capture images at a resolution of 300 dots per inch (dpi).

card 1 A punched card. **2** A sheet of insulating material on which electronic components can be mounted.

card cage The metal supporting frame for circuit boards. See also **rack.**

card code The combination of punched holes that represent characters on a punched card.

card column A line of punched information about one character, parallel to the shorter side of the card.

card edge connector A series of metal tracks ending at the edge and on the surface of a card, allowing it to be plugged into an edge connector to provide electrical contact (for data transmission, etc.).

card extender A card containing only conducting tracks, inserted between a motherboard connector and an expansion card, allowing the expansion card to be worked on and examined easily, outside the card cage.

card feed A device which draws punched cards into a reader automatically.

card field The part of a card column reserved for one type of data.

card format The way in which columns and rows are arranged to represent data fields or characters in a punched card.

card frame or **card chassis** A frame containing a motherboard into which printed circuit boards can be plugged to provide a flexible system. See also **rack.**

card image A section of memory that contains an exact representation of the information on a card.

card index A series of cards with information written on them, kept in special order so that the information can be found easily.

card loader A short program that transfers data from a punched card into main memory.

card punch (CP) A machine that punches the holes in punched cards.

card reader or **punched card reader** A device that transforms data on a punched card to a form that can be recognized by the computer.

card row The punch positions parallel to the longer edge of a card.

carriage The mechanical section of a typewriter or printer that correctly feeds or moves the paper that is being printed.

carriage control Codes that control the movements of a printer carriage. For example, carriage control codes can be used to move the paper forward two lines between each line of text.

carriage return (CR) A code, signal or key to move to the beginning of the next line of print or display.

carrier Continuous high frequency waveform that can be modulated by a signal. Data is transmitted in a modem and in many local area networks by modulating a continuous carrier signal.

carrier sense multiple access - collision detection (CSMA-CD) A network communications protocol that prevents two sources transmitting at the same time by waiting for a quiet moment, then attempting to transmit.

carrier signalling Simple data transmission (by switching on and off a carrier signal according to binary data). This is used for low-speed transmissions — usually up to 300bps. High speed transmission requires more sophisticated techniques, such as phase or quadrature modulation.

carrier system A method of transmitting several different signals on one channel by using different carrier frequencies.

carrier wave The waveform used as a carrier.

carry 1 To move (something such as data) from one place to another. **2** An (extra) digit due to an addition result being greater than the number base used. For example, when 5 and 7 are added, there is an answer of 2 and a carry which is put in the next column, giving 12. A **carry bit** or **flag** is an indicator in a status or flag byte which shows that a carry has occurred. The **carry complete signal** from an adder circuit indicates that all carry operations have been completed. A **carry look ahead** can predict if a carry will be generated by a sum and add it in, removing the delay found in an adder with ripple-through carry. **Carry time** is the time it takes to transfer a carry digit to the next higher digit position. See also **cascade carry.**

cartesian coordinates A positional system that uses two axes at right angles to represent a point which is located with two numbers, giving a position on each axis.

cartesian structure A data structure whose size is fixed and the elements are in a linear order. Compare with **polar coordinates.**

cartridge A removable cassette, containing a disk or tape or program or data (usually stored in ROM). A drive system which uses a disk or tape in a cartridge is called a **cartridge drive. Cartridge fonts** are contained in a ROM cartridge which can be plugged into a printer, providing a choice of new typefaces, but still limited to the typefaces and styles included in the cartridge. Compare **resident fonts.**

cascade carry A carry generated in an adder from an input carry signal.

cascade connection A number of devices or circuits arranged in series, the output of one driving the input of the next.

cascade control A system made up of a series of control units, each controlling the next.

case change A key used to change from upper to lower case on a keyboard.

cassette A standard-sized container used to store and protect magnetic tape, used for example, to back up the information from a computer.

cassette recorder A machine to transfer audio signals onto magnetic tape.

cassette tape A narrow reel of magnetic tape housed in a solid case for protection. Using cassette tape allows data to be stored for future retrieval; it is used instead of a disk system on small computers or as a slow, serial access, high-capacity back-up medium for large systems.

CAT 1 (computer aided or **assisted training)** Using a computer to demonstrate to and assist pupils in learning a skill. **2 (computer aided** or **assisted testing)** Using a computer to test equipment or programs to find any faults.

catalogue To make a catalogue of items stored, as for example, a catalogue of all terminals, with their location, call sign and attribute table.

catastrophe A serious fault, error or breakdown of equipment, usually leading to serious damage and shutdown of a system.

catastrophic error An error that causes a program to crash or files to be accidentally erased.

catastrophic failure A complete system failure or crash.

catena 1 A number of items in a chained list. **2** A series of characters in a word.

catenate To join together two or more sets of data.

cathode The negative electrical terminal of a device or battery. The opposite is **anode.**

cathode ray tube (CRT) A device used for displaying characters or figures or graphical information, similar to a TV set. A cathode ray tube has a long persistence phosphor screen coating that retains an image for a long time.

Cathode ray tubes are used in television sets, computer monitors and VDUs; a CRT consists of a vacuum tube, one end of which is flat and coated with phosphor, the other end containing an electron beam source. Characters or graphics are visible when the controllable electron beam strikes the phosphor, causing it to glow.

CBL (computer based learning) A learning process mainly using a computer.

CBMS (computer based message system) The use of a computer system to allow users to send and receive messages from other users (usually in-house). See also **BBS**.

CBT (computer based training) Using a computer system to train students.

CCD see **charge coupled device**

CCD memory Capacitors used with MOS transistors to store data, allowing either serial or random access.

CCP (command console processor) Software which interfaces between a user's terminal and system BIOS.

CCU see **communications control unit**

CD see **compact disk**

CD-ROM (compact disk-read only memory) A small plastic disk that is used as a high capacity ROM device, data is stored in binary form as holes etched into the metal-coated surface which are then read by a laser.

cell 1 A single function or number in a spreadsheet program. **2** A single memory location, capable of storing a data word, accessed by an individual address.

cellar Temporary storage for data or registers or tasks, in which items are added and retrieved from the same end of the list in a LIFO order.

central computer see **host computer**

centralized data processing Data processing facilities located in a centralized place that can be accessed by other users.

centralized computer network A network with processing capabilities provided by a central computer.

central memory (CM) The area of memory whose locations can be directly and immediately addressed by the CPU.

central processing element (CPE) A short (2, 4 or 8 bit) word length module that can be used to produce large word CPUs using bit slice techniques.

central processing unit (CPU) or **central processor** A group of circuits which perform the basic functions of a computer, made up of three parts: the control unit, the arithmetic and logic unit and the input/output unit.

central terminal A terminal which controls the communications between a central or host computer and remote terminals.

centre 1 To align the read/write head correctly on a magnetic disk or tape. **2** To place a piece of text in the centre of the paper or display screen.

centre holes Locating holes punched along the centre of paper tape.

centre operator A person who looks after central computer operations.

centre sprocket feed The centre sprocket holes that line up with coding hole positions on punched tape.

Centronics interface A parallel printer interface devised by Centronics Inc. Videotexncharacter standard defined by the Conference of European Post Telephone and Telegraph.

ceramic capacitor see **capacitor**

CGA (colour graphics adapter) A popular microcomputer medium-resolution colour display system. See also **EGA.**

chad Waste material produced from holes punched in tape or card.

chadded or **chadless tape** Punched tape that retains chad by not punching holes through completely.

chain 1 A series of files or data items linked sequentially, or a series of instructions to be executed sequentially. A **command chain** is a list of commands in a file executed sequentially by a batch mode system. **2** A physical link, such as a **daisy chain,** a method of connecting equipment with a single cable passing from one machine or device to the next (rather than separate cables to each device). **2** To link files or data items in series by storing a pointer to the next file or item at each entry. For example, more than 1,000 articles or chapters can be chained together when printing. See also **catena.**

chain code A series of words, each word being derived (usually shifted by one bit) from the previous word.

chain delivery mechanism A mechanical system to move paper from machine to machine.

chained or **threaded file** A file in which an entry will contain data and an address to the next entry that has the same data content (allowing rapid retrieval of all identical data records).

chained list A list in which each element contains data and an address to the next element in the list.

chained record A data record in a chained file.

chaining To execute a very large program by executing small segments of it at a time; this allows programs larger than memory capacity to be run.

chaining search A search of a file of elements arranged in a chained list.

chain list A list of data with each piece of information providing an address for the next consecutive item in the list.

chain printer A printer whose characters are located on a continuous belt.

change dump A printout of locations where data has been changed.

change file A file containing records that are to be used to update a master file.

change over To switch from one computer system to another.

change record A record containing new data which is to be used to update a master record.

change tape Magnetic tape containing recent changes or transactions to records which is used to update a master file.

channel A physical connection between two points that allows data to be transmitted (such as a link between a CPU and a peripheral).

channel capacity The maximum rate of data transmission over a channel.

channel command An instruction to a channel or control unit, providing control information such as data selection or routes.

channel isolation The separation of channels measured as the amount of crosstalk between two channels (low crosstalk is due to good channel isolation).

channel overload The transmission of data at a rate greater than the channel capacity.

channel synchronizer An interface between a central computer and peripherals, providing a channel, channel command interpretation and status signals from the peripherals.

channel queue 1 A queue of requests to use a channel. **2** A queue of data that has yet to be sent over a channel.

channel-to-channel connection A direct link between the main I/O channels of two computers, allowing high speed data transfer.

chapter 1 A section of a main program that can be executed in its own right, without the rest of the main program being required. **2** A sequence of frames on a video disk.

character A graphical symbol which appears as a printed or displayed mark, such as one of the letters of the alphabet, a number or a punctuation mark. A **cancel character** is a control code used to indicate that the last data transmitted was incorrect. A **check character** is an additional character inserted into transmitted data to serve as an error detection check, its value is dependent on the text.

character assembly The method of designing characters with pixels on a computer screen.

character blink A character whose intensity is switched on and off (as an indicator).

character block The pattern of dots that will make up a character on a screen * printer.

character byte A byte of data containing the character code and any error check bits.

character check A check digit or operation, made to ensure that a character code protocol and format are correct.

character code A system in which each character is represented by a unique number. The ASCII code is the most frequently used character coding system.

character density The number of characters that can be stored or displayed per unit area.

character display A device that displays data in alphanumeric form.

character fill Writing one character to every location within an area of memory (for clearing and resetting the memory).

character generator ROM that provides the display circuits with a pattern of dots which represent the character (block). The ROM used as a character generator can be changed to provide different fonts.

character machine A computer in which the number of bits which make up a word is variable, and varies according to the type of data.

character orientated A computer that addresses character locations rather than words.

character printer A device that prints characters one at a time; a daisy wheel printer is a character printer.

character recognition A system that optically reads written or printed characters into a computer, using various algorithms to ensure that characters are correctly recognized. See also **OCR.**

character repertoire A list of all the characters that can be displayed or printed.

character representation The combination of bits used for each character code.

character rounding Process of making a displayed character more pleasant to look at (within the limits of pixel size) by making sharp corners and edges appear smooth.

character set A list of all the characters that can be displayed or printed.

character string Storage allocated for a series of alphanumeric characters. Compare with **numeric string.**

characters per inch (cpi) The number of printed characters which fit within the space of one inch.

characters per second (cps) The number of characters which (something) can transmit or print per second.

characteristic 1 A value of exponent in a floating point number. For example, the floating point number 1.345×10^3, has a characteristic of 3. **Characteristic overflow** is an exponent value of a floating point number that is greater than the maximum allowable. **2** The measurements or properties of a component.

charge 1 The number of or excess of or lack of electrons in a material or component. **2** To supply a device with an electric charge.

charge-coupled device (CCD) An electronic device operated by charge.

charge-coupled device memory Capacitors used (with MOS transistors) to store data, allowing serial and random access.

chart A diagram showing information as a series of lines or blocks, etc. see also **bar chart.**

chassis A metal frame that houses the circuit boards together with the wiring and sockets required in a computer system or other equipment. See also **rack.**

check 1 A short fault or pause in a process (that does not stop the process). **2** A verification. A **character check** checks that a character code protocol and format are correct.

check bit One bit of a binary word that is used to provide a parity check.

check character An additional character inserted into transmitted text to serve as an error detection check for the text, its value is dependent on the text.

check digit or **number** An additional digit inserted into transmitted text to monitor and correct errors.

checkerboarding (Virtual page) memory organization that has resulted in odd pages or spread-out pages or segments of memory being filled, wasting memory by leaving unusable gaps inbetween.

check indicator Hardware or software device that shows that received text is not correct and a check has failed.

checking program Software that finds errors in program or data syntax, format and coding.

check key A series of characters derived from a text used to check for and correct errors.

check point A point within a program where data and program status can be recorded or displayed.

check point dump A printout of data and program status at a check point.

check register A temporary storage for received data before it is checked against the same data received via another path or method.

checksum or **check total** A program which checks that data is correct, by summing it and comparing the sum with a stored value. The data must have been corrupted if the checksum is different.

chip A device consisting of a small piece of a crystal of a semiconductor onto which are etched or manufactured (by doping) a number of components such as transistors, resistors and capacitors, which together perform a function.

chip architecture The design and layout of components on a chip.

chip card A plastic card with a memory and microprocessor device embedded in it, so that it can be used for electronic funds transfer or identification of a user.

chip count The number of chips on a PCB or in a device.

chip select line A connection to a chip that will enable it to function when a signal is present.

chip-set A number of chips which together will carry out a function.

chop see **binary**

chord keying The action of pressing two or more keys at the same time to perform a function. If, for example, the operator wants to access a second window, he will press CONTROL and F2; pressing SHIFT and character delete keys will delete a line of text.

chronological order The arrangement of records or files according to their dates.

CIM 1 (computer input from microfilm) The coordinated use of microfilm for computer data storage and the method of reading the data. **2 (computer integrated manufacture)** The use of computers in every aspect of design and manufacturing.

cipher A system of transforming a message into an unreadable form with a secret key (the message can be read normally after it has passed through the cipher a second time).

cipher key A secret sequence of characters used with a cipher system to provide a unique ciphertext.

cipher system A formula used to transform text into a secret form.

ciphertext The data output from a cipher. The opposite is **plaintext.**

CIR (current instruction register) CPU register that stores the instruction that is currently being executed.

circuit A number of electronic components connected together in such a way as to carry out a particular function.

circuit board or **card** An insulating board used to hold components which are then connected together electrically to form a circuit.

circuit capacity The information carrying capacity of a particular circuit.

circuit diagram The graphical description of a circuit.

circuitry A collection of circuits.

circular buffer A computer-based queue that uses two markers, for top and bottom of the line of stored items (the markers move as items are read from or written to the stack).

circular file A data file that has no visible beginning or end, each item points to the location of the next item with the last pointing back to the first.

circular list A list in which each element contains data and an address to the next element in the list with the last item pointing back to the first.

circular shift The rotation of bits in a word with the previous last bit inserted in the first bit position.

circulating register A shift register whose output is fed back to its input to form a closed loop.

circulating storage A storage device that maintains stored data as a series of pulses, that move along the length of the medium, being regenerated and re-input when they reach the end. Circulating storage devices are not often used now, being slow (serial access) and bulky: typical devices are acoustic or mercury delay lines.

CISC (complex instruction set computer) CPU design whose instruction set contains a number of long, complex instructions, that makes program writing easier, but reduces execution speed. Compare with **RISC.**

cladding A protective material surrounding a conducting core. If the cladding is chipped, fibre-optic cable will not functon well.

clamp To find the voltage of a signal.

clapper The mechanical part of a dot matrix printer that drives the printing needles onto the ribbon to print a character on the paper.

clean disk A disk which is not dirty or which has no errors or or which has no programs.

clean machine A computer that contains only the minimum of ROM based code to boot its system from disk, any languages required must be loaded in.

clean page A page (of memory) that has not been changed since it was read.

clear 1 To wipe out or erase or set to zero a computer file or variable * section of memory. 2 To release a communications link when transmissions have finished. **Clear to send (CTS)** is the RS232C signal that a line or device is ready for data transmission.

click 1 A short sound, often used to indicate that a key has been pressed. 2 The action of pressing a key or button on a keyboard. 3 To press a key or a button on a keyboard or the mouse. A designer can use a mouse to enlarge a frame by clicking inside its border.

clock 1 A machine which shows the time. Most micros have built-in clocks which can appear in the corner of the screen. 2 A circuit that generates pulses used to synchronize equipment. 2 To synchronize signals or circuits with a clock pulse.

clock cycle The time period between two consecutive clock pulses.

clocked signals Signals that are synchronized with a clock pulse.

clock pulse A regular pulse used for timing or synchronizing purposes.

clock rate The number of pulses that a clock generates every second.

clock track A line of marks on a disk or tape which provides data about the read head location.

clone A computer or circuit that behaves in the same way as the original it was copied from. The computer with the greatest number of clones is the IBM Personal Computer. Clones often work in the same way, use the same software, accept the same add-in hardware as the original, but cost less.

close To shut down access to a file or disk drive. The instruction is **close file.**

closed loop A number of computer instructions that are repeated.

closed subroutine A number of computer instructions in a program that can be called at any time, with control being returned on completion to the next instruction in the main program.

closed user group (CUG) Restricting the entry to a database or bulletin board or system (about or on a certain topic or subject) to certain known and registered users, usually by means of a password. See also **user group.**

cluster A number of terminals or stations or devices or memory locations grouped together in one place, controlled by a **cluster controller.**

clustering A series of elements, occurring in a sequential line within a hash table.

CM (central memory) An area of memory whose locations can be directly and immediately addressed by the CPU.

CMI see **computer managed instruction**

CML see **computer managed learning**

CMOS (complementary metal oxide semiconductor) An integrated circuit design and construction method (using a pair of complementary p- and n-type transistors). The final package uses very low power but is relatively slow and sensitive to static electricity as compared to TTL integrated circuits; their main use is in portable computers where battery power is being used.

CNC (computer numeric control) A machine operated automatically by computer. See also **numerical control.**

coalesce To merge two or more files.

co-axial cable A cable made up of a central core, surrounded by an insulating layer then a second shielding conductor. Co-axial cable is used for high frequency, low loss applications such as TV aerials.

COBOL (Common Ordinary Business Oriented Language) A programming language mainly used for writing business applications.

code 1 The rules used to convert instructions or data from one form to another. **Computer code** or **machine code** is a programming language that consists of commands in binary code that can be directly understood by the central processing unit, without the need for translation. **2** A sequence of computer instructions. **3** A system of signs or numbers or letters which mean something. A **chain code** is a series of words, each word being derived (usually shifted by one bit) from the previous word. A **cyclic code** is a coding system in which the binary representation of decimal numbers changes by only one bit at a time from one number to the next. **4** To convert instructions or data into another form. **5** To write a program in a programming language.

code conversion The rules used to change characters coded in one form, to another.

code area A section of main memory in which program instructions are stored.

code line One written or displayed computer program instruction.

code element A voltage or signal used to represent binary digits.

coercivity The magnetic field required to remove any flux saturation effects from a material.

coherent Referring to waveforms which are all in phase. For example, a laser produces **coherent light. A coherent bundle** is a number of optical fibres, grouped together so that they are all the same length and produce coherent signals from either end.

coincidence circuit or **element** An electronic circuit that produces an output signal when two inputs occur simultaneously or two binary words are equal. See also **AND.**

cold fault A computer fault or error that occurs as soon as it is switched on.

cold standby A backup system that will allow the equipment to continue running, but with the loss of any volatile data. Compare with **hot, warm standby.**

cold start Switching on a computer or to run a program from its original start point. Compare **warm start.**

collate To compare and put items in order.

collect transfer To load a register with bits from a number of different locations.

collision detection Detecting and reporting of the coincidence of two actions or events (usually on a network or communications line or cache). **CSMA-CD (carrier sense multiple access-collision detection)** is a network communications protocol that prevents two sources transmitting at the same time by waiting for a quiet moment on the channel, then attempting to transmit.

colon A printing sign (:), which shows a break in a string of words. A **semicolon** (;) marks the end of a program line or statement in some languages (such as C and Pascal).

colour cell The smallest area on a CRT screen that can display colour information.

colour display A display device able to represent characters or graphics in colour.

colour graphics adapter (CGA) A popular microcomputer colour display system. See also **EGA.**

colour monitor A screen that can display information in colour (particularly useful for graphics and games).

column A series of characters, printed one under the other. A **card column** is a line of punched information about one character, parallel to the shorter side of the card. **Column parity** is a parity check carried out on every punched card or tape column.

columnar graph A graph on which values are shown as vertical or horizontal bars.

COM (computer output on microfilm) Recording the output from a computer directly onto microfilm.

COMAL (Common Algorithmic Language) A structured programming language similar to BASIC.

combinational circuit An electronic circuit consisting of a number of connected components.

combinational logic A logic function made up from a number of separate logic gates.

combined head A transducer that can read and write data from the surface of a magnetic storage medium, such as a floppy disk.

combined station A high-level data link control station that processes commands and responses.

combined symbol matching (CSM) An efficient optical character recognition system.

command 1 An electrical pulse or signal that will start or stop a process. **2** A word or phrase which is recognized by a computer system and starts or terminates an action. For example, the command to execute a program may be RUN. A **channel command** instructs a channel or control unit, providing control actions such as data filtering or routes. A **command code** starts or stops an instruction or action in a CPU.

command console processor (CCP) A software interface between a user's terminal and the BIOS of a computer.

command control language A programming language that allows equipment to be easily controlled.

command-driven program A program which requires the user to enter instructions at every stage. Compare with **menu-driven.**

command file A sequence of frequently used commands stored in a file. See also **batch file.**

command file processor An execution of a user's command file, allowing the user to create a customized simple operating environment or to carry out a series of frequently used commands.

command interface A cue and prompts used by a program to inform and accept from a user required inputs (this can be user-friendly such as a WIMP environment, or not so friendly, such as a question mark).

command language A programming language made up of procedures for various tasks, that can be called up by a series of commands.

command line A program line that contains a command instruction.

command prompt A symbol displayed to indicate a command is expected.

command register A register that stores the instruction to be carried out or that is being processed.

command window An area of a screen where commands are entered.

comment Helpful notes in a program to guide the user. For example, BASIC allows comments to be written after a REM instruction.

comment field A section of a command line in an assembly language program that is not executed but provides notes and comments.

common channel signalling One channel used as a communications link to a number of devices or circuits.

common hardware Hardware items that can be used for a variety of tasks.

common language Data or program instructions in a standardized form that can be understood by other processors or compilers/interpreters.

common mode noise External noise on all power and ground lines.

Common Ordinary Business Oriented Language (COBOL) A programming language mainly used in business applications.

common software Useful (routines) that can be used by any program.

common storage area Memory or storage area used by more than one program. A file server memory is mainly common storage area, with a section reserved for the operating system.

communicating word processor A word processor workstation which is also able to transmit and receive data (using a modem).

communications The process by which data is transmitted and received, by means of telephones, satellites, radio or any medium capable of carrying signals.

communications buffer A terminal or modem that is able to store transmitted data.

communications channel A physical link over which data can be transmitted.

communications computer A computer used to control data transmission in a network.

communications control unit An electronic device that controls data transmission and routes in a network.

communications executive The main set of programs that ensure that protocol, format and device and line handlers are correct for the type of device or line in use.

communications interface adapter An electronic circuit that allows a computer to communicate with a modem.

communications link A physical path that joins a transmitter to a receiver.

communications link control A processor that provides various handshaking and error detection functions for a number of links between devices.

communications network A group of devices such as terminals and printers that are interconnected with a central computer, allowing the rapid and simple transfer of data.

communications network processor The processor that provides various interfacing and management services, such as buffering or code conversion, between a computer and communications link control.

communications port A connection to a computer's input/output port, allowing a device to communicate with it.

compact cassette Magnetic recording tape contained inside a standard plastic box, used in home personal computers for data storage.

compact code The minimum number of program instructions required to perform a task.

compact disk (CD) A small, metal coated plastic disk that contains audio signals in digital form etched onto the surface.

compact disk player A machine that reads the digital data from the surface of a CD and converts it back to its original form.

compact disk ROM (CD-ROM) A small plastic disk that is used as a high capacity ROM device, data is stored in binary form as holes etched on the metal-coated surface which are then read by a laser. A compact disk ROM can store as much data as a dozen hard disks.

compacting algorithm A formula used for reducing the amount of space required by text.

companding (compressing and expanding) Two processes which reduce or compact data before transmission * storage then restore packed data to its original form.

compandor (compressor/expander) A device used for companding signals.

comparator A logical device whose output is true if there is a difference between two inputs.

compatible 1 Two hardware or software devices that function correctly together. Hardware is often designed to be IBM-compatible. **2** A hardware or software device that functions correctly with other equipment or is a clone.

compatibility (of two hardware or software devices) The ability to function together. By conforming to the standards of another manufacturer or organization, compatibility of hardware or software allows programs or hardware to be interchanged with no modifications.

compilation The translation of an encoded source program into machine code. A **compilation error** is a syntax error found during compilation. **Compilation time** is the length of time it takes for a computer to compile a program. Compare with **decompilation.**

compile To convert a high level language program into a machine code program that can be executed by itself.

compile and go A computer program not requiring operator interaction that will load, compile and execute a high level language program.

compile phase The time during a program run, when the instructions are compiled.

compiler (program) A piece of software that converts an encoded program into a machine code program. A **cross-compiler** compiles programs for one computer whilst running on another. Compare with **interpreter.**

compiler diagnostics Features in a compiler that help the programmer to find any faults.

compiler language A high-level language (such as C, Pascal) that will convert a source program that follows the language syntax into a machine code version, then run it.

complement 1 The inversion of a binary digit. **2** The result after subtracting a number from one less than the radix. The complement is found by changing the 1's to 0's and 0's to 1's. **3** To invert a binary digit. A **complemented digit** has had a complement performed on it.

complementary operation A logical operation that results in the logical NOT of a function.

complementary metal oxide semiconductor (CMOS) An integrated circuit design and construction method (using a pair of complementary p- and n-type transistors).

complementation A number system used to represent positive and negative numbers.

complete operation An operation that retrieves the necessary operands from memory, performs the operation, returns the results and operands to memory and reads the next instruction to be processed.

complex instruction set computer (CISC) CPU design whose instruction set contains a number of long, complex instructions, that makes programming easier, but reduces execution speed. Compare **reduced instruction set computer (RISC)**.

complexity measure A measure of the system resources used in an operation or job.

component 1 A piece of machinery or section which will be put into a final product. **2** An electronic device that affects an electrical signal.

component density The number of electronic components per unit area on a PCB. Component density has increased as production has become more expert, and can be so high, that no expansion connectors can be fitted.

component error An error introduced by a malfunctioning device or component rather than incorrect programming.

composite circuit An electronic circuit made up of a number of smaller circuits and components.

composite video signal A single video signal containing synchronizing pulse and video signal in a modulated form.

compound logical element A logical circuit or function that produces an output from a number of inputs.

compound statement A number of program instructions in one line of program.

compress To squeeze something to fit into a smaller space.

compression Varying the gain of a device depending on input level to maintain an output signal within certain limits.

compressor 1 An electronic circuit which compresses a signal. **2** A program or device that provides data compression.

compute To calculate or to do calculations.

computational error A mistake made in calculating.

computer A machine that receives or stores or processes data very quickly according to a stored program.

computer-aided or **computer-assisted** Using a computer to make work easier. This is done in several ways: **computer-aided** or **assisted design (CAD)** uses computers and graphics terminals to help designers in their work. **Computer-aided** or **assisted engineering (CAE)** uses computers to help engineers solve problems or calculate design or product specifications. **Computer-aided** or **assisted instruction (CAI)** uses computers to assist teachers in teaching a subject and **computer-aided** or **assisted learning (CAL)** does the same to assist pupils to learn a subject. **Computer-aided** or **assisted manufacture (CAM)** uses computers to control machinery or to assist in a manufacturing process. In **computer-aided** or **assisted testing (CAT)** computers test equipment or programs to find any faults. **Computer-aided** or **assisted training (CAT)** uses computers to demonstrate to and assist pupils in learning a skill.

computer animation Using a computer to display a series of generated images displayed in sequence to simulate motion.

computer applications The tasks and uses that a computer can carry out in a particular field or job.

computer architecture 1 The layout and interconnection of a computer's internal hardware and the logical relationships between CPU, memory and I/O devices. **2** A way in which the CPU, terminals, printers and network connections are arranged.

computer-based learning (CBL) Learning mainly using a computer.

computer-based message system (CBMS) The use of a computer system to allow users to send and receive messages from other users (usually in-house).

computer-based training (CBT) The use of a computer system to train students.

computer bureau An office which offers to do work on its computers for companies which do not have their own computers.

computer code A programming language that consists of commands in binary code that can be directly understood by the central processing unit, without the need for translation.

computer conferencing Connecting a number of computers or terminals together to allow a group of users to communicate.

computer crime Theft, fraud or other crimes involving computers.

computer dating The use of a computer to match single people who may want to get married.

computer department A department in a company which manages the company's computers.

computer engineer A person who maintains or programs or designs computer equipment.

computer error A mistake made by a computer.

computer file A section of information on a computer (such as the payroll, list of addresses, customer accounts).

computer generations A way of defining the advances in the field of computing. The development of computers has been divided into a series of "generations": **first generation:** computers constructed using valves having limited storage; **second generation:** computers where transistors were used in construction; **third generation:** use of integrated circuits in construction; **fourth generation:** most often used at present, using low cost memory and IC packages; **fifth generation:** future computers using very fast processors, large memory and allowing direct human input/output (speech, etc.).

computer graphics Information represented graphically on a computer display.

computer image processing Analysis of information in an image, usually by electronic means or using a computer, also used for recognition of objects in an image.

computer independent language A programming language that will operate on any computer that has a correct compiler or interpreter.

computer input from microfilm (CIM) The use of microfilm for computer data storage, and the method of reading the data.

computer-integrated manufacturing (CIM) The coordinated use of computers in every aspect of design and manufacturing.

computer-integrated systems The coordinated use of computers and other related equipment in a process. Computer-integrated systems may, for example, allow both batch pagination of very long documents with alteration of individual pages.

computerize To change from a manual system to one using computers, such as stock control or an invoicing system.

computerization The action of introducing a computer system or of changing from a manual to a computer system.

computer language A system of words or symbols which allows communication with computers (such as one that allows computer instructions to be entered as words which are easy to understand, and then translates them into machine code). There are three main types of computer languages: machine code, assembly language, and high-level and low-level languages. **Assembly language** uses mnemonics to represent machine code instructions. **Machine code** is the basic binary patterns that instruct the processor to perform various tasks. A **high-level language (HLL)** is a language that is easy to learn and allows the user to write programs using words and commands that are easy to understand

and look like English words, the program is then translated into machine code, with one HLL instruction often representing more than one machine code instruction. A **low-level language (LLL)** is a language which is fast, but long and complex to program in, where each instruction represents a single machine code instruction. The higher the level the language is, the easier it is to program and understand, but the slower it is to execute. The following are the commonest high-level languages: ADA, ALGOL, APL, BASIC, C, COBOL, COMAL, CORAL, FORTH, FORTRAN, LISP, LOGO, PASCAL, PL/1, POP-2, PROLOG.

computer listing A printout of a list of items taken from data stored in a computer.

computer literacy Understanding the basic principles of computers, related expressions and concepts, and being able to use computers for programming or applications.

computer-literate A person who is able to understand how to use a computer, the expressions and concepts used.

computer logic The way in which the various sections of the CPU, memory and I/O are arranged (in hardware).

computer mail or **electronic mail** Messages sent between users of a bulletin board or network.

computer-managed instruction (CMI) Using a computer to assist students in learning a subject.

computer-managed learning (CML) Using a computer to teach students and assess their progress.

computer manager A person in charge of a computer department.

computer network A number of computers, terminals and peripherals connected together to allow communications between each.

computer numeric control (CNC) The control of a machine by computer.

computer office system Computer and related peripherals used for office tasks (filing, word processing, etc.).

computer operator A person who operates a computer.

computer organization see **computer architecture**

computer output Data or information produced after processing by a computer.

computer output on microfilm (COM) Information output from a computer, stored directly onto microfilm.

computer power A measure of speed and capacity of a computer (several tests exist, such as FLOPS or benchmark timings).

computer program A series of instructions to a computer, telling it to do a particular piece of work.

computer programmer A person who writes computer programs.

computer-readable codes Codes which can be read and understood by a computer.

computer run Action of processing instructions in a program by a computer.

computer science The scientific study of computers, the organization of hardware and development of software.

computer system A central processor with storage and associated peripherals that make up a working computer.

computer time The time when a computer is being used (paid for at an hourly rate).

computer word The number of bits that make up a standard word within a CPU (usually 8,16 or 32 bits long).

computing power A measure of speed and ability of a computer to perform calculations.

computing speed The speed at which a computer calculates.

concatenate To join together two or more sets of data to produce one set.

concentrate To combine a number of lines or circuits or data to take up less space.

concertina fold Accordion fold or method of folding continuous paper, one sheet in one direction, the next sheet in the opposite direction, allowing the paper to be fed into a printer continuously with no action on the part of the user.

concurrent operating system An operating system software that allows several programs or activities to be processed at the same time. It is impossible for one processor to run more than one process simultaneously, unless there is more than one CPU within the system, and so processes that appear to run concurrently are actually being processed in turn, one section at a time.

concurrent programming Running several programs apparently simultaneously, achieved by executing small sections from each program in turn.

condition 1 The state of a circuit or device or register **2** To modify data that is to be transmitted so as to meet set parameters, as for example, conditioning of raw data to a standard format.

condition code register A register that contains the state of the CPU after the execution of the last instruction. See also **flag.**

conditional breakpoint A breakpoint inserted into a program, which when reached gives the programmer the option to jump to one of a number of sections, depending on data or program status.

conditional jump or **branch** or **transfer** A programming instruction that provides a jump to a section of a program if a certain condition is met. As an example, a conditional branch will select routine one if the response is yes and routine two if no.

conditional statement A program instruction that will redirect program control according to the outcome of an event.

conductor A substance (such as a metal) which conducts electricity. Copper is a particularly good conductor. See also **semiconductor.**

conferencing Teleconferencing or holding a meeting of people in different places, using the telephones to allow each person to communicate with the others. You can also have **computer conferencing** when a number of computers or terminals are connected together to allow a group of users to communicate.

confidence level The likelihood that a number will lie within a range of values.

configure To select hardware, software and interconnections to make up a special system. So, a terminal can be configured to display graphics or a keyboard can be configured to produce special accents.

configuration The way in which the hardware and software of a computer system are planned and set up.

configuration state The state of a computer that allows it or the system or a program to be configured.

configured-in A device whose configuration state indicates it is ready and available for use.

configured-off or **configured out** A device whose configuration state indicates it is not available for use.

conform To work according to set rules. Software will not run if it does not conform to the operating system standards.

congestion A state that occurs when communication or processing demands are greater than the capacity of a system.

conjunct One of the variables in an logical AND function.

conjunction A logical function whose output is true if all inputs are true.

connect To link together two points in a circuit or communications network. A **connect charge** is the charge incurred for the time a user spends on-line to a system.

connection A link or something which joins two things together. A **parallel connection** is a connector on a computer allowing parallel data to be transferred. Normally eight bits are transferred in parallel across eight lines. This is faster, but requires one line for each bit, while a **serial connection** sends the bits of a byte one after the other along a single line.

connective A symbol between two operands that describes the operation to be performed.

connector A physical device with a number of metal contacts that allow devices to be easily linked together. A **card edge connector** is a series of metal tracks ending at the edge and on the surface of a circuit board, allowing it to be plugged into an edge connector to provide electrical path (for data transmission, etc.). See also **female, male.**

connect time The length of time a user is logged onto an interactive system.

console A unit which allows an operator to communicate with a computer system. It will usually consist of an input device such as a keyboard, and an output device such as a printer or CRT.

constant An item of data, whose value does not change (as opposed to a variable).

constant length field A data field that always contains the same number of characters.

consumables The small, cheap, extra items required in the day-to-day running of a computer system (such as paper and printer ribbons).

contact 1 The section of a switch or connector that provides an electrical path when it touches another conductor. A circuit may not work if the contact is dirty. **2** To try to call a user or device in a network.

contact bounce see **bounce, de-bounce**

content-addressable file or **location** A method of storing data in which each item may be individually accessed.

content-addressable memory (CAM) or **associative storage** A method of data retrieval which uses part of the data rather than an address to locate the data.

contention A situation that occurs when two or more devices are trying to communicate with the same piece of equipment.

contention bus A communication control system in which a device must wait for a free moment before transmitting data.

contention delay The length of time spent waiting for equipment to become free for use.

contiguous file A file stored in a series of adjacent disk sectors.

contiguous graphics Graphic cells or characters that touch each other. Most display units do not provide contiguous graphics: their characters have a small space on each side to improve legibility.

continuation page The page or screen of text that follows on from a main page.

continuous data stream A high speed serial data transmission, in which data words are not synchronized, but follow on immediately from each other.

continuous feed A device which feeds continuous stationery into a printer.

continuous loop An endless piece of recording or projection tape.

continuous signal An analog continuously variable signal.

continuous stationery Paper made as one long sheet, folded, with perforations, used in computer printers.

continuous wave A high frequency waveform that can be modulated to carry data. See also **carrier.**

control block A reserved area of computer memory that contains control data.

control bus A set of connections to a microcomputer that carry the control signals between CPU, memory and input/output devices.

control cards (In a punched card system) the first cards which contain the processor control instructions.

control character Special character that provides a control sequence rather than a alphanumeric character.

control computer A dedicated computer used to control a process or piece of equipment.

control cycle Events required to retrieve, decode and execute an instruction stored in memory.

control data Data that controls the actions of a device.

control-driven Computer architecture where instructions are executed once a control sequence has been received.

control field The storage area for control instructions.

control instruction A program instruction that controls the actions of a device.

control language Commands that describe the identification of and resources required by a job that a computer has to process.

controller A hardware or software device that controls a peripheral (such as a printer) or monitors and directs the data transmission over a local area network.

control memory or **ROM** A section of memory which decodes control instructions into microinstructions which operate the computer or microcontroller.

control mode The state of a device in which control signals can be received to select options or functions.

control panel The main control switches and status indicators of a computer.

control program/monitor or **control program for microcomputers (CP/M)** An old-fashioned but still popular operating system for microcomputers.

control register A storage location only used for control data.

control sequence A series of codes containing a control character and various arguments, used to carry out a process or change mode in a device.

control signals Electrical signals transmitted to control the actions of a circuit.

control statement 1 A program instruction that directs a CPU to provide controlling actions or controls the operation of the CPU. 2 A program instruction that redirects a program (to another branch etc.).

control systems Systems used to check that a computer system is working correctly.

control token A special sequence of bits transmitted over a LAN to provide control actions to the server or network circuitry.

control total A result of summing certain fields in a computer file to provide error detection.

control transfer The redirection of the CPU when a jump or call instruction is encountered.

control unit (CU) A section of central processor that selects and executes instructions.

control word A word that defines the actions (in a particular process) that are to be followed.

convention Well-known standards or rules which are followed, ensuring hardware or software compatibility.

conversational (mode) A computer system that provides immediate responses to a user's input. See also **interactive mode,** and compare with **batch mode.**

conversion equipment A device that will convert data from one format to another (suitable for another system) without changing the content.

conversion program 1 A program that converts programs written for one computer into a suitable form for another. 2 A program that converts data format, coding, etc. for use in another program.

conversion tables or **translation tables** A list of source codes or statements and their equivalent in another language or form. Conversion tables may be created and used in conjunction with the customer's data to convert it to a supplier's systems codes.

converter or **convertor** A device or program that translates data from one form to another. Used, for example, when moving old data to a new system.

coordinate To organize complex tasks, so that they fit together efficiently. As in multitasking, where the operating system has to coordinate all the file and resource requests from each task.

coordinates Values used to locate a point on a graph or map.

coordinate graph A means of displaying one point on a graph, using two values referring to axes which are usually at right angles to each other.

coprocessor An extra, specialized processor, such as an array or numerical processor that can work with a main CPU to increase execution speed.

copy To make a second document which is like the first; to duplicate original data. It is important to remember that data should be copied to back-up storage at the end of a keyboarding session.

copy protect A method of preventing copies of a disk being made. Many commercial programs are copy protected to ensure users do not make illegal copies.

copy protection Preventing copies being made. It is possible for a hard disk to crash because of copy protection.

copyright A legal right (lasting for fifty years after the death of an artist whose work has been published) which a writer or programmer has in his own work, allowing him not to have it copied without the payment of royalties.

Copyright Act Act of Parliament making copyright legal, and controlling the copying of copyright material

CORAL (common real-time applications language) A computer programming language used in real-time operating systems.

core The central conducting section of a cable. **Core memory** or **core store** is the central memory of a computer. A **core program** is stored in core memory.

coresident (Two or more programs) stored in main memory at the same time.

coroutine A section of a program or procedure that can pass data and control to another coroutine then halt itself.

corrective maintenance Actions to trace, find and repair a fault after it has occurred.

correspondence print quality The quality of print from a computer printer that is acceptable for business letters (that is daisy-wheel rather than dot-matrix printing).

corrupt 1 Data or program that contains errors. **2** To introduce errors into data or a program. Among other causes, power loss during disk access can corrupt data.

corruption (of data) Errors introduced into data, due to noise or faulty equipment. Acoustic couplers suffer from data corruption more than the direct connect form of modem.

counter A register or variable whose contents are increased or decreased by a set amount every time an action occurs.

coupler see **acoustic coupler**

CP see **card punch**

cpi see **characters per inch**

CP/M (control program/monitor) A popular operating system for microcomputers.

CPM see **critical path method**

cps (characters per second) The number of characters printed or processed every second.

CPU (central processing unit) A group of circuits which perform the basic functions of a computer made up of three parts, the control unit, the arithmetic and logic unit and the input/output unit. These are known as the **CPU elements.**

CPU cycle The period of time taken to fetch and execute an instruction (usually a simple ADD instruction) used as a measure of computer speed.

CPU handshaking The interfacing signals between a CPU and a peripheral or I/O device.

CPU time The total period of time that a CPU is used actually to process instructions. In a file handling program CPU time might be minimal, since data retrieval from disk would account for a large part of the program run; in a mathematical program, the CPU time could be much higher in proportion to the total run time.

CR see **carriage return, card reader**

crash 1 A failure of a component or a bug in a program during a run, which halts and prevents further use of the system. **2** (of a computer or program) To come to an sudden stop. A disk which uses a head protection or data corruption protection system is said to be **crash-protected.** It is sometimes possible to recover data from a crashed hard disk before reformatting, if the crash was caused by a bad sector on the disk rather than contact between the r/w head and disk surface.

CRC see **cyclic redundancy check**

create To make. To make a new file the operator moves to the CREATE NEW FILE instruction on the menu.

crippled leapfrog test A standard leapfrog test that uses a single memory location rather than a changing location.

critical path analysis The definition of tasks or jobs and the time each requires arranged in order to achieve certain goals. Also called PERT (Program Evaluation and Review Techniques).

critical path method (CPM) The use of analysis and projection of each critical step in a large project to help a management team.

critical resource A resource that can only be used by one process at a time.

CR/LF see **carriage return/line feed**

cross-assembler An assembler that produces machine-code code for one computer whilst running on another. A **cross-compiler** compiles programs for one computer whilst running on another. Cross-compilers and assemblers are used to compile programs for micros, but are run on larger computers to make the operation faster.

cross-check Validation of an answer by using a different method of calculation.

cross-reference generator A section of an assembler or compiler or interpreter that provides a list of program labels, variables or constants with their location within the program.

crossover To change from one system to another.

crosstalk The interference in one channel due to another nearby channel * signal (caused by badly isolated signals).

CRT (cathode ray tube) A device used for displaying characters or figures or graphical information, similar to a TV set. Cathode ray tubes are used in television sets, computer monitors and VDUs; a CRT consists of a vacuum tube, one end of which is flat and coated with phosphor, the other end containing an electron beam source. Characters or graphics are visible when the controllable electron beam strikes the phosphor causing it to glow.

cruncher, crunching see **number**

cryogenic memory A storage medium operating at very low temperatures (4K) to use the superconductive properties of a material.

cryptography The study of encryption and decryption methods and techniques. The rules which are used to encipher and decipher data are **cryptographic algorithms. A cryptographic key** is the number or code that is used with a cipher algorithm to personalize the encryption and decryption of data. The study and methods of breaking ciphers is **cryptanalysis.**

crystal A small slice of quartz crystal which vibrates at a certain frequency, used as a very accurate clock signal for computer or other high precision timing applications (a **crystal oscillator**).

CSM (combined symbol matching) An effecient optical character recognition system.

CSMA-CD see **carrier sense multiple access-collision detection**

CTR or **CTRL (control)** The control key or key on a computer terminal that sends a control character to the computer when pressed.

CTS (clear to send) RS232C signal that a line or device is ready for data transmission.

CU see **control unit**

cue A prompt or message displayed on a screen to remind the user that an input is expected.

CUG (closed user group) Restricting the entry to a database or bulletin board system (on a certain topic or subject) to certain known and registered users usually by means of a password.

current address The address being used (accessed) at this time.

current address register (CAR) CPU register that stores the address that is currently being accessed.

current instruction register (CIR) CPU register that stores the instruction that is currently being executed

cursor A marker on a display device which shows where the next character will appear. Cursors can take several forms, such as a square of bright light, a bright underline or a flashing light.

cursor control keys Keys on a keyboard that allow the cursor to be moved in different directions.

cursor home Movement of the cursor to the top left hand corner of the screen.

cursor pad A group of cursor control keys.

customer engineering The maintenance and repair of a customer's equipment.

customize To modify a system to the customer's requirements.

cut Removing a piece from a file or text; a piece removed from a file or text. Taking pieces of text from one point and inserting them at another (often used in DTP packages for easy page editing) is called **cut and paste.**

cut sheet feeder A mechanism that automatically feeds single sheets of paper into a printer.

CWP see (**communicating word processor**)

cybernetics The study of the mechanics of human or electronic machine movements, and the way in which electronic devices can be made to work and imitate human actions.

cycle 1 A period of time when something leaves its original position and then returns to it. **2** One completed operation in a repeated process. **3** To repeat an operation or series of instructions until instructed to stop.

cycle availability A period of time in a cycle, during which data can be accessed or transmitted.

cycle index The number of times a series of instructions have been or have to be repeated.

cycle shift To shift a pattern of bits within a word, with the bit(s) that are shifted off the end being inserted at the beginning of the word.

cycle stealing A memory access operation by a peripheral that halts a CPU for one or more clock cycles whilst data is being transferred from memory to the device.

cycle time The time between the start and stop of an operation, especially between addressing a memory location and receiving the data, and then ending the operation. Compare **address time.**

cyclic access Access to stored information that can only occur at a certain point in a cycle.

cyclic check An error detection method that uses or examines a bit of data every n bits (one bit examined then n bits transmitted, then another bit examined, etc.)

cyclic code see **gray code**

cyclic decimal code A cyclic code that is used to represent decimal digits.

cyclic redundancy check (CRC) An error detection code for transmitted data.

cyclic shift The rotation of bits in a word with the previous last bit inserted in the first bit position.

cylinder The tracks in a multi-disk device that can be accessed without moving the read/write head.

cypher see **cipher**

D

D The hexadecimal (base 16) figure equivalent to decimal number 13.

3D see **three-dimensional**

DAC or **d/a converter (digital to analog converter)** A circuit that outputs an analog number which is proportional to an digital input signal, and so converts a digital input to an analog form. A d/a converter allows the computer to work outside the computer environment, by driving a machine, imitating speech, etc.

DAD (digital audio disk) A method of recording sound by converting and storing signals in a digital form on magnetic disk.

daisy chain 1 A method of connecting equipment with a single cable passing from one machine or device to the next (rather than separate cables to each device). **2** To connect equipment using the daisy chain method.

daisy chain bus A communications bus that joins one device to the next, each device being able to receive or transmit or modify data as it passes through to the next device in line.

daisy chain interrupt A line joining all the interrupt outputs of a number of devices to a CPU.

daisy chain recursion A series of subroutines in a program that each call another in the series, (the first routine calls the second routine which calls the third routine, etc.).

daisy-wheel A wheel-shaped printing head, with characters on the end of spokes. A **daisy-wheel printer** or **daisy-wheel typewriter** has characters arranged in this way on interchangeable wheels. Daisy-wheel printers produce better quality text than a dot-matrix printer, but are slower.

DAMA see **demand assigned multiple access**

dark trace tube A CRT with a dark image on a bright background.

DASD (direct access storage device) A storage medium whose memory locations can be directly read * written to.

DAT (digital audio tape) A method of recording sound by converting and storing signals in a digital form on magnetic tape.

data A collection of facts made up of numbers, characters and symbols, stored on a computer in such a way that it can be processed by the computer. Data is different from information in that it is facts stored in machine-readable form. When the facts are processed by the computer into a form which can be understood by people, the data becomes information.

data access management Regulating the users who can access stored data.

data acquisition Gathering data about a subject.

data adapter unit A device that interfaces a CPU to one or more communications channels.

data administrator The control section of a database management system.

data aggregate A collection of items of data that are related.

data analysis Extracting information and results from data.

data area The amount of storage space that contains data (rather than instructions).

databank 1 A large amount of data (usually on one theme) stored in a structured form. **2** Personal records stored in a computer.

database An integrated collection of files of data stored in a structured form in a large memory, which can be accessed by one or more users at different terminals.

database administrator (DBA) A person in charge of running and maintaining a database system.

database language A series of languages, such as data description language, that make up a database management system.

database machine A hardware and software combination designed for the rapid processing of database information.

database management system (DBMS) or **database manager** A series of programs that allow the user to create and modify databases easily.

database mapping A description of the way in which the records and fields in a database are related.

database schema The way in which a database is organized and structured.

database system A series of programs that allows the user to create, modify, manage and use a database (often includes features such as a report writer or graphical output of data).

data block All the data required for or from a process.

data break A memory access operation by a peripheral that halts a CPU for one or more cycles whilst data is being transferred from memory to the device.

data buffer A temporary storage location for data received by a device that is not yet ready to accept it.

data bus A bus carrying the data between a CPU and memory and peripheral devices.

data capture The act of obtaining data (either by keyboarding or by scanning, or often automatically from a recording device or peripheral).

data carrier 1 Any device or medium capable of storing data. **2** A waveform used as a carrier for data signals.

data carrier detect (DCD) An RS232C signal from a modem to a computer indicating a carrier wave is being received.

data cartridge A cartridge that contains stored data. See **cartridge, cassette.**

data chaining A method of storing individual facts so that one stored record holds the address of the next in the list.

data channel A communication link able to carry data signals (as opposed to a link that carries speech or audio signals).

data check An error in reading data due to a fault with the magnetic medium.

data circuit A circuit which allows bi-directional data communications.

data cleaning Removing errors from data.

data collection The act of receiving data from various sources (either directly from a data capture device or from a cartridge) and inserting correctly in order into a database.

data communications The transmission and reception of data rather than speech or images.

data communications buffer A buffer in a receiver that allows a slow peripheral to accept data from a fast computer, without slowing either down.

data communications equipment (DCE) Equipment (such as a modem) which receives or transmits data.

data communications network A number of computers, terminals, operators and storage units connected together to allow data transmission between devices or files or users.

data compacting Reducing the space taken by data by coding it in a more efficient way.

data compression A means of reducing size of data by removing spaces, empty sections and unused material from the blocks of data.

data concentrator A device which combines intermittent data from various lines and sends it along a single line in one go.

data connection A link which joins two devices allowing data transmission.

data control The management of data to and from a database or processing system.

data corruption Errors introduced into data due to noise or faulty equipment.

data delimiter A special symbol or character that marks the end of a file or data item.

data description language (DDL) Part of database system software which describes the structure of the system and data.

data dictionary/directory (DD/D) Software which gives a list of types and forms of data contained in a database.

data division One part of a (COBOL) program giving full definitions of the data types and structures.

data-driven A type of computer architecture in which instructions are executed, once the relevant data has been received.

data element see **data item**

data element chain A series of more than one data element treated as a single element.

data encryption Encrypting data using a cipher system

data encryption standard (DES) A standard for a block data cipher system.

data entry A method of entering data into a system (usually using a keyboard but also direct from disks after data preparation).

data error An error due to incorrect or illegal data.

data field A part of a computer instruction that contains the location of the data.

data file A file with data in it (as opposed to a program file).

data flow The movement of data through a system. A **data flow diagram (DFD)** shows the movement of data through a system in diagrammatic form.

data flowchart A diagram used to describe a computer or data processing system.

data format A series of rules defining the way in which data is stored or transmitted.

datagram A packet of information in a packet switching system that contains its destination address and route.

data hierarchy A data structure which is organized hierarchically.

data highway A bus carrying data signals between a CPU and peripherals. See also **bus.**

data independence A database structure which can be changed without affecting what the user sees.

data input Data transferred into a computer (from an I/O port or peripheral). A **data input bus** or **DIB** is used when transferring data from one section of a computer to another, such as between memory and CPU.

data integrity The protection of data against damage or errors.

data item One unit of data such as the quantity of items in stock, a person's name, age or occupation.

data level The position of a data item within a database structure.

data link A connection between two devices to allow the transmission of data.

data link control The protocol and rules used to define the way in which data is transmitted or received.

data link layer One layer in the ISO/OSI defined network that sends packets of data to the next link and deals with error correction.

data logging Automatic data collection.

data management The maintenance and upkeep of a database.

data manipulation language (DML) Database software that allows the user to access, store and change data.

data medium A medium which allows data to be stored or displayed (such as a VDU or magnetic disk or screen).

data migration Data transfer (directed by a user's instruction) from an on-line device to an off-line device.

data name A group of characters used to identify one item of data.

data network A networking system which transmits data.

data origination The conversion of data from its original form to one which can be read by a computer.

data path A bus or connections over which data is transmitted.

dataplex To multiplex data signals.

data pointer A register containing the location of the next item of data.

data preparation The conversion of data into a machine-readable form before data entry.

data processing (DP or dp) Selecting data and operating on it to produce useful information; the sorting or organizing of data files. A **data processing manager** runs the computer services department in a company.

data protection A means of making sure that data is private and secure. This can basically be split into two areas — preventing an intruder from getting access to a terminal (with locks, secure rooms, etc.) or by allowing public access, but using passwords, etc., to retrict access to selected users.

data rate The maximum rate at which data is processed or transmitted in a synchronous system, usually equal to the system clock rate.

data record One single record containing data for use with a program.

data reduction The production of compact, useful data from raw data.

data register An area within a CPU used to store data temporarily before it is processed.

data reliability A measure of the number of data words with errors compared to the total number of words.

data retrieval The process of searching, selecting and reading data from a stored file.

data routing Defining the path to be taken by a message in a network.

data security The protection of data against corruption or unauthorized users.

data services Public services (such as the telephone system) which allow data to be transmitted over them (for example, using a modem).

dataset ready (DSR) An RS232C signal from a modem to a computer indicating it is ready for use, the signal occurs after a DTR signal is received. Note that **dataset** is American English for a modem.

data signals Electrical or optical pulses or waveforms that represent binary data.

data signalling rate The total amount of data that is transmitted through a system per second.

data sink The device in a data terminal which receives data.

data source The device in a data terminal which sends data

data station A point that contains a data terminal and a data circuit.

data storage A medium which is able to store large quantities of data. See also **backing store.**

data stream Data transmitted serially one bit or character at a time.

data strobe A signal in the control bus that indicates that valid data is on the data bus.

data structure A number of related items that are treated as one by the computer (in an address book record, the name, address and telephone number form separate entries which would be processed as one by the computer).

data switching exchange A device used to direct and switch data between communicatins lines.

data tablet see **graphics tablet**

data terminal A device at which a communications path starts or finishes and is able to display and transmit or receive data. Such devices are known as **data terminal equipment** or **DTE.** A signal from a device to indicate that it is ready to send data is **data terminal ready (DTR).**

data transaction One complete operation on data.

data transfer rate The rate at which data is moved from one point to another.

data translation The conversion of data from one system format to another.

data transmission The process of sending data from one location to another over a data link.

data type Data which can be stored in a register (such as string, number, etc.).

data validation The process of checking data for errors and relevance in a situation.

data vetting The process of checking data as it is input for errors and validity.

data word An amount of data stored as a single word.

data word length The number of bits that make up a word in a computer.

daughter board A small add-on board that connects to a system mother board or expansion card.

DBA (database administrator) A person in charge of running and maintaining a database system.

DBMS (database management system) A series of programs that allow the user to create and modify databases.

DC see **direct current**

DC signalling A method of communications using pulses of current over a wire circuit, like a telegraph system.

DCD (data carrier detect) An RS232C signal from a modem to a computer indicating a carrier is being received.

DCE see **data communications equipment**

DD see **double density**

DDC (direct digital control) A machine operated automatically by machine.

DD/D (data dictionary/directory) Software which gives a list of types and forms of data contained in a database.

DDE (direct data entry) Keying-in data directly onto magnetic tape or disk.

DDL see **data description language**

DDP (distributed data processing) Operations to derive information from data which is kept in different places.

dead A computer or piece of equipment that does not function.

dead halt or **drop dead halt** A program instruction from the user or an error, that causes the program to stop without allowing recovery.

dead keys The keys on a keyboard that cause a function rather than a character to occur, such as the shift key.

deadlock A situation when two users want to access two resources at the same time, one resource is assigned to each user but neither can use the other. Also called **deadly embrace.**

dead time The period of time between two events in which nothing happens, to ensure that they do not interfere with each other.

deallocate To free resources previously allocated to a job or process or peripheral. For example, when a TSR is deactivated, it deallocates any RAM it had reserved.

debit A bit transmission rate that is twice the baud rate.

deblock To return a stored block of data to its original form (of individual records).

de-bounce Preventing a single touch on a key giving multiple key contact.

de-bounce circuit An electronic circuit that prevents a key contact producing more than one signal when pressed.

debug To test a program and locate and correct any faults or errors. The software that helps a programmer find faults or errors in a program is a **debugger.**

decade Ten items or events. A **decade counter** is an electronic device which is able to count actions or events from 0-9 before resetting to zero and starting again.

decay 1 The rate at which the electronic impulse or the amplitude of a signal fades away. The time taken for an impulse to fade is the **decay time. 2** To decrease gradually in amplitude or size.

decay time The time taken for an impulse to fade.

decentralized computer network A network in which the control is shared between several computers.

decentralized data processing Data processing and storage carried out at each location rather than in one central location.

decimal (notation) Arithmetic operations and number representation using the decimal system.

decimal point A dot which indicates the division between the whole unit digits and the smaller (fractional) parts of a decimal number (such as 4.75).

decimal system A number system using the digits 0 - 9.

decimal tabbing Adjusting a column of numbers so that the decimal points are vertically aligned.

decimal tab key A key for entering decimal numbers (using a word processor) so that the decimal points are automatically vertically aligned.

decimal-to-binary conversion To convert a decimal (base ten) number into a binary (base two) number.

decipher To convert an encrypted or encoded message (**ciphertext**) into the original message (**plaintext**) again.

decision box A graphical symbol used in a flowchart to indicate that a decision is to be made and a branch or path or action carried out according to the result.

decision circuit or **element** A logical circuit that operates on binary inputs, whose output is dependent upon the inputs and the logical operation carried out.

decision or **descrimination instruction** A conditional program instruction that directs control by providing the location of the next instruction to be executed if a condition is met.

decision support system A suite of programs that help a manager reach decisions using previous decisions, information and other databases.

decision table A chart which shows the relationships between certain variables and actions available when various conditions are met.

decision tree A graphical representation of a decision table showing possible paths and actions if different conditions are met.

deck A pile of punched cards.

declare To define a computer program variable or to set a variable equal to a number. For example, a programmer may declare at the start of a program that X is equal to nine.

declaration or **declarative statement** A statement within a program that informs the compiler or interpreter of the form, type and size of a particular element, constant or variable.

decode To translate encoded data back to its original form.

decoder A program or device used to convert data into another form.

decoding Converting encoded data back into its original form.

decollate To separate continuous stationery into single sheets; to split two-part or three-part stationery into its separate parts (and remove the carbon paper). The machine used to do this is a **decollator.**

decompilation The conversion of a compiled program in object code into a source language.

decrement To subtract a set number (usually one) from a variable.

decrypt To convert encrypted data back into its original form. The action of doing this is **decryption.**

dedicated A program or procedure or system reserved for a particular use, so a **dedicated channel** is a communications line reserved for a special purpose and a **dedicated computer** is one which is only used for a single special purpose.

dedicated line A telephone line used only for data communications. See also **land line.**

dedicated logic A logical function implemented in hardware designed (usually for only one task or circuit.

dedicated word processor A computer which has been configured specially for word processing and which cannot run any other programs.

default A predefined course of action or value that is assumed unless the operator alters it.

default drive A disk drive that is accessed first in a multi-disk system to try and load the operating system or a program.

default option A preset value or option that is to be used if no other value has been specified.

default rate The baud rate (in a modem) that is used if no other is selected.

default response A value which is used if the user does not enter new data.

default value A value which is automatically used by the computer if no other value has been specified.

defect skipping A means of identifying and labelling defective magnetic tracks during manufacture so that they will not be used, and will instead point to the next good track that should be used.

defensive computing A method of programming that takes into account any problems * errors that might occur.

deferred addressing Indirect addressing, in which the location accessed contains the address of the operand to be processed.

deflection yokes Magnetic coils around a cathode ray tube used to control the position of the picture beam on the screen.

degauss To remove unwanted magnetic fields and effects from magnetic tape, disks or read/write heads. The device used to do this is a **degausser.**

degradation 1 The loss of picture or signal quality. **2** The loss of processing capacity because of a malfunction. **Graceful degradation** is allowing some parts of a system to continue to function after a part has broken down.

delay line A device that causes a signal to take a certain time to cross it. A **delay line store** was an old-fashioned method of storing serial data as sound or pulses in a delay line, the data being constantly read, regenerated and fed back into the input.

delay vector The time that a message will take to pass from one packet switching network node to another.

delete 1 To cut out words in a document. 2 To remove text or data from a storage device. When a file is deleted, it is not actually erased it but the space it occupies on the disk is made available for another file. This is done by instructing the operating system to ignore the file by inserting a special code in the file header and deleting the entry from the directory.

delete character A special code used to indicate data or text to be removed.

deletion 1 Making a cut in a document. 2 The text which is removed from a document.

deletion record A record containing new data which is to be used to update or delete data in a master record.

delimit To set up the size of data using delimiters. A **delimiter** is 1 a character or symbol used to indicate to a language or program the start or end of data or a record or information, or 2 the boundary between an instruction and its argument.

delta A type of connection used to connect the three wires in a 3-phase electrical supply.

delta clock A clock that provides timing pulses to synchronize a system, and will restart (with an interrupt signal) a computer or circuit that has had an error or entered an endless loop or faulty state.

delta-delta A connection between a delta source and load.

delta modulation A differential pulse coded modulation that uses only one bit per sample.

delta routing A means of directing data around a packet switching network.

demagnetize To remove stray or unwanted magnetic fields from a disk or tape * recording head. The device which demagnetizes is a **demagnetizer**.

demand assigned multiple access (DAMA) A means of switching in circuits as and when they are required.

demand multiplexing A time division multiplexing method which allocates time segments to signals according to demand.

demand paging System software that retrieves pages in a virtual memory system from backing store when it is required.

demand processing Processing data when it appears, rather than waiting.

demand reading/writing A direct data transfer between a processor and storage.

demand staging Moving files or data from a secondary storage device to a fast access device when required by a database program.

democratic network A synchronized network where each station has equal priority.

demodulation The recovery of an original signal from a received modulated carrier wave. The circuit that recovers a signal from a modulated carrier wave is a **demodulator.**

demonstration model A piece of equipment in a shop, which is used to show customers how the equipment works, and may then be sold off cheaply.

demultiplex To split one channel into the original signals that were combined at source. A **demultiplexor** separates out the original multiplexed signals from one channel.

denary notation The number system in base ten, using the digits 0 to 9.

denial a logical function which prevents something taking place. An **alternative denial** is a function whose output is false if all inputs are true, and true if any input is false. A **joint denial** is a function whose output is false if any input is true.

dense index A database index containing an address or entry for every item * entry in the database.

dense list A list that has no free space for new records.

density The amount of data that can be packed into a space on a disk * tape. If a disk has **double density** this means that the disk drive has double the storage capacity by doubling the number of bits which can be put on the disk surface. This makes a **double density disk (DD),** which can store two bits of data per unit area compared to a standard disk, using a modified write process.

deny access To refuse access to a circuit or system for reasons of workload or security.

deposit 1 A thin layer of a substance which is put on a surface. **2** To print out the contents of all or a selected area of memory. **3** To coat a surface with a thin layer of a substance. **4** To write data into a register or storage location.

deposition A process by which the surface of a semiconductor is coated with a thin layer of another substance (used during the process of manufacturing integrated circuits).

deque (double-ended queue) A queue in which new items can be added to either end.

derivation graph A structure within a global database that provides information on the rules and paths used to reach any element or item of data.

DES (data encryption standard) A standardized, popular block cipher system for data encryption.

descender The part of a character that goes below the line (such as the 'tail' of a 'g' or 'p'). Compare **ascender**.

de-scramble To reassemble an original message or signal from its scrambled form. The device which changes a scrambled message back to its original, clear form is a **de-scrambler.**

description list A list of data items and their attributes. See also **data description language, page description programming language.**

descriptor A code used to identify a filename or program name or pass code to a file.

desk check A dry run of a program.

desktop computer (system) A small microcomputer system that can be placed on a desk.

desktop publishing (DTP) The design, layout and printing of documents using special software, a small computer and a laser printer.

despool To print out spooled files.

despotic network A network synchronized and controlled by one single clock source.

destination The location to which data is sent.

destructive addition An addition operation in which the result is stored in the location of one of the operands used in the sum, so overwriting it.

destructive cursor A cursor that erases the text as it moves over it.

destructive read A read operation in which the stored data is erased as it is retrieved.

destructive readout A form of storage medium that loses its data after it has been read.

detail file A file containing records that are to be used to update a master file.

detected error An error noticed during a program run, but not corrected.

deterministic The result of a process that depends on the initial state and inputs.

development software A suite of programs that help a programmer write, edit, compile and debug new software.

development time The amount of time required to develop a new product.

device character control Control of a device using various characters or special combinations to instruct the device. Most printers can be controlled to produce text in italic, bold, etc., by using special codes embedded within the text. The **device control character** is the special code sent in a transmission to a device to instruct it to perform a special function.

device code A unique identification and selection code for each peripheral.

device driver A program or routine used to interface and manage an I/O device or peripheral.

device flag One bit in a device status word, used to show the state of one device.

device independent A programming technique that results in a program that is able to run with any peripheral hardware.

device priority The importance of a peripheral device assigned by the user or central computer which dictates the order in which the CPU will serve an interrupt signal from it.

device queue A list of requests from users or programs to use a device.

device status word (DSW) A data word transmitted from a device that contains information about its current status.

DFD (data flow diagram) A diagram used to describe the movement of data through a system.

diagnosis Finding a fault or discovering the cause of a fault, the result of diagnosing faulty hardware or software. **diagnostics** are the functions or tests that help a user find faults in hardware or software.

diagnostic aid A hardware or software device that helps to find faults. This can be a **diagnostic chip** that contains circuits to carry out tests on other circuits or chips, or a **diagnostic program** which is software that helps find faults in a computer system. A **diagnostic routine** is a routine in a program which helps to find faults in a computer system.

diagnostic message A message that appears on the screen to explain the type, location and probable cause of a software error or hardware failure.

diagnostic test A means of locating faults in hardware and software by test circuits or programs.

dialect A slight variation of a standard language, such as a certain manufacturer's dialect of BASIC.

dial into To call a telephone number which has a modem and computer at the other end. With the right access code it is possible to dial into a customer's computer to extract the files from a database.

dial-in modem An auto-answer modem that can be called at any time.

dialogue Communication between devices such as computers.

dialogue box On-screen message from a program to the user. These often contain instructions or help on what the user should do or enter next.

DIANE (Direct Information Access Network for Europe) Services offered over the Euronet network.

DIB (data input bus) The bus used when transferring data from one section of a computer to another, such as between memory and CPU.

dibit A digit made up of just two binary bits.

dichotomizing search A fast search method for use on ordered lists of data (the search key is compared with the data in the middle of the list and one half is discarded, this is repeated with the half remaining until only one data item remains).

dictionary 1 A data management structure which allows files to be referenced and sorted. 2 A part of a spelling checker program: the list of correctly spelled words against which the program checks a text.

dielectric An insulating material that allows an electric field to pass, but not an electric current.

differential PCM (differential pulse coded modulation) A pulse coded modulation method that uses the difference in size of a sample value and the previous one, requiring fewer bits when transmitting.

diffusion A means of transferring doping materials into an integrated circuit substrate.

digit A symbol or character which represents an integer that is smaller than the radix of the number base used. The decimal number system uses the digits 0123456789.

digit place or **position** The position of a digit within a number. See also **radix.**

digital Which represents data or physical quantities in numerical form (especially using a binary system in computer-related devices).

digital audio disk (DAD) A method of recording sound by converting and storing signals in a digital form on magnetic disk, providing very high quality reproduction. See also **compact disk.**

digital audio tape (DAT) A method of recording sound by converting and storing signals in a digital form on magnetic tape, providing very high quality reproduction.

digital cassette A high quality magnetic tape housed in a standard size cassette with write protect tabs, and a standard format leader.

digital circuit An electronic circuit that operates on digital information providing logical functions or switching.

digital computer A computer which processes data in digital form (that is data represented in discrete digital form, usually binary). Compare **analog computer.**

digital data Data represented in (usually binary) numerical form.

digital logic Applying Boolean algebra to hardware circuits.

digital optical recording (DOR) The recording of signals in binary form as small holes in the surface of an optical or compact disk which can then be read by laser.

digital output Computer output in digital form. Compare with **analog output.**

digital plotter A plotter whose pen position is controllable in discrete steps, so that drawings in the computer can be output graphically.

digital read-out Data displayed in numerical form, such as numbers on an LCD in a calculator.

digital recording The conversion of sound signals into a digital form and storing them on magnetic disk or tape usually in binary form.

digital representation Data or quantities represented using discrete quantities (i.e. digits).

digital resolution The smallest number that can be represented with one digit, the value assigned to the least significant bit of a word or number.

digital signal An electric signal that has only a number of possible states, as opposed to analog signals which are continuously variable.

digital signalling Control and dialling codes sent down a (telephone line) in digital form.

digital signature A unique identification code sent by a terminal or device in digital form.

digital speech see **speech synthesis**

digital system A system that deals with digital signals.

digital switching Operating communications connections and switches only by use of digital signals.

digital to analog converter or **D to A converter (DAC)** A circuit that converts a digital signal to an analog one (the analog signal is proportional to an input binary number).

digital transmission system Communications achieved by converting analog signals to a digital form then modulating and transmitting this (the signal is then converted back to analog form at the receiver).

digitize To change analog movement or signals into a digital form which can be processed by computers, etc. So a **digitized photograph** is one that has been scanned to produce an analog signal which is then converted to digital form and stored or displayed on a computer. The **digitizer** is the analog to digital converter which converts an analog movement or signal to a digital one which can be understood by a computer.

digitizing pad A sensitive surface that translates the position of a pen into numerical form, so that drawings can be entered into a computer.

DIL (dual-in-line package) A standard layout for integrated circuit packages using two parallel rows of connecting pins along each side.

dimensioning A program statement or instruction providing the definition of the size of something (usually an array or matrix).

diminished radix complement A number representation in which each digit of the number is subtracted from one less than the radix. See also **one's complement, nine's complement.**

DIN (Deutsche Industrienorm) German industry standards organization.

diode An electronic component that allows an electrical current to pass in one direction and not the other.

DIP (dual-in-line package) A standard layout for integrated circuit packages using two parallel rows of connecting pins along each side.

diplex The simultaneous transmission of two signals over the same line.

dipole A material or molecule or object that has two potentials, one end positive and the other negative, due to electron displacement from an applied electric field.

direct access The storage and retrieval of data without the need to read other data first. For **direct (access) address** see **absolute address.**

direct access storage device (DASD) A storage medium whose memory locations can be directly read * written to.

direct addressing A method of addressing where the storage location address given in the instruction is the location to be used.

direct change-over Switching a computerized system from one computer to another in one go.

direct code Binary code which directly operates the CPU, using only absolute addresses and values.

direct coding Program instructions written in absolute code.

direct connect A modem which plugs straight into the standard square telephone socket.

direct current (DC) A constant value electric current that flows in one direction.

direct data entry (DDE) Keying data directly onto a magnetic disk or tape.

direct digital control (DDC) Control of a machine automatically by a computer.

directed scan A file or array search method in which a starting point and a direction of scan is provided, either up or down from the starting point (an address or record number).

direct information access network for Europe (DIANE) The services offered over the Euronet network.

direct-insert routine or **subroutine** A routine which can be directly copied (i.e. inserted) into a larger routine or program without the need for a call instruction.

direct instruction A program command that contains an operand and the code for the operation to be carried out.

directive A programming instruction used to control the language translator, compiler, etc.

direct memory access (DMA) The direct, rapid link between a peripheral and a computer's main memory which avoids the use of accessing routines for each item of data required.

direct memory access channel A high speed data transfer link.

direct mode Typing in a command which is executed once return is pressed.

directory (disk) A list of names and information about files in a backing storage device. A disk directory shows file name, date and time of creation.

directory routing A means of directing messages in a packet switching network by a list of preferred routes at each node.

direct page register A register that provides memory page access data when a CPU is carrying out a direct memory access, to allow access to any part of memory.

direct transfer A bit for bit copy of the contents of one register into another register (including any status bits, etc.)

dirty bit A flag bit set by memory-resident programs (a utility or the operating system) to indicate that they have already been loaded into main memory.

disable To prevent a device or function from operating. For example, an operator might disable a keyboard by turning a key, so as to prevent anyone accessing his data.

disable interrupt A command to the CPU to tell it to ignore any interrupt signals.

disarmed state The state of an interrupt that has been disabled, and cannot accept a signal.

disassemble To translate machine code instructions back into assembly language mnemonics. The software that translates a machine code program back into an assembly language form is a **disassembler.**

disaster dump A system which dumps the current state of a program's registers, current data, etc., just before a fatal error or system crash.

disc see **disk**

discrete Values or events or energy or data which occurs in small individual units. A binary data word is made up of discrete bits.

discretionary Which can be used if wanted or not used if not wanted.

discrimination instruction A conditional program instruction that directs control by providing the location of the next instruction to be executed (if a condition is met). See also **branch, jump, call.**

disjointed A set of information or data that has no common subject.

disjunction A logical function that produces a true output if any input is true.

disjunctive search A search for data items that match at least one of a number of search requirements or keys.

disk A flat, circular plate coated with a substance that is capable of being magnetized. Data is stored on a disk by magnetizing selective sections to represent binary digits. The disk surface is divided into tracks and sectors which can be accessed individually; magnetic tapes cannot be accessed in this way. The two types of disk are the **floppy disk** or **floppy** or **FD** a flat, circular flexible disk which cannot store as much data as a hard disk, but is easily removed, and is protected by a flexible paper or plastic sleeve. Floppy disks are usually available in standard sizes of eight, five-and-a-quarter, three-and-a-half or three inch diameters. A **hard disk** is a rigid magnetic disk that is able to store many times more data than a floppy disk, and usually cannot be removed from the disk drive. See also **Winchester.**

disk access The operations required to read from or write to a magnetic disk, including device selection, sector and track address, movement of read/write head to the correct location, access location on disk.

disk-based (operating system) An operating system held on floppy or hard disk.

disk cartridge A protective case containing a removable hard disk.

disk controller An integrated circuit or circuits used to translate a request for data by the CPU into control signals for the disk drive (including motor control and access arm movement). An add-on card that contains all the electronics and connectors to interface a disk drive to a CPU is a **disk-controller card.**

disk crash A fault caused by the read/write head touching the surface of the disk.

disk drive A device that spins a magnetic disk and controls the position of the read/write head.

diskette A light, flexible disk that can store data in a magnetic form, used in most personal computers.

disk file A number of related records or data items stored under one name on disk.

disk formatting The initial actions required when setting up a blank disk. This usually consists of writing track and sector markers and other control information to the first (system) track.

disk index holes 1 Holes around the hub of a disk that provide rotational information to a disk controller. 2 A number of holes providing sector location indicators on a hard-sectored disk.

diskless system A computer or system which does not use disks for data storage.

disk map A display of the organization of data on a disk.

disk operating system (DOS) 1 A section of the operating system software that controls disk and file management. 2 An operating system (usually for microcomputers) that is stored on disk.

disk pack A number of disks on a single hub, each with its own read/write head.

disk sector The smallest area on a magnetic disk that can be addressed by a computer.

disk storage Using disks for backing storage.

disk track One of a series of (thin) concentric rings on a magnetic disk, which the read/write head accesses and along which data is stored in separate sectors.

disk unit A disk drive.

disorderly close-down A system crash that did not provide enough warning to carry out an orderly close-down.

dispersion A logical function whose output is false if all inputs are true, and true if any input is false.

displacement An offset used within an indexed address.

display 1 A device on which information or images can be presented visually. A **gas discharge** or **plasma** or **electroluminescent display** is a flat, lightweight display screen that is made up of two flat pieces of glass covered with a grid of conductors, separated by a thin layer of gas which luminesces when a point of the grid is selected by two electrical signals. A **liquid crystal display (LCD)** is the standard display used in laptop computers, being thin light and cheap. This display generates no light, and uses pixels which are blackened as required, so needs good light for viewing. **Light emitting diode (LED)** display produces a bright clear display, normally only one line or a few characters long. **2** To show information on a screen. See also **visual display unit.**

display adapter A device which allows information in a computer to be displayed on a CRT (the adapter interfaces with both the computer and CRT).

display attribute A variable which defines the shape or size or colour of text or graphics displayed.

display character A graphical symbol which appears as a printed or displayed item, such as one of the letters of the alphabet or a number.

display character generator ROM that provides the display circuits with a pattern of dots which form the character.

display colour The colour of characters in a videotext display system.

display controller A device that accepts character or graphics codes and instructions, and converts them into dot-matrix patterns that are displayed on a screen.

display format A number of characters that can be displayed on a screen, given as row and column lengths.

display highlights To emphasise certain words or paragraphs by changing character display colour.

display line An allowable horizontal printing position for characters in a line of text.

display mode A way of referring to the character set to be used, usually graphics or alphanumerics.

display processor The processor that changes data to a format suitable for a display controller. See also **graphics coprocessor.**

display register A register that contains character or control or graphical data that is to be displayed.

display resolution The number of pixels per unit area that a display can clearly show.

display screen The physical part of a Visual Display Unit or terminal or monitor, which allows the user to see characters or graphics (usually a Cathode Ray Tube, but sometimes LCD or LED displays are used).

display scrolling The movement of a screenful of information up or down one line or pixel at a time.

display size A character size greater than 14 points, used in composition and headlines rather than normal text.

display space The memory or amount of screen available to show graphics or text.

display unit A computer terminal or piece of equipment that is capable of showing data or information, usually by means of CRT.

distort To introduce unwanted differences between a signal input and output from a device.

distribute To send out data or information to users in a network or multiuser system.

distributed adaptive routing Directing the route taken by messages in a packet network switching system by an exchange of information between nodes.

distributed database system A data system in which the data is kept on different disks in different places.

distributed data processing (DDP) The operations to derive information from data which is kept in different places.

distributed file system A system that uses files stored in more than one location or backing store but are processed at a central point.

distributed intelligence A decentralized system in which a number of small micros or mini-computers carry out a set of fixed (tasks rather than one large computer).

distributed (data) processing A system of processing in a large organization with many small computers at different workstations instead of one central computer.

distributed system A computer system which uses more than one processor in different locations, all connected to a central computer.

distribution The act of sending information out to various users or nodes, especially via a network. For **distribution network** see **LAN, WAN.**

distribution point The point from which cable television or telephone signals are split up from a main line and sent to individual users' homes.

dittogram A printing error caused by repeating the same letter twice.

dividend The operand that is divided by a divisor in a division operation. The dividend is divided by the divisor to form the quotient and a remainder.

DMA (direct memory access) A direct, rapid link between a peripheral and a computer's main memory, which avoids the use of accessing routines for each item of data read.

DMA controller Interface and associated circuitry that controls high-speed data transfer between a high-speed peripheral and main memory, usually the controller will also halt or cycle steal from the CPU.

DMA cycle stealing The action of a CPU allowing the DMA controller to send data over the bus during clock cycles when it performs internal or NOP instructions.

DML see **data manipulation language**

DMM see **digital multimeter**

do-nothing (instruction) A programming instruction that does not carry out any action (except increasing the program counter to the next instruction address.

document A file containing text.

document assembly or **document merge** Creating a new file by combining two or more sections or complete documents.

document processing Processing of documents such as invoices by a computer.

document reader A device which converts written or typed information to a form that a computer can understand and process.

document recovery A program which allows a document which has been accidentally deleted to be recovered.

document retrieval system An information storage and retrieval system that contains complete documents rather than just quotes or references.

dollar sign A printed or written character ($) used in some languages to identify a variable as a string type.

dongle A coded circuit or chip that has to be present in a system before a piece of copyright software will run.

dopant A chemical substance that is diffused or implanted onto the substrate of a chip during manufacture, to provide it with n- or p-type properties. A piece of semiconductor which has had a dopant added to it is said to be **doped.**

DOR (digital optical reading) Recording signals in binary form as small holes in the surface of an optical or compact disk which can then be read by laser.

DOS see **disk operating system**

dot command One method of writing instructions with a full stop followed by the command, used mainly for embedded commands in word-processor systems.

dot matrix Forming characters using a pattern of dots within a rectangular matrix.

dot-matrix printer A printer in which the characters are made up by a series of closely spaced dots. It produces a page line by line; a dot-matrix printer can be used either for printing using a ribbon or for thermal or electrostatic printing.

dots per inch (d.p.i. or dpi) A standard means used to describe the resolution capabilities of a page printer or scanner. 300 d.p.i. is now the normal industry standard for a laser printer, but some laser printers offer high resolution printing — up to 400 dpi.

double buffering Using two buffers, allowing one to be read while the other is being written to.

double density A system to double the storage capacity of a disk drive by doubling the number of bits which can be put on the disk surface.

double-density disk A disk that can store two bits of data per unit area, compared to a standard disk.

double ended queue (deque) A queue in which new items can be added to either end.

double-length or **double precision arithmetic** Using two data words to store a number, providing greater precision.

double-sided disk A disk which can store information on both sides of its surface.

double-sided disk drive A disk drive which can access data stored on double-sided disks.

double-sided printed circuit board A circuit board with conducting tracks on both sides.

doublet or **diad** A word made up of two bits.

double word Two bytes of data handled as one word, often used for address data.

down (of computers or programs) Not working. The period of time during which a computer or system is not working or usable is called **downtime**.

download 1 To receive a program or section of data from a remote computer via a telephone line. **2** To load data from a mainframe to a small computer. **3** To send font data stored on disk to a printer (where it will be stored in temporary memory or RAM).

downloadable fonts Fonts or typefaces stored on a disk, which can be downloaded or sent to a printer and stored in temporary memory or RAM.

downward compatibility The ability of a complex computer system to work with a simple computer. A mainframe is downward compatible with a micro.

dp or **DP (data processing)** To operate on data to produce useful information or to sort and organize data files.

d.p.i. or **dpi (dots per inch)** A standard method used to describe the resolution capabilities of a dot-matrix or laser printer or scanner. 300 dpi is now the normal industry standard for a laser printer.

DPM see **data processing manager**

draft A rough copy of a document before errors have been corrected.

draft printing Low quality, high speed printing. Most dot-matrix printers have two modes of operation: a high-speed draft printing mode and a lower-speed letter quality mode.

drag To move (a mouse) with a mouse button or control key pressed, so that an image is moved around the screen. Normal operation of a mouse, with no button pressed, just moves a pointer around the screen.

drain 1 Electrical current provided by a battery or power supply connection to a FET. **2** To remove or decrease power or energy from a device such as a battery.

DRAM (dynamic random access memory) see **RAM** Changes in the characteristics of a circuit with time orchanging temperature.

drive The part of a computer which operates a tape or disk. A **disk drive** spins a magnetic disk and controls the position of the read/write head. A **tape drive** carries the magnetic tape over the recording and playback heads.

driver or **handler** A program or routine used to interface and manage an input/output device or other peripheral.

DRO (destructive readout) A form of storage medium that loses its data after it has been read.

drop dead halt or **dead halt** A program instruction from the user or an error that causes the program to stop without allowing recovery.

drop in A small piece of dirt that is on a disk or tape surface, which does not allow data to be recorded on that section.

drop out 1 The failure of a small piece of tape or disk to be correctly magnetized for the accurate storage of data. **2** The loss of transmitted signals due to attenuation or noise.

drum (magnetic) An early type of magnetic computer storage consisting of a coated cylinder.

drum plotter A computer output device that consists of a movable pen and a piece of paper around a drum that can be rotated, creating patterns and text when both are moved in various ways.

dry cell A battery that cannot be recharged. Compare with **rechargeable battery.**

dry contact A faulty electrical connection, often causing an intermittent fault.

dry joint A faulty or badly made electrical connection.

dry run To run a program with test data to check everything works.

DSE see **data switching exchange**

DSR (data set ready) A signal sent from a device to indicate that it is ready to accept data, this signal occurs after a DTR signal is received.

DSW (device status word) A data word transmitted from a device that contains information about its current status.

DTE (data terminal equipment) A device at which a communications path starts or finishes.

DTP (desktop publishing) The design, layout and printing of documents using special software, a desktop computer and a laser printer.

DTR (data terminal ready) A signal from a device that indicates that it is ready to send data.

D-type flip-flop A flip-flop device with one input and two outputs.

dual-in-line package (DIL or DIP) A standard layout for integrated circuit packages using two parallel rows of connecting pins along each edge.

dual port memory Memory with two sets of data and memory lines to allow communications between CPUs.

dual processor A computer system with two processors for faster program execution.

dual systems Two computer systems, working in parallel on the same data, with the same instructions, to ensure high reliability.

duct A pipe containing cables, providing a tidy and protective surrounding for a group of cables.

dumb terminal A peripheral that can only transmit and receive data from a computer, but is not capable of processing data. Compare **intelligent terminal.**

dummy instruction An instruction in a program that is only there to satisfy language syntax or to make up a block length but which does not carry out any actions.

dummy variable A variable set up to satisfy the syntax of a language, but which is replaced when the program is executed.

dump 1 Data which has been copied from one device to another for storage. 2 A printout of the contents of all or selected data in memory. 3 To move data from one device or storage area to another. 4 To transfer data from volatile memory to a disk for storage.

dump and restart Software that will stop a program execution, dump any relevant data or program status then restart the program.

dump point A point in a program at which the program and its data are saved onto backing store to minimize the effects of any future faults.

duodecimal number system A number system with a radix of twelve.

duplex The simultaneous transmission of two signals over one line.

duplex circuit An electronic circuit used to transmit data in two directions simultaneously.

duplex computer Two identical computer systems used in an on-line application, with one used as a backup in case of failure of the other.

duplex operation The simultaneous transmission of data over a single line in two directions. See also **half-duplex, full duplex, simplex.**

duty-rated Referring to the maximum number of operations which a device can perform in a set time to a certain specification.

dyadic operation A binary operation using two binary operands.

dynamic Referring to data which can change with time. See also **volatile.**

dynamic allocation A system in which resources are allocated during a program run, rather than being determined in advance.

dynamically redefinable character set A computer or videotext character set that can be changed as and when required.

dynamic buffer A buffer whose size varies with demand.

dynamic data structure A structure of a data management system which can be changed * adapted.

dynamic dump A memory dump that is carried out periodically during a program run. This is usually used to keep track of progress, or to monitor a program for any potential problems.

dynamic memory or **dynamic RAM** Random access memory (RAM) that requires its contents to be updated regularly.

dynamic multiplexing A time division multiplexing method which allocates time segments to signals according to demand.

dynamic relocation (program) A program that is moved from one section of memory to another during its run-time without affecting it or its data.

dynamic stop A pause in a process where the system informs the user that some action must be taken before the processing can continue.

dynamic storage allocation To allocate memory to a program when it needs it rather than reserving a block before it has run.

dynamic subroutine A subroutine whose function must be defined each time it is called. Compare **static.**

E

E The hexadecimal (base 16) number equivalent to decimal number 14.

EAN (European article number) A numbering system for bar codes (the European version of UPC).

EAPROM (electrically alterable programmable read-only memory) A version of an EAROM device which can be programmed.

EAROM see **electrically alterable read-only memory**

earth wire A connecting wire between an electrical device and the earth, representing zero potential.

EBCDIC (extended binary coded decimal interchange code) An eight bit binary character coding system.

EBNF (extended Backus-Naur form) A flexible way of defining the syntax of a language. See also **BNF.**

echo check A system in which each character received at a terminal is returned to the transmitter and checked to ensure accurate data transmission.

ECL (emitter coupled logic) High-speed logic circuit design using the emitters of the transistors as output connections to other stages.

ECMA see **European Computer Manufacturers Association** The **ECMA symbols** are a standard set of symbols used to draw flowcharts.

EDAC (error detection and correction) A forward error correction system used for data communications.

edge board or **edge card** A printed circuit board that has a series of contact strips along one edge allowing it to be inserted into an edge connector.

edge connector A long connector with a slot containing metal contacts to allow it to make electrical contact with an edge card.

edge detection An algorithm and routines used in image recognition to define the edges of an object.

edge notched card A paper card which has punched holes along an edge to represent data.

edge-triggered A process or circuit which is clocked or synchronized by the changing level (the edge) of a clock signal rather than the level itself.

edit To change, correct and modify text or programs. The sequence of characters or keys that must be pressed to accomplish a function in an editor program are the **edit commands.**

editing run Processing to check that new data meets certain requirements before actually analysing the data and its implications.

editing terms The command words and instruction sequences used when editing a file or data with an editor.

edit key A key that starts a function that makes an editor easier to use.

editor or **editor program** Software that allows the user to select sections of a file and alter, delete or add to them.

edit window The area of the screen in which the user can display and edit text or graphics.

EDP (electronic data processing) Data processing using computers and electronic devices.

EDP capability A word processor that is able to carry out certain data processing functions.

EDS (exchangeable disk storage) A disk drive that uses a removable disk pack (as opposed to a fixed disk). Some normally fixed hard disk drives are able to use exchangeable disk storage packs.

EEPROM see **electrically erasable programmable read-only memory**

EEROM see **electrically erasable read-only memory**

effective address The address resulting from the modification of an address.

effective instruction The resulting instruction executed after the modification of an original instruction.

effective search speed The rate of finding a particular section of information from a storage device.

effective throughput The average throughput of a processor.

EFT (electronic funds transfer) A system in which computers are used to transmit money to and from banks. **EFTPOS (electronic funds transfer point-of-sale)** is a terminal at a POS (point-of-sale) that is linked to a central computer which automatically transfers money from the customer's account to the shop's.

EGA (enhanced graphics adapter) A popular microcomputer high-resolution colour display standardized system.

EIA (Electronic Industry Association) interface A standard defining interface signals, transmission rate and power, usually used to connect terminals to modems.

eight-bit system An old, small, cheap, low-power home computer in which the CPU can process eight-bit words.

eight-bit byte or **octet** A byte made up of eight binary digits. Compare with **sixteen, thirty-two bit.**

eight-inch disk A high-capacity floppy disk which is eight inches in diameter. This size of floppy disk has now largely been replaced by five-and-a-quarter inch and three-and-a-half inch floppy disks.

eight-inch drive A disk drive that can read and write to eight-inch disks.

eighty-column screen A screen that can display eighty characters horizontally. An eighty-column screen is the most popular of terminal screen formats.

eighty-track disk A disk formatted so as to contain eighty tracks.

either-or operation A logical function that produces a true output if any input is true.

either-way operation A data transmission in one direction at a time over a bidirectional channel.

elapsed time The time taken by the user to carry out a task on a computer.

elastic banding A method of defining the limits of an image on a computer screen by stretching a boundary around it (usually using a mouse).

elastic buffer A buffer whose size changes according to demand.

electrically alterable, programmable read-only memory (EAPROM) A version of an EAROM that can be programmed.

electrically alterable read-only memory (EAROM) A read-only memory chip whose contents can be programmed by applying a certain voltage to a write pin, and can only be erased by light or a reverse voltage (the contents are not volatile with time).

electrically erasable programmable read-only memory (EEPROM) ROM storage chip which can be programmed and erased using an electrical signal.

electrically erasable read-only memory (EEROM) EAROM memory chip whose contents can be programmed by applying a certain voltage to a write pin, and can be erased by light * a reverse voltage.

electrode The part of an electric circuit or device that collects, controls or emits electrons.

electrographic printer see **ELECTROSTATIC PRINTER**

electroluminescence The light emitted from a phosphor dot when it is struck by an electron or charged particle.

electroluminescing Emitting light due to electroluminescence.

electroluminescent display A flat, lightweight display screen that is made up of two pieces of glass covered with a grid of conductors, separated by a thin layer of gas which luminesces when a point of the grid is selected by two electric signals.

electromagnet A device that consists of a core and a coil of wire that produces a magnetic field when current is passed through the coil.

electromagnetic interference The corruption of data due to nearby electrically generated magnetic fields.

electromagnetic spectrum The frequency range of electromagnetic radiation (from light to radio wave).

electromagnetic radiation An energy wave consisting of electric and/or magnetic fields. Electromagnetic radiation requires no medium to support it, travels approximately at the speed of light and can support frequency ranges from light to radio waves.

electromechanical switching A connection of two paths by an electrically operated switch * relay.

electromotive force (EMF) A difference in electrical potential across a source of electric current.

electron beam recording (EBR) 1 The production of microfilm images by means of an electron beam. 2 Recording the output from a computer directly onto microfilm using an electron beam.

electron gun An electronic component that emits a large number of electrons (usually by heating a filament of metal). The source of an electron beam is located inside a cathode ray tube. Black and white monitors have a single beam gun, while colour monitors contain three, one for each primary colour (Red, Green and Blue) used.

electronic composition Text manipulation by computer before typesetting. Electronic composition systems were the predecessors of full desktop publishing systems.

electronic data processing (EDP) Data processing using computers and electronic devices.

electronic data processing compatibility The ability of a word processor to carry out certain data processing functions.

electronic digital computer A digital computer constructed with electronic components (the basic form uses a CPU, main memory, backing storage and input/output devices; these are all implemented with electronic components and integrated circuits).

electronic industry association (EIA) interface A standard defining interface signals, transmission rate and power usually used to connect terminals to modems.

electronic filing A system of storing documents which can be easily retrieved.

electronic funds transfer (EFT) Using a computer to transfer money to and from banks.

electronic funds transfer point-of-sale (EFTPOS) A terminal at a POS (point-of-sale) that is linked to a central computer which automatically transfers money from the customer's account to the shop's.

electronic keyboard A keyboard that generates characters electronically in response to a switch making contact when pressed, rather than by mechanical means.

electronic lock A security device, usually in the form of a password (used to protect a file or piece of equipment from unauthorized use).

electronic mail (E-mail) The process of sending and receiving messages over a telephone network, usually using a bulletin board.

electronic mailbox A system for storing messages sent by electronic mail until the person to whom they were sent is ready to accept them. Normally in a bulletin-board or electronic mail system, each user has his own unique mailbox to which other users may send messages.

electronic money Smart cards or phonecards, etc., which take the place of money.

electronic office An office where all the work is done using computers, which store information, communicate with different workstations, etc.

electronic pen or **stylus** or **wand** A light pen or wand; a stylus used to draw on a graphics tablet.

electronic point-of-sale (EPOS) A system that uses a computer terminal at a point-of-sale site for electronic funds transfer or stock control as well as product identification, etc.

electronic publishing 1 Use of desktop publishing packages and laser printers to produce printed matter. **2** Using computers to write and display information, such as viewdata.

electronics The science of applying the study of electrons and their properties to manufactured products, such as components, computers, calculators or telephones.

electronic shopping Shopping from the home, using computerized catalogues and paying by credit card, all by means of a home computer terminal.

electronic signature A special code which identifies the sender of a coded message. Electronic signatures are used with authentication systems to ensure that the sender is genuine and authentic.

electronic smog Excessive stray electromagnetic fields and static electricity generated by large numbers of electronic equipment: this can damage equipment or an operator's health.

electronic stylus or **wand** see **light pen**

electronic traffic Data transmitted in the form of electronic pulses.

electrosensitive paper A metal-coated printing paper, which can display characters using localized heating with a special dot-matrix print head. This sort of paper is used in an electrothermal printer.

electrostatic printer A type of printer which forms an image on the paper by charging certain regions to provide character shapes, etc., and using ink with an opposite charge which sticks to the paper where required.

electrostatic screen A metal cage surrounding sensitive equipment (and connected to earth) to protect it from interference.

electrostatic storage Data stored in the form of small electric charged regions on a a dielectric material.

electrothermal printer A printer that uses a printing head with a dot-matrix of heating elements to form characters on electrosensitive paper.

elegant programming Writing a well-structured program using the minimum number of instructions.

elimination factor During a search, the section of data that is not used.

else rule A program logical rule used with an IF-THEN instruction to provide an alternative if the IF-THEN condition is not met. For example, IF X=20 THEN PRINT 'X is 20' ELSE PRINT 'X not 20'.

E-mail or **email** see **electronic mail**

embedded code Sections or routines written in machine code, inserted into a high-level program to speed up or perform a special function.

embedded command A printer command (such as indicating that text should be in italic) inserted into the text and used by a word-processing system when producing formatted printed text.

embedded computer or **system** A dedicated computer controlling a machine; a dedicated computer within a larger system that performs one fixed function.

embrace see **deadly**

emf see **electromotive force**

EMI (electromagnetic interference) The corruption of data due to nearby electrically generated magnetic fields.

emitter-coupled logic (ECL) High-speed logic circuit design using the emitters of the transistors as output connections to other stages.

empty or **null list** A list with no elements.

empty medium A blank but formatted storage medium that is ready to receive data.

empty set A reserved area for related data items, containing no data. Also called a **null** or **void set.**

empty slot 1 A packet of data in a packet-switching LAN that is carrying no information. **2** An unused expansion edge connector on a motherboard.

empty or **null string** A variable containing no characters.

emulate To copy or behave like something else. A laser printer, for example, may emulate a wide range of office impact printers.

emulation The behaviour by one computer or printer which is exactly the same as another, which allows the same programs to be run and the same data to be processed.

emulation facility A feature of hardware or software which emulates another system.

emulator Software or hardware that allows a machine to behave like another.

emulsion laser storage Digital storage technique using a laser to expose light-sensitive material.

enable To use an electronic signal to start a process or access a function (on a chip or circuit). The signal that starts a process * allows one to take place is an **enabling signal.**

encipher To convert plaintext into a secure coded form by means of a cipher system.

encode To apply the rules of a code to a program or data. An iscaddevice that can translate data from one format to another.

encoding The process of translation of a message or text according to a coding system. The **encoding format** is the method of coding data stored on a magnetic disk in such a way as to avoid a series of similar bits.

encrypt To convert plaintext to a secure coded form, using a cipher system. If an encrypted text is sent along ordinary telephone lines, no one will be able to understand it.

encryption The conversion of plaintext to a secure coded form by means of a cipher system. The standard for block data cipher systems is **data encryption standard (DES).**

end about carry The most significant digit is added into the least significant place (used in BCD arithmetic).

end about shift Data movement to the left or right in a word, the bits falling outside the word boundary are discarded and replaced with zeros.

endless loop A continuous piece of recording tape or number of computer instructions that are continuously repeated.

end of address (EOA) A transmitted code which indicates that address data has been sent.

end of block (EOB) A code which indicates that the last byte of a block of data has been sent through a communications link.

end of data (EOD) A code which indicates that the end of a stored data file has been reached.

end of document or **end of file (EOF)** A marker after the last record in a file.

end of job (EOJ) A code used in batch processing to indicate that a job has been finished.

end of medium (EM) A code that indicates the end of usable physical medium.

end of message (EOM) A code used to separate the last character of one message from the first of another message.

end of record (EOR) A code that indicates the end of a record.

end of run routines Routines carried out before a program run finishes to perform certain system housekeeping functions.

end of tape A code used to indicate the end of a magnetic tape.

end of text (EOT or **ETX)** A code sent after last character of text.

end of transmission (EOT) A sequence of characters that indicate that all the data from a terminal or peripheral has been transmitted.

end user A person who will use the device or program or product, usually the keyboard operator.

enhanced dot matrix A clearer character or graphics printout (using smaller dots and more dots per inch).

enhanced graphics adapter (EGA) A popular standardized system of high-resolution colour display for microcomputers. An **EGA screen** is a high-resolution colour monitor that can display EGA system signals and graphics.

enhanced small device interface (ESDI) An interface standard between a CPU and peripherals such as disk drives.

enhancement An add-on facility which improves the output or performance of equipment.

enhancer A device or software which enhances a process or product.

enquiry (ENQ) A request for data or information from a device or database; accessing data in a computer memory without changing the data.

enquiry character A special control code that is a request for identification or status or data from a remote terminal.

enter To type in information on a terminal or keyboard. The **enter key** is the key on a keyboard which is pressed to indicate the end of an input or line of text.

entity The subject to which the data stored in a file or database refers.

entry 1 A single record or data about one action or object in a database or library. 2 The point in a program where data input is required or possible.

entry condition A condition that must be satisfied before a routine can be entered.

entry instruction The first instruction executed in a called subroutine.

entry point An address from which a program or subroutine is to be executed.

entry time A point in time when a program or job or batch will be executed by the operating system scheduler.

enumerated type Data storage or classification using numbers to represent chosen convenient labels. If 'man', 'horse', 'dog', 'cat' are the items of data, stored by the machine simply as 0, 1, 2, 3, they can still be referred to in the program as man, horse, etc., to make it easier for the user to recognize them.

envelope A transmitted byte of data containing error and control bits. The shape of the initial section of a signal is the **attack envelope. Envelope detection** is a technique of signal recovery from a modulated waveform.

environment 1 The condition in a computer system of all the registers and memory locations. 2 The appearance and method of working of an operating system or application that is presented to the user. New operating systems are adopting a graphical environment to simplify use and speed training.

EOA see **end of address**

EOB see **end of block**

EOD see **end of data**

EOF see **end of file**

EOJ see **end of job**

EOM see **end of message**

EOR see **end of record**

EOT see **end of text** or **end of transmission**

EPOS (electronic point-of-sale) A system that uses a computer terminal at a point-of-sale site for electronic funds transfer or stock control as well as product identification.

EPROM see **electrically programmable read-only memory; erasable programmable read-only memory**

equality A logical function whose output is true if either of two inputs is true, and false if both inputs are the same.

equipment failure A hardware fault, rather than a software fault

equivalence Logical operation that is true if all the inputs are the same.

equivalence function or **operation** 1 AND function. 2 A logical function whose output is true if both inputs are the same. The **equivalence gate** is the gate which performs an equivalence function.

erase 1 To set all the digits in a storage area to zero. **2** To remove any signal from a magnetic medium.

erase head A small magnet that clears a magnetic tape or disk of recorded signals.

erase character A character which means "do nothing".

erasable storage or **erasable memory 1** A storage medium that can be re-used. **2** Temporary storage.

erasable programmable read-only memory (EPROM) A read-only memory chip that can be programmed by a voltage applied to a write pin and data applied to its output pins, usually erasable with ultraviolet light.

eraser A device that erases the contents of an EPROM (usually using UV light).

ERCC (error checking and correcting) A memory which checks and corrects errors.

EROM see **erasable read-only memory** (the same as **EAROM**)

error ambiguity An error due to an incorrect selection from ambiguous data.

error burst A group of several consecutive errors (in a transmission).

error checking code A general term used to describe all error correcting and error detecting codes.

error code A code that indicates that a particular type of error has occurred.

error condition A state that is entered if an attempt is made to operate on data containing errors.

error control Routines that ensure that errors are minimised and any errors that occur are detected and dealt with rapidly.

error correcting code A coding system that allows bit errors occurring during transmission to be rapidly corrected by logical deduction methods rather than re-transmission. See also **Gray code.**

error correction Hardware or software that can detect and correct an error in a transmission.

error detecting codes A coding system that allows errors occurring during transmission to be detected but is not complex enough to correct the errors.

error detection Using special hardware or software to detect errors in a data entry or transmission, then usually ask for re-transmission.

error detection and correction (EDAC) A forward error correction system for data communications.

error diagnosis Finding the cause of an error.

error diagnostics Information and system messages displayed when an error is detected to help a user diagnose and correct it.

error handling or **management** Routines and procedures that diagnose and correct errors or minimise the effects of errors, so that a system will run when an error is detected.

error interrupt An interrupt signal sent due to an error in hardware or software.

error logging The recording of errors that have occurred.

error message A report that an error has occurred.

error propagation One error causing another.

error rate 1 The number of mistakes per thousand entries or per page. **2** The number of corrupt bits of data in relation to the total transmission length.

error recovery Software or hardware that can continue after an error has occurred.

error routine A short routine within a main program that handles any errors when they occur.

error trapping Detecting and correcting errors before they cause any problems.

ESC The escape character code or key on a computer.

escape character A character used to represent an escape code.

escape codes A transmitted code sequence which informs the receiver that all following characters represent control actions.

escape key (ESC) A key on a keyboard which allows the user to enter escape codes to control the computer's basic modes or actions.

ESDI (enhanced small device interface) An interface standard between a CPU and peripherals such as disk drives.

etch To use an acid to remove selected layers of metal from a printed circuit board.

ETX see **end of text**

even A quantity or number that is a multiple of two. The first three even numbers are 2, 4, 6.

even parity (check) An error checking method that only transmits an even number of binary ones in each word. Compare **odd parity**.

event-driven A computer program or process where each step of the execution relies on external actions.

except gate A logical function whose output is true if either of two inputs is true, and false if both inputs are the same.

excess-3 code A code in which decimal digits are represented by the binary equivalent of three greater than the number. For example, the excess-3 code representation of 6 is 1001.

exchange To swap data between two locations.

exchange selection A sorting method which repeatedly exchanges various pairs of data items until they are in order.

exchangeable disk storage (EDS) A disk drive using a removable disk pack (as opposed to a fixed disk).

exclusive NOR (EXNOR) Logical function whose output is true if all inputs are the same level, and false if any are different.

exclusive NOR gate An electronic implementation of the EXNOR function.

exclusive OR (EXOR) A logical function whose output is true if any input is true, and false if all the inputs are the same.

exclusive OR gate An electronic implementation of the EXOR function.

executable form A program translated or compiled into a machine code form that a processor can execute.

execute To run or carry out a computer program or process. The **execute cycle** is the series of events required to fetch, decode and carry out an instruction stored in memory. See also **fetch-execute cycle.**

execute mode The state of a computer that is executing a program. Compare with **direct mode.**

execute phase A section of the execute cycle when the instruction is carried out.

execute signal A signal that steps the CPU through the execute cycle.

execute statement A basic operating system command to start a program run.

execute time see **execution time**

execution The carrying out of a computer program or process.

execution address A location in memory at which the first instruction in a program is stored.

execution cycle A period of time during which the instruction is executed.

execution error An error detected while a program is being run, due to bad inputs or a faulty program.

execution phase see **execute phase**

execution time 1 The time taken to run or carry out a program or series of instructions. 2 The time taken for one execution cycle.

executive control program see **operating system**

executive instruction An instruction used to control and execute programs under the control of an operating system. See also **supervisor instruction.**

executive program or **supervisor program** The master program in a computer system that controls the execution of other programs.

exhaustive search A search through every record in a database.

exit To stop program execution or to leave a program and return control to the operating system or interpreter.

exit point The point in a subroutine where control is returned to the main program.

exjunction A logical function whose output is true if either (of two) inputs is true, and false if both inputs are the same.

EXNOR (exclusive NOR) A logical function whose output is true if all inputs are the same level, false if any are different.

EXNOR gate An electronic implementation of the EXNOR function. See also **NOR.**

EXOR (exclusive OR) A logical function whose output is true if any input is true, and false if the all inputs are the same.

EXOR gate An electronic implementation of the EXOR function. See also **OR.**

expandable system A computer system that is designed to be able to grow (in power or memory) by hardware or software additions.

expansion card or **expansion board** A printed circuit board that is connected to a system to increase its functions or performance.

expansion slot A connector inside a computer into which an expansion card can be plugged.

expert system Software that applies the knowledge, advice and rules defined by experts in a particular field to a user's data to help solve a problem.

explicit address An address provided in two parts, one is the reference point, the other a displacement or index value.

exponent A number indicating the power to which a base number is to be raised.

extended arithmetic element The section of a CPU that provides hardware implementations of various mathematical functions.

extended binary coded decimal interchange code (EBCDIC) An 8-bit character coding system.

extended BNF (EBNF) A flexible way of defining the syntax of a language.

extending serial file A stored file that can be added to or that has no maximum size.

extensible language A computer programming language that allows the user to add his own data types and commands.

extension memory Storage which is located outside the main computer system but which can be accessed by the CPU.

external clock A clock or synchronizing signal supplied from outside a device.

external data file A file containing data for a program that is stored separately from it.

external device 1 An item of hardware (such as a terminal or printer) which is attached to a main computer. **2** Any device that allows communications between the computer and itself, but which is not directly operated by the main computer.

external disk drive A device not built into the computer, but which is added to increase its storage capabilities.

external interrupts An interrupt signal from a peripheral device indicating that attention is required.

external memory Memory which is located outside the main computer system confines but which can be accessed by the CPU.

external registers A user's registers that are located in main memory rather than within the CPU.

external schema A user's view of the structure of data or a program.

external sort A method of sorting which uses a file stored in secondary memory, such as a disk, as its data source and uses the disk as temporary memory during sorting.

external storage or **external store** A storage device which is located outside the main computer system but which can be accessed by the CPU.

extracode Short routines within the operating system that emulate a hardware function.

extract To remove required data or information from a database.

extract instruction An instruction to select and read required data from a database or file.

extrapolation The process of predicting future quantities or trends by the analysis of current and past data.

F

f (femto-) A prefix meaning equal to one thousandth of a million millionth (10^{-15}).

F The hexadecimal (base 16) number equivalent to decimal number 15.

face see **typeface**

faceted code Code which indicates various details of an item, by assigning each one a value.

facia see **fascia**

facility A communications path between two or more locations, with no ancillary line equipment.

facsimile An exact copy of an original.

facsimile character generator A means of displaying characters on a computer screen by copying preprogrammed images from memory.

facsimile transmission (FAX) A method of sending and receiving images in digital form over a telephone or radio link.

factor Any number in a multiplication that is the operand.

factorial The product of all the numbers below and including a number. For example, **4 factorial** (written 4!) is 1x2x3x4 = 24.

factorize To break down a number into two whole numbers which when multiplied will give the original number. For example, when factorized, 15 gives the factors 1, 15 or 3, 5.

fail safe system A system that has a predetermined state it will go to if a main program or device fails, so avoiding a total catastrophe that a complete system shutdown would produce.

fail soft system A system that will still be partly operational even after a part of the system has failed. See also **graceful degradation.**

failure logging A section of the operating system that automatically saves the present system states and relevant data when an error or fault is detected.

failure rate The number of times a certain type of failure occurs within a specified period of time.

failure recovery The ability to resume a process or program after a failure has occurred and has been corrected.

fall back Special or temporary instructions or procedures or data used in the event of a fault or failure. **Fall back routines** are procedures which are executed by a user when a machine or system has failed. Resuming a program after a fault has been fixed, from the point at which fall back routines were called is **fall back recovery.**

false A logical term, equal to binary 0, the opposite of true.

false code Code that contains values not within specified limits.

false drop or **false retrieval** Unwanted files retrieved from a database through the use of incorrect search codes.

false error An error warning given when no error has occurred.

FAM see **fast access memory**

family 1 A range of different designs of a particular typeface. **2** A range of machines from one manufacturer that are compatible with other products in the same line from the same manufacturer.

fan 1 A mechanism that circulates air for cooling. **2** A spread of data items or devices. **3** To cool a device by blowing air over it. **4** To spread out a series of items or devices

fanfold or **accordion paper** A method of folding continuous paper, one sheet in one direction, the next sheet in the opposite direction, allowing the paper to be stored conveniently and fed into a printer continuously.

fan-in The maximum number of inputs that a circuit or chip can deal with.

fan-out The maximum number of outputs that a circuit or chip can drive without exceeding its power dissipation limit.

farad (F) SI unit of capacitance, defined as coulombs over volts.

Faraday cage A wire or metal screen, connected to ground, that completely encloses sensitive equipment to prevent any interference from stray electromagnetic radiation.

far end see **receiving end**

fascia plate The front panel on a device.

fast access memory (FAM) Storage locations that can be read from or written to very rapidly.

fast core High speed, low access time working memory for a CPU. A fast core can be used as a scratchpad.

fast line A special telecommunications line which allows data to be transmitted at 48K or 96K baud rates.

fast peripheral A peripheral that communicates with the computer at very high speeds, limited only by the speed of the electronic circuits, as opposed to a slow peripheral such as a card reader, where mechanical movement determines speed.

fast time-scale An operation in which the time-scale factor is less than one.

fatal error A fault in a program or device that causes the system to crash.

father file A backup of the previous version of a file. See also **grandfather, son.**

fault A situation where something has gone wrong with software or hardware, causing it to malfunction. See also **bug, error.**

fault detection An automatic process which logically or mathematically determines that a fault exists in a circuit.

fault diagnosis A process by which the cause of a fault is located.

fault location program A routine that is part of a diagnostic program that identifies the cause of faulty data or equipment.

fault time A period of time during which a computer system is not working or usable.

fault tolerance The ability of a system to continue functioning even when a fault has occurred.

fault-tolerant A system or device that is able to continue functioning even when a fault occurs.

fault trace A program that checks and records the occurrences of faults in a system.

faulty sector A sector of a magnetic disk that cannot be written to or read from correctly.

fax or **FAX** see **facsimile copy, facsimile transmission**

fd or **FD 1 (full duplex)** Data transmission over a single channel in two directions simultaneously. **2** Floppy disk.

fdc see **floppy disk controller**

fdx or **FDX** see **full duplex**

FEDS (fixed and exchangeable disk storage) A magnetic disk storage system that contains some removable disks, such as floppy disks and some fixed or hard disk drives.

feed 1 A device which puts paper or tape into and through a machine, such as a printer or photocopier. Printers take continuous stationery, but if a **front feed** or **sheet feed attachment** is attached, this will allow individual sheets of paper to be fed in automatically. **2** To put paper into a machine or information into a computer.

feeder 1 A channel that carries signals from one point to another. **2** A mechanism that automatically inserts the paper into a printer.

feeder cable A main transmission line that carries signals from a central point for distribution.

feed holes Punched sprocket holes along the edge of continuous paper.

feed reel The reel of tape which is being fed into a machine.

female connector A connector with connecting sockets into which the pins or plugs of a male connector can be inserted.

female socket A hole into which a pin or plug can be inserted to make a connection.

femto- (f) A prefix meaning equal to ten exponent minus fifteen (10^{-15}). A **femto second** is one thousandth of a picosecond.

FEP (front end processor) A processor placed between an input source and the central computer, whose function is to preprocess received data to relieve the workload of the main computer.

ferric oxide or **ferrite** A substance (iron oxide) used as tape or disk coating. It can be magnetized to store data or signals. The **ferrite core** was a small bead of magnetic material that ccoul hold an electromagnetic charge, used in old core memory.

FET (field effect transistor) An electronic device that can act as a variable current flow control, an external signal varies the resistance of the device and current flow by changing the width of a conducting channel.

fetch A command that retrieves the next instruction from memory.

fetch cycle The events that retrieve the next instruction to be executed from memory (by placing the program counter contents on the address bus).

fetch-execute cycle The events required to retrieve, decode and carry out an instruction stored in memory.

fetch instruction A computer instruction to select and read the next instruction or data to be processed.

fetch phase A section of the fetch-execute cycle that retrieves and decodes the instructions from memory.

fetch protect To restrict access to a section of memory.

fetch signal A signal that steps the CPU through the fetch cycle.

FF see **form feed, flip-flop**

fibre optics Light transmission through thin strands of glass or plastic, which allows data to be transmitted.

fibre optic cable or **connection** Fine strands of glass or plastic protected by a surrounding material, used for transmission of light signals. Fibre optic connections can enable nodes up to one kilometre apart to be used.

fibre ribbon A fabric-based ribbon used in many impact printers.

field 1 A section (of a data file) containing individual data items in a record. **2** An area of force and energy distribution, caused by magnetic * electric energy sources. **3** A method of building up a picture on a television screen. **Field blanking** is the short interval during which video or television signal field synchronizing pulses are transmitted.

field effect transistor (FET) An electronic device that can act as a variable current flow control; an external signal varies the resistance of the device and current flow by changing the width of a conducting channel.

field frequency The number of field scans per second.

field flyback The return of electron beam to top left hand corner of a screen.

fielding The arrangement of field allocations inside a record and file.

field label A series of characters used to identify a field or its location.

field length A number of characters that a field can contain.

field marker or **separator** A code used to indicate the end of one field and the start of the next.

field programmable device see **PLA**

field programming Writing data into a PROM. See also **blow.**

field strength The amplitude of the magnetic or electric field at one point in that field.

field sweep The vertical movement of an electron beam over a video or television screen.

field sync pulse A pulse in a video signal that makes sure that the receiver's field sweep is in sync.

FIFO (first in first out) A storage read/write method in which the first item stored is the first read. Compare **LIFO.**

FIFO memory A type of memory using a FIFO access scheme. Two computers may operate at different rates, but can transmit data using a FIFO memory.

FIFO queue A temporary (queue) storage, in which the first item written to the queue is the first to be read.

fifth generation computers The next stage of computer system design using fast VLSI circuits and powerful programming languages to allow human interaction.

figures shift 1 A transmitted code that indicates to the receiver that all following characters should be read as upper case. **2** A mechanical switch which allows a typewriter to print or keyboard to produce special characters and symbols located on the same keys as the numbers.

file A section of data on a computer (such as payroll, address list, customer accounts), in the form of individual records which may contain data, characters, digits or graphics.

file activity ratio The ratio of the number of different records accessed within a file compared to the total number in store.

file cleanup Tidying and removing out of date or unnecessary data from a file.

file collating Putting the contents of a file into order.

file control block A list (in main memory) of files in use within the system.

file conversion Changing the format or structure of a file system, usually when using a new program or file handling routine.

file creation Writing file header information onto a disk and writing an entry into the directory.

file deletion Erasing a file from storage. See also **delete.**

file descriptor A code or series of characters used to identify a file.

file directory A list of names and information about files in a backing storage device.

file extent An actual area or number of tracks required to store a file.

file gap A section of blank tape or disk that indicates the end of a file.

file handling routine A short computer program that manages the reading/writing and organization of stored files.

file identification A unique label or name used to identify and locate a file stored on baking store.

file index A sorted table of the main entries in a file, with their address, allowing the rapid location of entries.

file label One or more characters used to identify a file.

file layout The set of rules defining an internal file structure.

file maintenance The process of updating a file by changing, adding or deleting entries.

file management (system) The section of a DOS that allocates disk space to files, keeping track of the sections and their sector addresses.

file manager The routines used to create, locate and maintain files on backing store.

file merge To combine two data files, but still retaining an overall structure. One file created from several files written one after the other, with no order preserved is a **file merger.**

filename A word used to identify a particular stored file; a unique identification code allocated to a program.

filename extension Additional information after a filename, indicating the type * use of the file. For example, the filename extensions .BAK or .SYS indicates that the file is a backup or a system file.

file organization see **file layout**

file processing Applying a set of rules or search limits to a file, in order to update or find information.

file protection 1 Software or a physical device used to prevent any accidental deletion or modification of a file or its records. **2** Hardware or software organization of a computer system to protect users' files from unauthorized access.

file protect tab A plastic tab on a disk which prevents accidental erasure of a file.

file purge Erasing the contents of a file.

file-recovery utility Software that allows files that have been accidentally deleted or damaged to be read again. Lost files cannot be found without a file-recovery utility.

file security A hardware or software organization of a computer system to protect users' files from unauthorized access.

file server A small microcomputer and large backing store device that is used for the management and storage of a user's files in a network.

file set A number of related files treated as one unit.

file sort To put the contents of a file into order.

file storage The physical means of preserving data in a file, such as a disk drive or tape machine.

file store Files that are available in main memory at any time.

file structure The way in which a (data) file is organized.

file transfer Moving a file from one area of memory to another or to another storage device.

file update 1 Any recent changes or transactions to a file. **2** A new version of software which is sent to users of an existing version.

file validation Checking that a file is correct.

filing system Software which organizes files.

fill To put characters into gaps in a field so that there are no spaces left.

fill character A character added to a string of characters to make up a required length.

film optical scanning device for input into computers (FOSDIC) A storage device for computer data using microfilm.

find A command to locate a piece of information.

find and replace A feature in a word-processor that allows certain words or sections of text to be located and replaced with others.

finite-precision numbers The use of a fixed number of bits to represent numbers, which results in a limited precision.

firmware A computer program or data that is permanently stored in a hardware memory chip, such as a ROM or EPROM. Compare with **hardware, software.**

first-level address A computer storage address that directly, without any modification, accesses a location or device.

first fit A routine or algorithm that selects the first, largest section of free memory in which to store a virtual page, rather than fragment the page over a number of small free areas.

first generation computer One of the original computers made with valve-based electronic technology, around 1951.

first generation image A master copy of an original image, text or document.

first in first out (FIFO) A temporary queue where the first item stored is the first read.

fixed and exchangeable disk storage (FEDS) A magnetic disk storage system that contains some removable disks, such as floppy disks and some fixed or hard disk drives.

fixed cycle operation 1 A process in which each operation is allocated a certain, fixed time limit. **2** Actions within a process that are synchronized to a clock.

fixed data Data written to a file or screen for information or identification purposes and which cannot be altered by the user.

fixed disk A hard disk or magnetic disk which cannot be removed from the disk drive.

fixed field An area in a stored record that can only contain a certain amount of data.

fixed head disk (drive) A disk which uses a separate immovable read/write head over each disk track, making access time very short.

fixed-length record A record whose size cannot be changed.

fixed-length word A preset number of bits that make up a computer word.

fixed-point notation A number representation that retains the position of the digits and decimal points in the computer, so limiting the maximum manageable numbers. Storage of fixed point numbers has two bytes allocated for the whole number and one byte for the fraction part. **Fixed-point arithmetic** rules and methods use fixed-point numbers. Compare with **floating point.**

fixed program computer A hardwired computer program that cannot be altered and is run automatically.

fixed routing A communications direction routing that does not consider traffic or efficient paths.

fixed word length A computer whose word size (in bits) cannot be changed.

flag 1 A way of showing the end of field or of indicating something special in a database. **2** A method of reporting the status of a register after a mathematical or logical operation. For example, if the result is zero, the zero flag is set. **3** To attract the attention of a program while it is running to provide a result or to report an action or to indicate something special.

flag bit A single bit of a word used as a flag for certain operations.

flag code A code sequence which informs the receiver that following characters represent control actions.

flag event A process or state or condition that sets a flag.

flagging Putting an indicator against an item so that it can be found later.

flag register A register that contains the status and flag bits of a CPU.

flag sequence A sequence of codes sent on a packet switching network as identification of the start and finish of a frame of data

flash A/D A parallel, high speed A/D converter.

flashing character A character whose intensity is switched on and off as an indicator.

flatbed A printing or scanning machine that holds the paper or image on a flat surface while processing. Scanners are either flatbed models or platen type, paper-fed models; paper cannot be rolled through flatbed scanners. In a **flatbed plotter** the pen draws diagrams under the control of a computer onto a flat piece of paper.

flat file A two-dimensional file of data items.

flat pack An integrated circuit package whose leads extend horizontally, allowing the device to be mounted directly onto a PCB without the need for holes.

flex The wire or cable used to connect an appliance to the mains electricity supply.

flexible array An array whose size and limits can be altered.

flexible disk (cartridge) see **floppy disk**

flexible machining system (FMS) A computer numeric control (CNC) or control of a machine by a computer.

flexible manufacturing system (FMS) The use of CNC machines, robots and other automated devices in manufacturing.

flexibility The ability of hardware or software to adapt to various conditions or tasks.

flip-flop (FF) An electronic circuit or chip whose output can be one of two states, which is determined by one or two inputs, and can be used to store one bit of digital data.

flippy A disk that is double-sided but used in a single-sided drive, so it has to be turned over to read the other side.

float The addition of the origin address to all indexed or relative addresses to check the amount of memory a program will require.

float factor The location in memory at which the first instruction of a program is stored.

floating address A location specified in relation to a reference address.

floating head see **flying head**

floating point arithmetic Arithmetic operations on floating point numbers.

floating point (notation) A numerical notation in which a fractional number is represented with a point after the first digit and a power of ten, so that any number can be stored in a standard form. For example, the fixed number 56.47 in floating-point arithmetic would be 0.5647 and a power of 2.

floating point number A number represented using floating point notation.

floating point operation (FLOP) A mathematical operation carried out on a floating point number. Often, FLOPs are used as an indication of the speed of a CPU whose throughput is then measured in millions of FLOPs per second (or MFLOPS).

floating point processor A specialized CPU that can process floating point numbers very rapidly. Using a floating point processor speeds up the processing of graphics software.

floating symbolic address A symbol or label that identifies a particular instruction or word, regardless of its location.

floating voltage A voltage in a network or device that has no related ground or reference plane.

float relocate To convert floating addresses to absolute addresses.

flooding A rapid, reliable but not very efficient means of routing packet-switched data, in which each node sends the data received to each of its neighbours.

FLOP see **floating point operation**

FLOPs per second A measure of computing power as the number of floating point operations that a computer can execute every second.

floppy disk or **floppy** or **FD** A secondary storage device, in the form of a flat, circular flexible disk onto which data can be stored in a magnetic form. A floppy disk cannot store as much data as a hard disk, but is easily removed, and is protected by a flexible paper or plastic sleeve. Floppy disks are usually available in standard sizes of eight, five-and-a-quarter, three-and-a-half or three inch diameters. 5.25 and 3.5 inch disks are the commonest.

floppy disk controller (FDC) The combination of hardware and software devices that control and manage the read/write operations of a disk drive from a computer.

floppy disk drive or **unit** A disk drive for floppy disks and ancillary electronics as a separate assembly.

floppy disk sector The smallest area on a magnetic (floppy) disk that can be individually addressed by a computer.

floppy tape or **tape streamer** A continuous loop of tape, used for backing storage.

flow control The management of the flow of data into queues and buffers, to prevent spillage or lost data.

flowchart or **flow diagram 1** A chart which shows the arrangement of the steps in a process * program. A diagram used to describe a computer or data processing system structure is a **data flowchart. 2** To describe a process, its control and routes graphically.

flowchart symbols Special symbols used to represent devices, decisions and operations in a flowchart.

flow diagram see **flowchart**

flow direction The order in which events occur in a flowchart.

flowline The lines connecting flowchart symbols, showing the direction of flow within a flowchart.

flush To clear or erase all the contents of a queue, buffer, file or section of memory.

flush buffers An operation to erase any data remaining in a buffer, ready for a new job or after a job has been aborted.

flush left or **flush right** see **justify left, justify right**

flutter Fluctuations of tape speed due to mechanical or circuit problems, causing signal distortion.

flyback The return of the electron picture beam from the end of a scan to the beginning of the next.

flying head A hard disk read/write head that is wing-shaped to fly just above the surface of the spinning disk.

FMS (flexible machining system, flexible manufacturing system) A computer numeric control (CNC) or control of a machine by a computer.

FNP see **front end network processor**

folding A hashing method that generates an address by splitting the key into parts and adding them together.

font or **fount** A set of characters all of the same style, size and typeface.

font change A function (usually in a word processing or desktop publishing package) to change the style of characters used on a display screen.

font disk A floppy disk that contains the data to drive a character generator to make up the various fonts on a computer display.

footer or **footing** A message at the bottom of all the pages in a printed document (such as the page number). Compare **header.**

footprint The area that a computer takes up on a desk.

forbidden character or **combination** A bit combination in a computer word that is not allowed according to the rules defined by the programmer or system designer.

forced page break An embedded code (within text) which indicates the start of a new page.

foreground colour The colour of characters and text displayed on a screen.

foreground/background modes A computer system in which two modes for program execution are possible: foreground mode for interactive user programs, background mode for housekeeping and other necessary system programs.

foreground processing or **foregrounding** The region of a multitasking operating system in which high priority jobs or programs are executed.

foreground program A high priority program in a multitasking system, whose results are usually visible to the user. Compare **background.**

forest A number of interconnected data structure trees.

form feed A command to a printer to move to the next sheet of paper.

form handling equipment Peripherals (such as a decollator) which deal with output from a printer.

form letter A standard letter into which personal details of each addressee are inserted, such as name, address and job title.

form mode A display method on a data entry terminal, the form is displayed on the screen and the operator enters relevant details.

form stop A sensor in a printer which indicates when the paper has run out.

format 1 The specific method of arranging text or data; a way of arranging data on disk. **2** The precise syntax of instructions and arguments. **3** To set up a blank disk so that it is ready for data, by writing control and track location information on it. **4** To define the areas of a disk reserved for data and control.

format mode The use of protected display fields on a screen to show a blank form or page which cannot be altered, but into which a user can enter information.

formatted dump Text or data printed in a certain format.

formatter Hardware or software that arranges text or data according to certain rules.

formula A set of mathematical rules applied to solve a problem.

formula portability A feature in a spreadsheet program to find a value in a single cell from data in others, with the possibility of using the same formula in other cells.

formula translator see **FORTRAN**

for-next loop A loop or routine that is repeated until a condition no longer occurs. For example, **for X=1 to 5: print X: next X** - this will print out 1 2 3 4 5.

FORTH A high-level programming language mainly used in control applications.

FORTRAN (FOrmula TRANslator) A high-level programming language developed in the first place for scientific use.

forty-track disk A floppy disk formatted to contain forty tracks of data.

forward error correction A method of detecting and correcting certain error conditions with the use of redundant codes.

forward mode To add a number or index or displacement to an origin.

FOSDIC (film optical scanning device for input into computers) A storage device for computer data using microfilm.

fount or **font** A set of characters all of the same style, size and typeface.

four-address instruction A program instruction which contains four addresses within its address field, usually the location of the two operands, the result and the location of the next instruction.

four-plus-one address An instruction that contains the locations of four registers and the location of the next instruction.

Fourier series A mathematical representation of waveforms by a combination of fundamental and harmonic components of a frequency.

fourth generation computers Computer technology using LSI circuits, developed around 1970 and still in current use.

fourth generation languages Languages that are user-friendly and have been designed with the non-expert in mind.

fraction 1 A part of a whole unit, expressed as one figure above another (such as °, , etc.). 2 The mantissa of a floating point number.

fractional part The mantissa of a floating point number.

fragmentation Allocation of main memory to a number of files, which has resulted in many small, free sections or fragments that are too small to be of any use, and so waste a lot of space.

frame 1 Space on magnetic tape for one character code. 2 A packet of transmitted data including control and route information.

frame flyback The return of the electron beam the bottom right to the top left corner of the screen to start building up a new field.

frame grabber A high speed digital sampling circuit that stores a television picture frame in memory so that it can then be processed by a computer.

frame store The digital storage of analog TV signals on disk.

framework The basic structure of a database or process or program.

free 1 Available for use or not currently being used; spare bytes available on disk or in memory. 2 To erase or remove or backup programs or files to provide space in memory.

free running mode An interactive computer mode that allows more than one user to have simultaneous use of a program.

free wheeling A transmission protocol in which the computer transmitting receives no status signals from the receiver.

freedom of information Being able to examine computer records (referring both to government activities and to records kept about individuals).

frequency The number of cycles or periods of a regular waveform that are repeated per second. The frequency of the main clock that synchronizes a computer system is the **clock frequency**.

frequency changer An electronic circuit that shifts the frequency of a signal up or down.

frequency divider An electronic circuit that reduces the frequency of a signal by a multiple of two.

frequency division multiplexing (FDM) Transmission of several independent signals along a single channel, achieved by shifting each signal up in frequency by a different amount.

frequency domain The effects of a certain circuit on the frequency range of a signal.

friction feed A printer mechanism in which the paper is advanced by holding it tightly between two rollers (as opposed to tractor feed, which pulls on the sprocket holes).

FROM see **fusible read only memory**

front panel The panel with the main computer system control switches and status indicators. Also called the **fascia.**

front-end processor (FEP) A processor placed between an input source and the central computer, whose function is to preprocess received data to relieve the workload of the main computer.

full adder A binary addition circuit that can produce the sum of two inputs and can also accept a carry input, producing a carry output if necessary.

full duplex The transmission of data down a channel in two directions simultaneously. See also **duplex, half-duplex, simplex**

fully connected network A situation in which each node in a network is connected with all the others.

fully formed characters Characters produced by a printer in a single action.

full-size display A large screen VDU which can display a whole page of text (usually in A3 or A4 format).

full subtractor A binary subtractor circuit that can produce the difference of two inputs and can also accept a carry input, producing a carry output if necessary.

function 1 A mathematical formula, where a result is dependent upon several other numbers. **2** A sequence of computer program instructions in a main program that perform a certain task. **3** A special feature available on a computer or word-processor. For example, a word-processor may have a spelling-checker function but no built-in text-editing function.

functional diagram A drawing of the internal workings and processes of a machine * piece of software.

functional specification A specification which defines the results which a program is expected to produce.

functional unit Hardware or software that works as it should.

function code Printing codes that control an action rather than representing a character.

function digit A code used to instruct a computer as to which function or branch in a program to follow.

function key or **programmable function key** A key or switch that has been assigned a particular task or sequence of instructions. Function keys often form a separate group of keys on the keyboard, and have specific functions attached to them. They may be labelled F1, F2, etc.

function table A list that gives the relationship between two sets of instructions or data.

fuse An electrical protection device consisting of a small piece of metal, which will melt when too much power passes through it.

fusible link A small link in a PLA that can be blown to program the device permanently.

fusible read only memory (FROM) PROM that is made up of a matrix of fusible links which are selectively blown to program it.

fuzzy logic or **fuzzy theory** A type of logic applied to computer programming, which tries to replicate the reasoning methods of the human brain.

G

G (giga) Prefix meaning one thousand million. In computing G refers to 2^{30}, equal to 1,073,741,824.

GaAs see **gallium arsenide**

gain The amount by which a signal amplitude is changed as it passes through a circuit, usually given as a ratio of output to input amplitude.

gain access to a file To be able to access a file. The user cannot usually gain access to confidential information in a file without a password.

gallium arsenide (GaAs) A semiconductor compound, a new material for chip construction, that allows faster operation than silicon chips.

game paddle A device held in the hand to move a cursor or graphics in a computer game.

ganged Mechanically linked devices that are operated by a single action. A **ganged switch** is a series of switches that operate on different parts of a circuit, but which are all switched by a single action. A ganged switch is used to select which data bus a printer will respond to.

gap 1 The space between recorded data (on a medium). 2 The space between a read head and the magnetic medium.

gap character or **gap digit** An extra character or digit added to a group of characters (for parity or another purpose, but not data or instructions).

garbage Data or information that is no longer required because it is out of date or contains errors.

garbage collection Reorganization and removal of unwanted or out of date files and records; clearing a section of memory of a program or its data that is not in use.

garbage in garbage out (GIGO) An expression meaning that the accuracy and quality of information that is output depends on the quality of the input. GIGO is sometimes taken to mean "garbage in gospel out": i.e. that whatever wrong information is put into a computer, people will always believe that the output results are true.

gas discharge display or **gas plasma display** A flat, lightweight display screen that is made of two flat pieces of glass covered with a grid of conductors, separated by a thin layer of a gas which luminesces when one point of the grid is selected by two electric signals. Mainly used in modern portable computer displays, but the definition is not as good as in cathode ray tube displays.

gate A logical electronic switch whose output depends on the states of the inputs and the type of logical function implemented.

gate array A number of interconnected logic gates built into an integrated circuit to perform a complex function.

gate circuit An electronic component that implements a logical function.

gate delay or **propagation time** The time taken for a gate to produce an output after it has received inputs.

gateway Hard or software protocol translation device that allows users working in one network to access another.

gather To receive data from various sources (either directly from a data capture device or from a cartridge) and sort and insert in correct order into a database. To **gather write** is to write a group of separate records as one block of data.

gender changer A device for changing a female connection to a male or vice versa.

general purpose computer A computer whose processing power may be applied to many different sorts of applications, depending on its hardware or software instructions.

general purpose interface bus (GPIB) A standard for an interface bus between a computer and laboratory equipment.

general purpose program A program or device able to perform many different jobs or applications.

general register or **general purpose register (gpr)** A data register in a computer processing unit that can store items of data for many different mathematical or logical operations.

generate To use software or a device to produce codes or a program automatically. A **generated address** is a location used by a program that has been produced by instructions within the program itself. An error occurring due to inaccuracies in data used (such as a sum total error due to a series of numbers which are rounded up) is a **generated error.**

generation 1 Producing data or software or programs using a computer. **2** The distance between a file and the original version, used when making backups. A father file is a first generation backup.

generator A program that generates new programs according to rules or specifications set out by the user.

generic Something that is compatible with a whole family of hardware * software devices from one manufacturer.

germanium A semiconductor material, used as a substrate in some transistors instead of silicon.

get An instruction to obtain a record from a file or database.

ghost cursor A second cursor which can be used in some programs.

giga- or **G** A prefix meaning one thousand million. A **gigabyte** is 10^9 bytes. In computing **giga** refers to 2^{30} , which is equal to 1,073,741,824.

GIGO (garbage in garbage out) An expression meaning that the accuracy and quality of information that is output depends on the quality of the input. GIGO is sometimes taken to mean "garbage in gospel out": i.e. that whatever wrong information is put into a computer, people will always believe that the output results are true.

GINO (graphical input output) A standard graphical control routine written in FORTRAN.

GKS (graphics kernel system) Standard for software command and functions describing graphical input/output to provide the same functions on any type of hardware.

glitch Anything which causes the sudden unexpected failure of a computer or equipment.

global exchange A replace function which replaces one piece of text (such as a word) with another throughout a whole text.

global knowledge All the knowledge about one problem or task.

global search and replace A word-processor search and replace function covering a complete file or document.

global variable A variable or number that can be accessed by any routine or structure in a program. Compare **local variable.**

go ahead A signal to indicate that a receiver or device is ready to accept information.

golf-ball A metal ball with characters on its surface, which produces printed characters by striking a ribbon onto paper. These are used in **golf-ball printers.** A golf-ball contains all the characters of a single typeface; to change the face, the ball is taken out and replaced by another. The main defect of a golf-ball typewriter when used as a printer, is that it is slower than a dot-matrix printer.

GOTO A programming command which instructs a jump. GOTO statements are frowned upon by software experts since their use discourages set, structured programming techniques. For example, GOTO 105 instructs a jump to line 105.

GPIB (general purpose interface bus) A standard for an interface bus between a computer and laboratory equipment.

gpr (general purpose register) A data register in a computer processing unit that can store items of data for many different mathematical or logical operations.

graceful degradation Allowing some parts of a system to continue to function after a part has broken down.

grandfather file The third most recent version of a backed up file, after father and son files.

grandfather cycle The period in which the grandfather file is retrieved and updated to produce a new father file, the old father file becoming the new grandfather file.

granularity The size of the default memory segments in a virtual memory system.

graph A diagram showing the relationship between two or more variables as a line or series of points.

graphic Representation of information in the form of pictures or plots instead of by text.

graphic data Stored data that represents graphical information (when displayed on a screen).

graphic display A computer screen able to present graphical information. The number of pixels that a computer is able to display on the screen is the **graphic display resolution.**

graphic language A computer programming language with inbuilt commands that are useful when displaying graphics.

graphics Pictures or lines which can be drawn on paper or on a screen to represent information.

graphics character A preprogrammed shape that can be displayed on a non-graphical screen instead of a character, used extensively in videotext systems to display simple pictures.

graphics kernel system (GKS) A standard for software command and functions describing graphical input/output to provide the same functions etc. on any type of hardware.

graphics library A number of routines stored in a library file that can be added to any user program to simplify the task of writing graphics programs.

graphics light pen A high-accuracy light pen used for drawing onto a graphics display screen.

graphics mode A videotext terminal whose displayed characters are taken from a range of graphics characters instead of text.

graphics pad or **tablet** A flat device that allows a user to input graphical information into a computer by drawing on its surface.

graphics processor A dedicated processor and memory used only to produce and control images on a display, to provide high speed graphics handling capabilities.

graphics software Prewritten routines that perform standard graphics commands such as line drawing, plotting, etc., that can be called from within a program to simplify program writing.

graphics terminal A special terminal with a high-resolution graphic display and graphics pad or other input device.

graphics VDU A special VDU which can display high-resolution or colour graphics as well as text.

Gray code A coding system in which the binary representation of decimal numbers changes by only one bit at a time from one number to the next. This is used in communications systems to provide error detection facilities.

green phosphor The most commonly used phosphor for monochrome screen coating, which displays green characters on a black background. A new popular screen type is paper-white, using a white phosphor to display black characters on a white background.

gremlin An unexplained fault in a system.

grey scale The shades which are produced from displaying what should be colour information on a monochrome monitor.

grid 1 A system of numbered squares used to help when drawing. **2** A matrix of lines at right angles allowing points to be easily plotted or located.

grid snap A feature of many graphics programs that locates points to the nearest grid location.

group A set of computer records that contain related information.

group mark or **marker** A code used to identify the start and end of a group of related records or items of data.

group poll Polling a number of devices at once.

guard band A section of magnetic tape between two channels recorded on the same tape.

guard bit One bit within a stored word that indicates to the computer whether it can be altered or if it is protected.

gulp A group of words, usually two bytes. See also **byte, nibble.**

gun or **electron gun** The source of an electron beam located inside a cathode ray tube. Black and white monitors have a single beam gun, while colour monitors contain three, one for each primary colour (Red, Green and Blue) used.

H

H & J see **hyphenation and justification**

hack 1 To experiment and explore computer software and hardware. **2** To break into a computer system for criminal purposes. A person who hacks into a computer system is a **hacker**.

half adder A binary adder that can produce the sum of two inputs, producing a carry output if necessary, but cannot accept a carry input.

half duplex Data transmission in one direction at a time over a bidirectional channel.

half-duplex modem A modem which works in one mode at a time (either transmitting or receiving).

half-height drive A disk drive whose front is half the height of a standard drive (half height drives, usually 5.25 inches, are now the norm on PCs).

half-intensity A character or graphics display at half the usual display brightness.

half space Paper movement in a printer by a half the amount of a normal character.

half word A sequence of bits occupying half a standard computer word, but which can be accessed as a single unit.

hall effect switch A solid state electronic switch operated by a magnetic field; these switches are often used in keyboards.

halt A computer instruction to stop a CPU carrying out any further instructions until restarted, or until the program is restarted, usually by external means (such as a reset button).

halt instruction A program instruction that causes a CPU to come to a stop, suspending all operations, usually until it is reset.

halt condition An operating state reached when a CPU reaches a fault or faulty instruction or halt instruction in the program that is being run.

Hamming code A coding system that uses check bits and checksums to detect and correct errors in transmitted data, mainly used in teletext systems.

Hamming distance The number of digits that are different in two equal length words.

hand-held computer A very small computer which can be held in the hand, useful for basic information input, when a terminal is not available.

handler or **driver** A section of the operating system or program which controls a peripheral.

handshake or **handshaking** Standardized signals between two devices to make sure that the system is working correctly, equipment is compatible and data transfer is correct (signals would include ready-to-receive, ready-to-send, data OK).

handshake I/O control The use of handshake signals meaning ready-to-send and ready-to-receive, that allow a computer to communicate with a slower peripheral.

hands off Working system where: (a) the operator does not control the operation, which is automatic or (b) the operator does not need to touch the device in use.

hands on Working system where the operator controls the operations by keying instructions on the keyboard.

hang To enter an endless loop and not respond to further instruction.

hangup The sudden stop of a working program (often due to the CPU executing an illegal instruction or entering an endless loop).

hard Parts of a computer system that cannot be programmed or altered.

hard card A board containing a hard disk drive and the required interfacing electronics, which can be slotted into a system's expansion connector.

hard copy Printed document or copy of information contained in a computer or system, in a form that is readable (as opposed to soft copy). A **hard copy interface** is the serial or parallel interface used to transmit data between a computer and a printer.

hard disk A rigid magnetic disk that is able to store many times more data than a floppy disk, and usually cannot be removed from the disk drive.

hard disk drive A unit used to store and retrieve data from a spinning hard disk (on the commands of a computer).

hard disk model A computer that contains a hard disk.

hard error A permanent error in a system.

hard failure A fault in hardware that must be mended before a device will function correctly.

hard-sectoring A method of permanently formatting a disk, where each track is split into sectors, sometimes preformatted by a series of punched holes around the central hub, where each hole marks the start of sector.

hardware The physical units, components, integrated circuits, disks and mechanisms that make up a computer or its peripherals.

hardware compatibility The architecture of two different computers that allows one to run the programs of the other without changing any device drivers or memory locations, or the ability of one to use the add-on boards of the other.

hardware configuration The way in which the hardware of a computer system is connected together and set up. This process is usually only carried out once, and is used to tell the operating system the peripherals and resources available to it.

hardware interrupt An interrupt signal generated by a piece of hardware rather than by software.

hardware reliability The ability of a piece of hardware to function normally over a period of time.

hardware security Making a system secure by means of hardware (such as keys, cards, etc.)

hardwired connection A permanent phone line connection, instead of a plug and socket.

hardwired logic A logical function or program, which is built into the hardware, using electronic devices, such as gates, rather than in software.

hardwired program A computer program built into the hardware, and which cannot be changed.

hartley A unit of information, equal to 3.32 bits, or the probability of one state out of ten equally probable states.

hash 1 To produce a unique number derived from the entry itself, for each entry in a database. **2** A hash mark.

hash code A coding system derived from the ASCII codes, where the code numbers for the first three letters are added up, giving a new number used as hash code.

hash index A list of entries sorted according to their hashed numbers.

hashing function An algorithm used to produce a hash code for an entry and ensure that it is different from every other entry.

hashmark or **hash mark** A printed sign (£) used as a hard copy marker or as an indicator.

hash table A list of all entries in a file with their hashed key address.

hash total A total of a number of hashed entries used for error detection.

hash value A number arrived at after a key is hashed.

hazard A fault in hardware due to incorrect signal timing.

hazard-free implementation A logical function design that has taken into account any hazards that could occur, and solved them.

HD (half duplex) Data transmission in one direction only, over a bidirectional channel.

HDLC see **high level data link control**

HDX see **half duplex**

head 1 A transducer that can read or write data from the surface of a magnetic storage medium, such as a floppy disk. Also called a **combined** or **read/write head. 2** Data that indicates the start address of a list of items stored in memory.

head alignment 1 The correct position of a tape or disk head in relation to the magnetic surface, to give the best performance and correct track location. **2** The location of the read head in the same position as the write head was (in relation to the magnetic medium).

head cleaning disk A special disk which is used to clean the disk read/write heads.

head crash A component failure in a disk drive, where the head is allowed to hit the surface of the spinning disk, causing disk surface damage and data corruption.

head demagnetizer A device used to remove any stray magnetic effects that might have built up on the tape head.

header 1 (In a local area network) a packet of data that is sent before a transmission to provide information on destination and routing. **2** Information at the beginning of a list of data relating to the rest of the data. **3** Words at the top of a page of a document (such as title, author's name, page number, etc.) See also **footer.**

header block A block of data at the beginning of a file containing data about file characteristics.

header card A punched card containing information about the rest of the cards in the set.

header label A section of data at the beginning of a magnetic tape, that contains identification, format and control information.

heading 1 A title or name of a document or file. **2** Header or words at the top of each page of a document (such as the title, the page number, etc.)

head park To move the read/write head in a (hard) disk drive to a safe position, not over the disk, so that if the unit is knocked or jarred the head will not damage the disk surface.

heap A temporary data storage area that allows random access. Compare with **stack.**

heat sensitive paper see **electrostatic printing**

heat-sink A metal device used to conduct heat away from an electronic component to prevent damage.

help A function in a program or system that provides useful information about the program in use. You hit the HELP key if you want information about what to do next.

Hertz SI unit of frequency, defined as the number of cycles per second of time. Hertz rate is the frequency at which mains electricity is supplied to the consumer. The Hertz rate in the USA and Canada is 60; in Europe it is 50.

heterogeneous network A computer network joining computers of many different types and makes.

heterogeneous multiplexing Communications multiplexing system that can deal with channels with different transmission rates and protocols.

heuristic A program or system which learns from past experience.

hex or **hexadecimal notation** A number system using base 16 and digits 0-9 and A-F.

hex dump A display of a section of memory in hexadecimal form.

hex pad A keypad with keys for each hexadecimal digit.

hidden defect A defect in a program which was not seen when the program was tested.

hidden files Important system files which are not displayed in a directory listing and cannot normally be read by a user.

hidden lines Lines which make up a three-dimensional object, but are obscured when displayed as a two-dimensional image.

hidden line algorithm A mathematical formula that removes hidden lines from a two-dimensional computer image of a 3-D object.

hidden line removal Erasing lines which should not be visible when looking at a two-dimensional image of a three-dimensional object.

hierarchy The way in which objects or data or structures are organized, usually with the most important or highest priority or most general item at the top, then working down a tree structure.

hierarchical communications system A network in which each branch has a number of separate minor branches dividing from it.

hierarchical computer network A method of allocating control and processing functions in a network to the computers which are most suited to the task.

hierarchical database A database in which records can be related to each other in a defined structure.

hierarchical directory A directory listing of files on a disk, showing the main directory and its files, branches and any sub-directories.

high density storage A very large number of bits stored per area of storage medium. For example, a hard disk is a high density storage medium compared to paper tape.

high-level data link control (HLDLC) ISO defined communications interface protocol which allows several computers to be linked.

high-level data link control station Equipment and programs which correctly receive and transmit standard HLDLC data frames.

high-level (programming) language (HLL) A computer programming language that is easy to learn and allows the user to write programs using words and commands that are easy to understand and look like English words. The program is then translated into machine code, with one HLL command often representing a number of machine code instructions. Compare with **low-level language.**

highlights Characters or symbols treated to make them stand out from the rest of the text, often by using bold type.

high order The digit with the greatest weighting within a number.

high-order language see **high-level language**

high pass filter A circuit that allows frequencies above a certain limit to pass, while blocking those below that frequency limit.

high performance equipment A very good quality or high specification equipment.

high priority program A program that is important or urgent and is processed before others.

high-resolution or **hi-res graphics** The ability of a monitor or screen to display or detect a very large number of pixels per unit area.

high specification or **high spec** A system with a high degree of accuracy or having a large number of features.

high speed carry A single operation in which a carry into an adder results in a carry out.

high-speed skip The rapid movement in a printer to miss the perforations in continuous stationery.

highway or **bus** A communications link consisting of a set of leads or wires which connect different parts of a computer hardware system and over which data is transmitted and received by various circuits inside the system.

hill climbing A method of achieving a goal in an expert system.

hi-res see **high resolution**

histogram A graph on which values are represented as vertical or horizontal bars.

hit on the line A short period of noise on a communications line, causing data corruption.

HLDLC see **high-level data link control**

HLL see **high-level language**

HMI (human-machine interface) Facilities provided to improve the interaction betweeen a user and a computer system.

hold To retain or keep a value or communications line or section of memory.

hold current The amount of electrical current that has to be supplied to keep a device in an operational state, but not actually operating.

holding loop A section of program that loops until it is broken by some action, most often used when waiting for a response from the keyboard or a device.

holdup 1 The time period over which power will be supplied by a UPS. 2 A pause in a program or device due to a malfunction.

Hollerith code A coding system that uses punched holes in a card to represent characters and symbols; the system uses two sets of twelve rows to provide possible positions for each code.

hologram An imagined three-dimensional image produced by the interference pattern when a part of a coherent light beam is reflected from an object and mixed with the main beam.

holographic image A hologram of a three-dimensional object.

holographic storage Storage of data as a holographic image which is then read by a bank of photocells and a laser (a new storage medium with massive storage potential).

holography The science and study of holograms and their manufacture.

home A starting point for the cursor on a screen, usually taken as the top left hand corner.

home banking A method of examining and carrying out bank transactions via a terminal and modem in the user's home.

home computer A microcomputer designed for home use, whose applications might include teaching, games, personal finance and word-processing.

home record A first or initial data record in a file.

homogeneous computer network A network made up of similar machines, that are compatible or from the same manufacturer.

homogeneous multiplexing A switching multiplexer system where all the channels contain data using the same protocol and transmission rate.

hood A cover which protects something. An **acoustic hood** is a soundproof cover put over a line printer to cut down its noise.

hooking Distortion of a video picture caused by tape head timing errors.

hopper A device which holds punched cards and feeds them into the reader.

horizontal blanking Preventing a picture signal reaching a television beam during the time it contains no picture information on its return trace.

horizontal check An error detection method for transmitted data. See also **cyclic check**.

horizontal wraparound The movement of a cursor on a computer display from the end of one line to the beginning of the next.

host adapter An adapter which connects to a host computer.

host computer 1 A main controlling computer in a multi-user or distributed system. 2 A computer used to write and debug software for another computer, often using a cross compiler. 3 A computer in a network that provides special services or programming languages to all users.

hot chassis A metal framework or case around a computer that is connected to a voltage supply rather than being earthed.

hot standby A piece of hardware that is kept operational at all times and is used as backup in case of system failure.

hot zone Text area to the left of the right margin in a word-processed document (if a word does not fit in completely, a hyphen is automatically inserted).

housekeeping Tasks that have to be regularly carried out to maintain a computer system (checking backups, deleting unwanted files, etc.). A **housekeeping routine** ia a set of instructions executed once, at the start of a new program, to carry out system actions such as clear memory, configure function keys or change screen display mode. See also **in-house**.

HRG (high resolution graphics) The ability of a monitor or screen to display a large number of pixels per unit area.

hub The central part of a disk, usually with a hole and ring which the disk drive grips to spin the disk.

huffman code A data compression code, where frequent characters occupy less bit space than less frequent ones.

human-computer or **human-machine interface (HMI)** Facilities provided to improve the interaction between a user and a computer system.

hunting The process of searching out a data record in a file.

hybrid circuit The connection of a number of different electronic components such as integrated circuits, transistors, resistors and capacitors in a small package, which since the components are not contained in their own protective packages, requires far less space than the individual discrete components.

hybrid computer A combination of analog and digital circuits in a computer system to achieve a particular goal.

hybrid interface A one-off interface between a computer and a piece of analog equipment.

hybrid system A combination of analog and digital computers and equipment to provide an optimal system for a particular task.

hyphen A printing sign (-) used to show that a word has been split. See also **hard, soft.**

hyphenation and justification or **H & J** Justifying lines to a set width, splitting the long words correctly at the end of each line.

Hz see **Hertz**

I

IAM (intermediate access memory) Memory storage that has an access time between that of main memory and a disk based system.

IAR (instruction address register) A register in a CPU that contains the location of the next instruction to be processed.

IAS (immediate access store) The high-speed main memory area in a computer system.

IBG see **interblock gap**

IC see **integrated circuit**

icand see **multiplicand**

icon or **ikon** A graphic symbol or small picture displayed on screen, used in an interactive computer system to provide an easy way of identifying a function. Icons are an integral part of many new graphical environments. For example, an icon for a graphics program is a small picture of a palette, a wordprocessor icon is the picture of the typewriter.

ID see **identification**

ID code A password or word that identifies a user so that he can access a system.

IDA see **integrated digital access**

identify To establish who someone is or what something is. A user has to identify himself to the system by using a password before access is allowed.

identification A procedure used by a host computer to establish the identity and nature of the calling computer or user (this could be for security and access restriction purposes or to provide transmission protocol information).

identification character A single character sent to a host computer to establish the identity and location of a remote computer or terminal.

identification division A section of a COBOL program source code, in which the identifiers and formats for data and variables to be used within the program are declared.

identifier A set of characters used to distinguish between different blocks of data or files.

identifier word A word that is used as a block or file identifier.

identity burst A pattern of bits before the first block of data on a magnetic tape that identifies the tape format used.

identity gate or **element** A logical gate that provides a single output that is true if the inputs are both the same.

identity number A unique number, used usually with a password to identify a user when logging into a system.

identity operation A logical function whose output is true only if all the operands are of the same value.

idle A machine or telephone line or other device which is not being used, but is ready and waiting to be used. **Idle time** is the period of time when a device is switched on but not doing anything.

idle character A symbol or code that means "do nothing" or a code that is transmitted when there is no data available for transmission at that time.

IDP see **integrated data processing**

IEE Institution of Electrical Engineers

IEEE Institute of Electrical and Electronic Engineers

IEEE bus An interface that conforms to IEEE standards.

IEEE-488 Interfacing standard as laid down by the IEEE, where only data and handshaking signals are used, mainly used in laboratories to connect computers to measuring equipment.

ier see **multiplier**

IF statement A computer programming statement, meaning do an action IF a condition is true (usually followed by THEN).

IF-THEN-ELSE A high-level programming language statement, meaning IF something cannot be done, THEN do this, or ELSE do that.

ignore character A null or fill character.

IH see **interrupt handler**

IIL see **integrated injection logic**

IKBS see **intelligent knowledge-based system**

ikon see **icon**

illegal character An invalid combination of bits in a computer word, according to preset rules.

illegal instruction An instruction code not within the repertoire of a language.

illegal operation An instruction or process that does not follow the computer system's protocol or language syntax.

image An exact duplicate of an area of memory.

image processing The analysis of information contained in an image, usually by electronic means or using a computer which provide the analysis or recognition of objects in the image, etc.

image processor Electronic or computer system used for image processing, and to extract information from the image.

image scanner An input device which converts documents or drawings or photographs into a digitized, machine-readable form.

image sensor A photoelectric device that produces a signal related to the amount of light falling on it (this scans horizontally over an image, reading in one line at a time).

image stability The ability of a display screen to provide a flicker-free picture.

image storage space The region of memory in which a digitized image is stored.

image table Two bit-mapped tables used to control input and output devices or processes.

imaging A technique for creating pictures on a screen (in medicine used to provide pictures of sections of the body, using scanners attached to computers).

immediate access store (IAS) A high-speed main memory area in a computer system.

immediate addressing Accessing data immediately because it is included within the instruction (usually held in the address field of the instruction).

immediate instruction A computer instruction in which the operand is included within the instruction, rather than an address of the operand location.

immediate mode Mode of operation in which a computer executes an instruction as soon as it is entered.

immediate operand An operand which is fetched at the same time as the instruction (within an immediate addressing operation).

immediate processing Processing data when it appears, rather than waiting for a synchronizing clock pulse or time. Compare with **batch.**

immunity see **interference**

impact printer A printer that prints text and symbols by striking an ink ribbon onto paper with a metal character, such as a daisy-wheel printer (as opposed to a non-impact printer like a laser printer). See also **daisy-wheel printer, dot matrix printer.**

impedance A measurement of the effect an electrical circuit has on signal current magnitude and phase when a steady voltage is applied.

implication A logical operation that uses an IF-THEN structure, if A is true and if B is true this implies that the AND function of A and B will be true.

implied addressing An assembler instruction that operates on only one register: this is preset at manufacture and the user does not have to specify an address.

import To bring something in from outside a system. For example, you can import images from a CAD package into a DTP program.

impulse A voltage pulse which lasts a very short time.

impulsive noise Interference on a signal caused by short periods of noise.

inbuilt A feature or device which is included in a system, such as a software package with inbuilt error correction.

inches-per-second (ips) A measurement of the speed of tape past the read/write heads.

in-circuit emulator A circuit that emulates a device or integrated circuit and is inserted into a new or faulty circuit to test it working correctly.

inclusion A logical operation that uses an IF-THEN structure, if A is true and if B is true this implies that the AND function of A and B will be true.

inclusive OR see **OR**

incoming message A message which is received in a computer.

incoming traffic The amount of data or messages received by a computer.

incompatible Systems which are not compatible or which cannot work together.

increment 1 The addition of a set number, usually one, to a register, often for counting purposes. **2** The value of the number added to a register. **3** To add something or to increase a number, as when a counter is incremented each time an instruction is executed. **4** To move forward to the next location. **5** To move a document or card forward to its next preset location for printing or reading.

incremental computer A computer that stores variables as the difference between their actual value and an absolute initial value.

incremental data Data which represents the difference of a value from an original value.

incremental plotter A graphical output device that can only move in small steps, with input data representing the difference between present position and the position required, so drawing lines and curves as a series of short straight lines.

indent 1 A space or series of spaces from the left margin, when starting a line of text. **2** To start a line of text with a space in from the left margin.

indeterminate system A system whose logical (output) state cannot be predicted.

index 1 A list of items in a computer memory, usually arranged alphabetically. **2** The address to be used that is the result of an offset value added to a start location. See **indexed addressing.**

index build The creation of an ordered list from the results of a database or file search.

indexed address The address of the location to be accessed which is found in an index register.

indexed addressing A method of addressing in which the storage location is addressed with a start address and an offset word, which is added to give the destination address.

indexed file A sequential file with an index of all entries and their addresses.

indexed instruction An instruction that contains an origin and offset that are added to provide the location to be accessed.

indexed sequential access method (ISAM) A data retrieval method using a list containing the address of each stored record, where the list is searched, then the record is retrieved from the address in the list.

indexed sequential storage A method of storing records in a consecutive order, but in such a way that they can be accessed rapidly.

index hole A hole in the edge of a hand-sectored disk.

indexing 1 The use of indexed addressing methods in a computer. **2** The process of building and sorting a list of records. If a computer is used to compile an index for a book by selecting relevant words or items from the text, and then putting them in order, together with page references, this is called **computer indexing.**

index page A videotext page that tells the user the locations of other pages or areas of interest.

index register (IR) An address register that is added to a reference address to provide the location to be accessed.

index value word An offset value added to an address to produce a usable address.

indicator chart A graphical representation of the location and use of indicator flags within a program.

indicator flag A register or single bit that indicates the state of the processor and its registers, such as a carry or overflow.

indicator light A light used to warn or to indicate the condition of equipment.

indirect addressing A way of addressing data, in which the first instruction refers to an address which contains a second address.

induced failure The failure of a device due to an external cause.

induced interference Electrical noise on a signal due to induced signals from nearby electromagnetic sources.

inequivalence A logical function whose output is true if either of two inputs is true, and false if both inputs are the same.

inference A deduction of results from data according to certain rules.

inference engine or **machine** A set of rules used in an expert system to deduce goals or results from data.

infinite loop A program loop which has no exit (except by ending the running of the program by switching off the machine or resetting).

infix notation A method of computer programming syntax where operators are embedded inside operands (such as C - D or X + Y). Compare with **prefix, postfix notation.**

informatics The science and study of ways and means of information processing and transmission.

information Data that has been processed or arranged to provide facts which have a meaning.

information bearer channel A communications channel that is able to carry control and message data, usually at a higher rate than a data only channel.

information content A measurement of the amount of information conveyed by the transmission of a symbol or character, often measured in shannons.

information flow control The regulation of access to certain information.

information input Information received from an input device.

information line A line running across the screen which gives the user information about the program running or the file being edited, etc.

information management system A computer program that allows information to be easily stored, retrieved, searched and updated.

information networks A number of databases linked together, usually by telephone lines and modems, allowing a large amount of data to be accessed by a wider group of users.

information output A display of information on an output device.

information processing Organizing, processing and extracting information from data.

information processor A machine that processes a received signal, according to a program, using stored information to provide an output (this is an example of a computer that is not dealing with mathematical functions).

information provider (IP) A company or user that provides an information source for use in a videotext system (such as the company providing weather information or stock market reports).

information rate The amount of information content per character multiplied by the number of characters transmitted per second.

information retrieval (IR) Locating quantities of data stored in a database and producing useful information from the data.

information retrieval centre An information search system, providing specific information from a database for a user.

information storage Storing data in a form which allows it to be processed at a later date.

information storage and retrieval (ISR) Techniques involved in storing information and retrieving data from a store.

information structure see **data structure**

information system A computer system which provides information according to a user's requests.

information technology (IT) The technology involved in acquiring, storing, processing and distributing information by electronic means (including radio, television, telephone, computers).

information theory The formulae and mathematics concerned with data transmission and signals.

information transfer channel A connection between a data transmitter and a receiver. See also **data terminal equipment.**

inherent addressing An instruction that contains all the data required for the address to be accessed with no further operation. Compare with **extended, indexed.**

inherited error An error that is the result of a fault in a previous process * action.

inhibit To stop a process taking place or to prevent an integrated circuit or gate from operating, (by means of a signal or command).

inhibiting input A signal at one input of a gate which blocks the output signal.

initial address An address at which the first instruction of a program is stored.

initial condition A condition that must be satisfied before a routine can be entered.

initial error An error in data that is the difference between the value of the data at the start of processing and its present actual value.

initial instructions A routine that acts as an initial program loader.

initial program header A small machine-code program usually stored in a read-only memory device that directs the CPU to load a larger program or operating system from store into main memory (such as a boot up routine that loads the operating system when a computer is switched on).

initial program loader (IPL) A short routine that loads a program (the operating system) from backing store into main memory.

initial value A starting point (usually zero) set when initializing variables at the beginning of a program.

initialize To set values or parameters or control lines to their initial values, to allow a program or process to be re-started.

injection logic see **integrated**

ink-jet printer A computer printer that produces characters by sending a stream of tiny drops of electrically charged ink onto the paper. The movement of the ink drops is controlled by an electric field; this is a non-impact printer with few moving parts.

inlay card An identification card inside a tape or disk box.

inline 1 The connection pins on a chip arranged in one or two rows. **2** The way in which unsorted or unedited data is processed.

inline program A program that contains no loops.

inline processing Processing data when it appears rather than waiting for a synchronizing or clock pulse.

inner loop A loop contained inside another loop. See also **nested loop**.

input (i/p or I/P) 1 To transfer data or information from outside a computer to its main memory. **2** The action of inputting information. **3** Data or information that is transferred into a computer. **4** Electrical signals which are applied to relevant circuits to perform an operation.

input area The section of main memory that holds data transferred from backing store until it is processed or distributed to other sections.

input block A block of data transferred to an input area.

input-bound or **limited** A program which is not running as fast as it could due to limiting input rate from a slower peripheral.

input buffer register A temporary store for data from an input device before it is transferred to main or backing store.

input device A device such as a keyboard or bar code reader, which converts actions or information into a form which a computer can understand and transfers the data to the processor.

input lead A lead which connects an input device to a computer.

input limited A program which is not running as fast as it could due to limiting input rate from a slower peripheral.

input mode The state of a computer which is receiving data.

input/output (I/O) Receiving or transmitting data between a computer and its peripherals, and other points outside the system.

input/output buffer A temporary storage area for data waiting to be output or data input.

input/output bus Electrical links allowing data and control signal transfer between a CPU and memory or peripheral devices.

input/output channel A link between a processor and peripheral allowing data transfer.

input/output control program The monitoring and control of I/O operations and data flow by a section of the operating system or supervisory program.

input/output controller An intelligent device that monitors, directs and controls data flow between a CPU and I/O devices.

input/output device or **unit** A peripheral (such as a terminal in a workstation) which can be used both for inputting and outputting data to a processor.

input/output executive A master program that controls all the I/O activities of a computer.

input/output instruction A computer programming instruction that allows data to be input or output from a processor.

input/output interface A circuit allowing controlled data input and output from a CPU, consisting usually of: input/output channel, parallel input/output port and a DMA interface.

input/output interrupt An interrupt signal from a peripheral device or to indicate that an input or output operation is required.

· **input/output library** A set of routines that can be used by the programmer to help simplify input/output tasks (such as printer drivers or port control routines).

input/output port A circuit or connector that provides an input/output channel to another device. For example, a joystick can be connected to an input/output port.

input/output processor (IOP) A processor that carries out input/output transfers for a CPU, including DMA and error correction facilities.

input/output referencing The use of labels to refer to specific input/output devices, the actual address of the device being inserted at run-time.

input/output register A temporary store for data received from main memory before being transferred to an I/O device (or data from an I/O device to be stored in main memory or processed).

input/output request (IORQ) A request signal from the CPU for data input or output.

input/output status word A word whose bits describe the state of peripheral devices (busy, free, etc.)

input port A circuit or connector that allows a computer to receive data from other external devices.

input register A temporary store for data received at slow speeds from an I/O device, the data is then transferred at high speed to main memory.

input routine A set of instructions which control an I/O device and direct data received from it to the correct storage location.

input section 1 An input routine. **2** An input area.

input statement A programming command that waits for data entry from a port or keyboard.

input storage see **input area**

input unit An input device.

input work queue A list of commands to be carried out in the order they were entered or in order of priority.

inquiry (ENQ) A request for data or information from a device or database; accessing data in a computer memory without changing the data.

inquiry character A special control code that is a request for identification or status or data from a remote terminal.

inquiry station A terminal that is used to access and interrogate files stored on a remote computer.

inquiry/response An interactive computer mode, in which a user's commands and inquiries are responded to very quickly.

insert To add new text inside a word or sentence.

inserted subroutine A series of instructions that are copied directly into the main program where a call instruction appears or where a user requires.

insert mode An interactive computer mode used for editing and correcting documents. This is a standard feature on most word-processing packages where the cursor is placed at the required point in the document and any characters typed will be added, with the existing text moving on as necessary.

install To set up a new computer system to the user's requirements or to configure a new program to the existing system capabilities.

instantaneous access An extremely short access time to a random access device.

instruction A word used in a programming language that is understood by the computer to represent an action. For example, the instruction PRINT is used in BASIC as an operand to display data. In a high level language the instructions are translated by the compiler or interpreter to a form that is understood by the central processing unit. An instruction that contains an origin and location of an offset that are added together to provide the address to be accessed is an **indexed instruction.** A computer programming instruction that allows data to be input or output from a processor is an **input/output instruction.**

instruction address The location of an instruction.

instruction address register (IAR) The register in a CPU that contains the location of the next instruction to be processed.

instruction area A section of memory that is used to store instructions.

instruction cache An area of high-speed memory which stores the next few instructions to be executed by a processor.

instruction character A special character that provides a control sequence rather than an alphanumeric character.

instruction codes A set of symbols or codes that a CPU can directly understand and execute.

instruction counter or **instruction address register (IAR)** or **program counter** The register in a CPU that contains the location of the next instruction to be processed.

instruction cycle A sequence of events and their timing that is involved when fetching and executing an instruction stored in memory. **Instruction cycle time** is the time taken for one instruction cycle.

instruction decoder A program which decodes machine code nstructions into CPU directives. It is usually hardwired.

instruction execution time The time taken to carry out an instruction.

instruction format The rules defining the way the operands, data and addresses are arranged in an instruction.

instruction modification Altering a part of an instruction (data or operator) so that it carries out a different function when next executed.

instruction pipelining To begin to process a second instruction while still processing the present one (this increases program speed of execution).

instruction processor A section of the central processing unit that decodes the instruction and performs the necessary arithmetic and logical functions.

instruction register (IR) A register in a central processing unit that stores an instruction during decoding and execution operations.

instruction repertoire or **set** The total number of instructions that a processor can recognize and execute.

instruction storage see **instruction area**

instruction time The amount of time taken for a central processing unit to carry out a complete instruction.

instruction word A fixed set of characters used to initiate an instruction.

integer A mathematical term to describe a whole number (it may be positive or negative or zero).

integer BASIC A faster version of BASIC that uses only integer mathematics and cannot support fractions.

integral An add-on device or special feature that is already built into a system, such as an integral disk drive.

integrated circuit (IC) A circuit where all the active and passive components are formed on one small piece of semiconductor, by means of etching and chemical processes. Integrated circuits can be classified as follows: **Small Scale Integration (SSI):** 1 to 10 components per IC; **Medium Scale Integration (MSI):** 10 to 500 components per IC; **Large Scale Integration (LSI):** 500 to 10,000 components per IC; **Very Large Scale Integration (VLSI):** 10,000 to 100,000 components per IC.

integrated database A database that is able to provide information for varied requirements without any redundant data.

integrated data processing (IDP) Organizational method for the entry and retrieval of data to provide maximum efficiency.

integrated device A device that is part of another machine or device.

integrated digital access (IDA) A system where subscribers can make two telephone calls and be linked (from their office or home) to a database, and send material by fax, all at the same time.

integrated digital network A communications network that uses digital signals to transmit data.

integrated emulator An emulator program run within a multitasking operating system.

integrated injection logic (IIL) A method of designing and constructing logical circuits on an integrated circuit to provide low power consumption with medium speed gates.

integrated modem A modem that is a internal part of the system.

integrated office An office environment in which all operations are carried out using a central computer (to store information, print, etc.).

integrated optical circuit An optoelectronic circuit that can generate, detect and transmit light for communications over optical fibres.

integrated services digital network (ISDN) An international digital communications network which can transmit sound, fax and data over the same channel.

integrated software Software such as an operating system or word-processor that is stored in the computer system and has been tailored to the requirements of the system.

integrated system A system that contains many peripherals grouped together in order to provide a neat, complete system.

integrity Reliability of data when it is being processed or stored on disk.

integrity of a file The fact that a file that has been stored on disk is not corrupted or distorted in any way.

intelligence The ability of a device to carry out processing or run a program.

intelligent A program or device that is capable of limited reasoning facilities, giving it human-like responses.

intelligent device A peripheral device that contains a central processing unit allowing it to process data.

intelligent knowledge-based system (IKBS) or **expert system** Software that applies the knowledge, advice and rules defined by an expert in a particular field to a user's data to help solve a problem.

intelligent spacer A facility in a word-processing system used to prevent words from being hyphenated or separated at the wrong point.

intelligent terminal A computer terminal which contains a CPU and memory, usually with a facility to allow the user to program it independently of the main CPU.

intelligent tutoring system A computer-aided learning system that provides responsive and interactive teaching facilities for users.

interactive A system or piece of software that allows communication between the user and the computer (in conversational mode).

interactive debugging system A software development tool that allows the user to run a program under test, set breakpoints, examine source and object code, examine registers and memory contents and trace the instruction execution.

interactive graphics A display system that is able to react to different inputs from the user. A space invaders game has interactive graphics, and the player controls the position of his spaceship on the screen with the joystick.

interactive mode or **processing** A computer mode that allows the user to enter commands or programs or data and receive immediate responses. See also **inquiry/response.**

interactive routine A computer program that can accept data from an operator, process it and provide a real-time reaction to it.

interactive system A system which provides an immediate response to the user's commands or programs or data.

interactive terminal A terminal in an interactive system which sends and receives information.

interactive video A system that uses a computer linked to a video disk player to provide processing power and real images or moving pictures. This system is often used in teaching to ask a student questions, which if answered correctly will provide him with a filmed sequence from the video disk.

interactive videotext Viewdata service that allows the operator to select pages, display them, ask questions or use a service such as teleshopping.

interblock gap (IBG) A blank magnetic tape between the end of one block of data and the start of the next in backing store.

intercharacter spacing A feature in some word-processors that provides variable spacing between words to create a justified line.

interface 1 A point at which one computer system ends and another begins. **2** A circuit or device or port that allows two or more incompatible units to be linked together in a standard communication system, allowing data to be transferred between them. So an **input/output interface** is a circuit allowing controlled data input and output from a CPU, consisting usually of: input/output channel, parallel input/output port and a DMA interface. **3** The section of a program which allows transmission of data to another program. **4** To modify a device by adding a circuit or connector to allow it to conform to a standard communications system. **5** To connect two or more incompatible devices together with a circuit, to allow them to communicate.

interface card An add-on board that allows a computer to interface to certain equipment or conform to a certain standard.

interface message processor A computer in a packet switching network that deals with the flow of data, acting as an interface processor.

interface processor A computer that controls data transfer between a processor and a terminal or network.

interface routines Software that allows programs or data for one system to run on another.

interfacing Hardware or software used to interface two computers or programs or devices.

interlace To build up an image on a television screen using two passes, each displaying alternate lines. This system uses two picture fields made up of alternate lines to reduce picture flicker effects.

interleaved Sections of two programs executed alternately to give the impression that they are running simultaneously.

interleaving 1 A processor dealing with slices or sections of processes alternately, so that they appear to be executed simultaneously. **2** Dividing data storage into sections so that each can be accessed separately.

interlock A security device which is part of the logon prompt and requires a password.

interlude A small initial routine at the start of a program that carries out housekeeping tasks.

intermediate access memory (IAM) Memory storage that has an access time between that of main memory and disk based systems.

intermediate code Code used by a computer or assembler during the translation of a high-level code to machine code.

intermediate file A series of records that contain partially processed data, that will be used at a later date to complete that task.

intermediate storage A temporary area of memory for items that are currently being processed.

intermittent error An error which apparently occurs randomly in a computer or communications system due to a program fault or noise.

These errors are very difficult to trace and correct due to their apparently random appearance.

internal arithmetic Arithmetic operations performed by the ALU of the main central processor (rather than by a coprocessor).

internal character code The representation of characters in a particular operating system.

internal format The way in which data and instructions are represented within a CPU or backing store.

internal language The language used in a computer system that is not under the direct control of the operator. Many compiled languages are translated to an internal language.

internally stored program A computer program code that is stored in a ROM device in a computer system (and does not have to be loaded from backing store).

internal memory or **store** A section of RAM and ROM to which the central processing unit is directly connected without the use of an interface (as in external memory devices such as disk drives).

internal sort A sorting program using only the main memory of a system.

International Standards Organization (ISO) The organization which regulates standards for many types of product.

International Standards Organization Open System Interconnection (ISO/OSI) Standardized ISO network design which is constructed in layered form, with each layer having a specific task, allowing different systems to communicate if they conform to the standard.

interpolation The calculation of intermediate values between two points.

interpret To translate what is said in one language into another.

interpreted language A programming language that is executed by an interpreter.

interpreter Software that is used to translate at the time of execution a user's high-level program into machine code. A compiler translates the high-level language into machine code and then executes it, rather than the real-time translation by an interpreter.

interpretative code Code used with an interpretative program.

interpretative program Software that translates at run-time high level interpretative code into machine code instructions.

interrupt 1 To stop something happening while it is happening. **2** Stopping of a transmission due to an action at the receiving end of a system. An **armed interrupt** is an interrupt line which has been made active (using an interrupt mask). **3** A signal which diverts a central processing unit from one task to another which has higher priority, allowing the CPU to return to the first task later.

interrupt disable To disable an interrupt by resetting a bit in the interrupt mask to zero.

interrupt enable To arm an interrupt by setting the appropriate bit in the interrupt mask.

interrupt handler (IH) Software routine that accepts interrupt signals and acts on them, such as running a special routine or sending data to a peripheral.

interrupt level The priority assigned to the interrupt from a peripheral.

interrupt line A connection to a central processing unit from outside the system that allows external devices to use the CPU's interrupt facility.

interrupt mask A byte or word whose bits represent the state of a number of interrupt lines. If a bit is set (on) the interrupt line is armed and active, if not set (off) the interrupt line will not register with the CPU.

interrupt priorities Deciding which interrupt is given highest priority.

interrupt request A signal from a device that indicates to the CPU that it requires attention.

interrupt servicing Carrying out some action when an interrupt is detected, such as running a routine.

interrupt stacking Storing interrupts in a queue and processing them according to priority.

intersection A logical function whose output is only true if both its inputs are true.

interword spacing Variable spacing between words in a text, used to justify lines.

intimate Software that operates and interacts closely with hardware in a system.

inverse Changing the logical state of a signal or device to its logical opposite.

inverse video A video effect created by swapping the background and foreground text display colours.

inversion Changing over the numbers in a binary word (one to zero, zero to one). The inversion of a binary digit takes place in one's complement.

invert To change all binary ones to zeros and zeros to ones.

inverted file A file with an index entry for each of the data items.

inverter A logical gate that provides an inversion function.

invitation An action by a processor to contact another device to allow it to send a message.

invitation to send (ITS) A special character transmitted to indicate to a device that the host computer is willing to receive messages.

invoke To start or run a program, often a memory resident utility.

I/O (input/output) Referring to the receiving or transmitting of data.

I/O bound A processor that is doing very little processing since its time is taken up reading or writing data from a I/O port.

I/O buffer A temporary storage area for data waiting to be input or output.

I/O bus Electrical links allowing data and control signal transfer between a CPU and memory or peripheral devices.

I/O channel A link between a processor and peripheral, allowing data transfer.

I/O device A peripheral, such as a terminal in a workstation, which can be used for both inputting and outputting data to a processor.

I/O file A file whose contents have been or will be transferred from storage to a peripheral.

I/O instruction A computer programming instruction that allows data to be input or output from a processor.

I/O mapping A method of assigning a special address to each I/O port that does not use any memory locations. Compare with **memory mapping.**

I/O port A circuit or connector that provides an input/output channel from a CPU to another device. See also **serial port, parallel port.**

IOP see **input/output processor**

IORQ see **input/output request**

i/p or **I/P** see **input**

ip (information provider) A company or user that provides an information source for use in a videotext system. An **ip terminal** is the special visual display unit that allows users to create and edit videotext pages before sending them to the main videotext page database.

IPL see **initial program loader**

ips see **inches per second**

IR see **information retrieval, index register, instruction register**

IS see **indexed sequential**

ISAM see **indexed sequential access method**

ISDN see **integrated services digital network**

ISO see **international standards organization**

ISO/OSI see **international standards organization open system interconnection**

isolated location A hardware storage location which cannot be directly accessed by a user's program, protecting it against accidental erasure.

ISR see **information storage and retrieval**

IT see **information technology**

italic A type of character font in which the characters slope to the right.

item size A number of characters or digits in an item of data.

iterate or **iterative routine** A loop or series of instructions in a program which repeat over and over again until the program is completed. The repeated application of a program to solve a problem is **iteration.**

iterative process A process that is continuously repeated until a condition is met.

ITS see **invitation to send**

J

jack A single pin plug.

jam 1 A process or mechanism which has stopped working due to a fault which blocks it. **2** (Of a device) to stop working because something is blocking its functioning.

jar To give a sharp knock to a device. Damage can be caused by turning off or jarring a PC while the disk read heads are moving; hard disks are particularly sensitive to jarring.

JCL (job control language) Commands that describe the identification of and resources required by a job that a computer has to process.

jitter A fault where there is rapid small up-and-down movement of characters or pixels on a screen of image bits in a facsimile transmission.

JK-flip-flop A flip-flop device with two inputs (J and K) and two complementary outputs that are dependent on the logical condition of the inputs.

job A task or number of tasks or work to be processed as a single unit.

job control file A file which contains instructions in a JCL.

job control language (JCL) Commands that describe the identification of and resources required by a job that a computer has to process.

job control program A short program made up of job control instructions loaded before a particular application is run, that sets up the system as required by the application.

job file A file containing jobs or job names waiting to be processed.

job mix The different jobs being executed at any one time in a system.

job number An identifying number which is given to a job in a queue, waiting to be processed.

job orientated language A programming language that provides specialized instructions relating to job control tasks and processing.

job orientated terminal A terminal designed for and used for a particular task.

job priority The importance of a job compared to others. The job with the highest priority will be executed first or fastest.

job processing To read in job control instructions from an input source and execute them.

job queue or **job stream** A number of tasks arranged in an order waiting to be processed in a multitasking or batch system. The arranging of the order in which jobs are processed is **job scheduling.**

job statement control The use of instructions and statements to control the actions of the operating system of a computer.

job step or **stream** One unit of processing involved in a task.

join 1 To combine two or more pieces of information to produce a single unit. 2 A logical function that produces a true output if any input is true.

join files An instruction to produce a new file consisting of one file added to the end of another.

joint denial A logical function whose output is false if any input is true.

journal 1 A record of all communications to and from a terminal. 2 A list of any changes or updates to a file.

journal file A stored record of every communication between a user and the central computer, used to help retrieve files after a system crash or fault.

joystick A device that allows a user to move a cursor around the screen by moving an upright rod connected to an I/O port on the computer. Joysticks are mostly used for computer games, CAD or desktop publishing packages. The electronic circuit and connector used to interface a joystick with a computer is a **joystick port.**

judder Any unwanted movement in a printing or facsimile machine that results in a distorted picture.

jumbo chip An integrated circuit made using the whole of a semiconductor wafer. These devices are very new and proving rather difficult to manufacture without faults to any of the thousands of gates on the surface; when working, these devices will be extremely powerful. See also **wafer scale integration.**

jump (instruction) 1 A programming command to end one set of instructions and direct the processor to another section of the program. 2 To direct a CPU to another section of a program.

jump operation A situation in which the CPU is sent from the instruction it is currently executing to another point in the program.

jump on zero A conditional jump executed if a flag or register is zero

jumper A temporary wire connection on a circuit board.

jumper-selectable A circuit or device whose options can be selected by positioning various wire connections. Sometimes DIP switches are used instead of jumpers to set the options in a device.

junction A connection between wires or cables. A **junction box** is a small box where a number of wires can be interconnected.

junk 1 Information or hardware which is useless or out-of-date or non-functional. 2 **to junk a file** is to erase or delete from storage a file that is no longer used.

justify 1 To change the spacing between words or characters in a document so that the left and right margins are straight. To prevent a word processor justifying a document is **justify inhibit.** See also **left justify, right justify.** 2 To shift the contents of a computer register by a set amount.

justification Moving data bits or characters to the left or right so that the lines have straight margins.

K

K 1 A symbol used to represent one thousand. **2** A symbol used in computing to represent 1,024, equal to 2^{10}. 1,024 is the strict definition in computer or electronics applications, being equal to a convenient power of two. **Kb (kilobit)** is a measure of 1,024 bits. **KB or K byte (kilobyte)** is the unit of measurement of the capacity of storage devices equal to 1,024 bytes. Abbreviations using K can also be taken to equal approximately one thousand, even in computing applications. 1KB is roughly equal to 1,000 output characters in a PC, for example.

Karnaugh map A graphical representation of states and conditions in a logic circuit.

kernel The basic, essential instruction routines required as a basis for any operations in a computer system.

kerning Slight overlapping of certain printed character areas to prevent large spaces between them, giving a neater appearance. Most high-powered desktop publishing systems allow the user to control character kerning to provide a more professional appearance.

key 1 A button on a keyboard that operates a switch. **2** An important object or group of characters in a computer system, used to represent an instruction or set of data. **3** A special combination of numbers or characters that are used with a cipher to encrypt or decrypt a message. **4** The identification code or word used for a stored record or data item. **5** To enter information by using a keyboard.

keyboard A number of keys fixed together in some order, used to enter information into a computer or to produce characters on a typewriter. See also **AZERTY, QWERTY.**

keyboard contact bounce A fault causing multiple signals from a key pressed just once, due to a faulty switch and key bounce.

keyboard encoder The way in which each key generates a unique word when pressed.

keyboarder A person who enters data via a keyboard.

keyboarding The action of entering data using a keyboard.

keyboard layout The way in which various function and character keys are arranged.

keyboard overlay A piece of paper placed over the keys on a keyboard describing their special functions for a particular application.

keyboard scan A method for a computer to determine if a key has been pressed by applying a voltage across each key switch (if the key is pressed a signal will be read by the computer).

keyboard send/receive (KSR) A terminal which has a keyboard and monitor, and is linked to a CPU.

keyboard to disk entry A system in which information entered on a keyboard is stored directly onto disk with no processing.

key click A sound produced by a computer to allow the operator to know that the key pressed has been registered.

keyed sequential access method (KSAM) A file structure that allows data to be accessed using key fields or key field content.

key field A field which identifies entries in a record.

key force The pressure required to close the switch in a key.

key in To enter text or commands via a keyboard.

key management The selection, protection and safe transmission of cipher keys.

key matrix The design of interconnections between keys on a keyboard.

key number The numeric code used to identify which key has been pressed.

key overlay A piece of paper placed over the keys on a keyboard describing their functions for a particular application.

keypad A group of special keys used for certain applications.

key punch A machine used for punching data into punched cards by means of a keyboard.

key rollover Using a buffer between the keyboard and computer to provide rapid key stroke storage for fast keyboarders who hit several keys in rapid succession.

key strip A piece of paper above certain keys used to remind the operator of their special functions.

keystroke The action of pressing a key. Keystrokes are often used to calculate keyboarding costs by counting each keystroke made, in a **keystroke count.**

keystroke verification A check made on each key pressed to make sure it is valid for a particular application.

key terminal The most important terminal in a computer system or one with the highest priority.

key-to-disk A system where data is keyed in and stored directly on disk without any processing.

key travel The distance a key has to be pressed before it registers.

keyword 1 A command word used in a programming language to provide a function. **2** An important or informative word in a title or document that describes its contents.

kHz (kiloHertz) Unit of frequency measurement equal to one thousand Hertz. See also **Hertz.**

kill To erase a file or stop a program during execution. So the command **kill file** will erase a stored file completely, and **kill job** halts a computer job while it is running.

kilo- A prefix meaning one thousand.

kilobaud 1,000 bits per second.

kilobit or **Kb** 1,024 bits of data.

kilobyte or **KB** or **Kbyte** A unit of measurement for the capacity of storage devices meaning 1,024 bytes of data.

kilohertz or **KHz** A unit of frequency measurement equal to one thousand Hertz

kilo instructions per second (KIPS) One thousand computer instructions processed every second, used as a measure of computer power.

kiloword or **KW** A unit of measurement of 1,024 computer words.

KIPS see **kilo instructions per second**

kludge or **kluge** 1 A temporary correction made to a badly written or constructed piece of software or to a keyboarding error. Software which has been temporarily repaired is said to be **kluged**. 2 Hardware which should be used for demonstration purposes only.

knowledge-based system A computer system that applies the stored reactions, instructions and knowledge of experts in a particular field to a problem. See also **expert system.**

knowledge engineering Designing and writing expert computer systems.

KSR (keyboard send/receive) A terminal which has a keyboard and monitor, and is linked to a CPU. Compare with **ASR.**

KW see **kiloword**

L

label 1 A word or other symbol used in a computer program to identify a routine or statement. 2 Character(s) used to identify a variable or piece of data or a file.

label field An item of data in a record that contains a label.

label record A record containing identification for a stored file.

lag 1 The time taken for a signal to pass through a circuit, such that the output is delayed compared to the input. 2 The time taken for an image to be no longer visible after it has been displayed on a CRT screen (this is caused by long persistence phosphor).

LAN or **lan (local area network)** A network in which the various terminals and equipment are all within a short distance of one another (at a maximum distance of about 500m, for example in the same building), and can be interconnected by cables. Compare with **WAN.**

LAN server A dedicated computer and backing storage facility used by terminals and operators of a LAN.

landline A permanent direct link using cables laid in the ground.

language A system of words or symbols which allows communication with computers (such as one that allows computer instructions to be entered as words which are easy to understand, and then translates them into machine code). There are three main types of computer languages: machine code, assembler and high-level language. **Assembly language** uses mnemonics to represent machine code instructions. **Machine code** is the basic binary patterns that instruct the processor to perform various tasks. A **high-level language (HLL)** is a language that is easy to learn and allows the user to write programs using words and commands that are easy to understand and look like English words, the program is then translated into machine code, with one HLL instruction often representing more than one machine code instruction. A **low-level language (LLL)** is a language which is fast, but long and complex to program in, where each instruction represents a single machine code instruction. The higher the level the language is, the easier it is to program and understand, but the slower it is to execute. The following are the commonest high-level languages: ADA, ALGOL, APL, BASIC, C, COBOL, COMAL, CORAL, FORTH, FORTRAN, LISP, LOGO, PASCAL, PL/1, POP-2, PROLOG.

language assembler A program used to translate and assemble a source code program into a machine executable binary form.

language compiler Software that converts an encoded source program into another machine code form, and then executes it.

language interpreter Any program that takes each consecutive line of source program and translates it into another machine code language at run-time.

language processor A language translator from one language to machine code (there are three types of language processor: **assembler, compiler** and **interpreter).**

language rules The syntax and format for instructions and data items used in a particular language.

language support environment Hardware and software tools supplied to help the programmer write programs in a particular language.

language translation Using a computer to translate text from one language to another. A program that converts code written in one language into equivalent instructions in another language is a **language translator.**

lapheld computer or **laptop computer** A computer that is light enough to carry but not so small as to fit in a pocket, usually containing a screen, keyboard and disk drive.

large-scale computer A high-powered large word-size computer system that can access high capacity memory and backing storage devices as well as multiple users.

large-scale integration (LSI) An integrated circuit with 500 to 10,000 components.

laser (light amplification by stimulated emission of radiation) A device that produces coherent light of a single wavelength in a narrow beam, by exciting a material so that it emits photons of light.

laser beam recording The production of characters on a light-sensitive film by a laser beam controlled directly from a computer.

laser beam communications The use of a modulated laser beam as a line-of-sight communications medium.

laser disk A plastic disk containing binary data in the form of small etched dots that can be read by a laser, used to record high quality TV images or sound in digital form.

laser emulsion storage A digital storage technique using a laser to expose light-sensitive material.

laser printer A high-resolution computer printer that uses a laser source to print high-quality dot matrix character patterns on paper (these have a much higher resolution than normal printers, usually 300 dpi or higher).

last in first out (LIFO) A queue system that reads the last item stored first. Compare with **first in first out.**

latch 1 An electronic component that maintains an output condition until it receives an input signal to change. **2** To set an output state. See also **flip-flop.**

latency The time delay between the moment when an instruction is given to a computer and the execution of the instruction or return of a result (such as the delay between a request for data and the data being transferred from memory).

lateral reversal Creating the mirror image of a picture by swapping left and right.

layer ISO/OSI standards defining the stages a message has to pass through when being transmitted from one computer to another over a network. The layers are: **application layer** — the program that requests a transmission; **data link layer** — layer that sends packets of data to the next link, and deals with error correction; **network layer** — layer that decides on the routes to be used, the costs, etc; **physical layer** — layer that defines the rules for bit rate, power, medium for transmission, etc.; **presentation layer** — section that agrees on format, codes and request for start/end of a connection; **session layer** — layer that makes the connection/disconnection between a transmitter and receiver; **transport layer** — layer that checks and controls the quality of the connection.

layout 1 A mock-up of a finished piece of printed work showing the positioning and sizes of text and graphics. **2** The rules governing the data input and output from a computer.

LBR (laser beam recording) Producing characters on a light sensitive film by laser beam directly controlled from a computer.

LCD (liquid crystal display) A liquid crystal that turns black when a voltage is applied, used in many watches, calculators and other small digital displays.

LCP (link control procedure) The rules defining the transmission of data over a channel.

lead in page A videotext page that directs the user to other pages of interest.

leader A section of magnetic tape or photographic film that contains no signal or images, used at the beginning of the reel for identification and to aid the tape machine to pick up the tape.

leader record An initial record containing information (such as titles, format, etc.) about following records in a file.

leading edge The first edge of a punched card that enters the card reader.

leading zero A zero digit (0) used to pad out the beginning of a stored number.

leaf The final node in a data tree structure.

leap-frog test A memory location test, in which a program skips from one location to another random location, writing data then reading and comparing for faults, until all locations have been tested.

learning curve The rate at which someone can acquire knowledge about a subject.

leased circuit An electronic circuit or communications channel rented for a period.

leased line A communications channel, such as a telephone line, which is rented for the exclusive use of the subscriber.

least recently used algorithm An algorithm which finds the page of memory that was last accessed before any other, and erases it to make room for another page.

least significant bit (LSB) The binary digit occupying the right hand position of a word and carrying the least power of two in the word (usually equal to two raised to zero 1).

least significant digit (LSD) The digit which occupies the right hand position in a number and so carries the least power (equal to the number radix raised to zero 1).

leaving files open A phrase meaning that a file has not been closed or does not contain an end of text marker; this will result in the loss of data since the text will not have been saved.

LED (light emitting diode) A semiconductor diode that emits light when a current is applied. LED displays are used to display small amounts of information, as in pocket calculators, watches, indicators, etc.

left justification 1 Shifting a binary number to the left hand end of the word containing it. **2** Making the left hand margin of the text even.

left justify A printing command that makes the left hand margin of the text even.

left shift A left arithmetic shift by one bit of data in a word, a binary number is doubled for each left shift.

leg One possible path through a routine.

legal A statement or instruction that is acceptable within language syntax rules.

length Line length is the number of characters which can be displayed horizontally on one line of a display (CRT displays often use an 80 character line length). **Length of filename** is the number of characters allowed for identification of a file.

letter-quality (LQ) printing A feature of some dot-matrix printers to provide characters of the same quality as a typewriter by using dots which are very close together. See also **near letter quality.**

level 1 The strength or power of an electrical signal. **2** The quantity of bits that make up a digital transmitted signal.

lexical analysis The stage in program translation when the compiling or translating software replaces program keywords with machine code instructions.

LF see **line feed**

library function A software routine that a user can insert into his program to provide the function with no effort.

library program 1 A number of specially written or relevant software routines, which a user can insert into his own program, saving time and effort. **2** A group of functions which a computer needs to refer to often, but which are not stored in main memory.

library routine Prewritten routine that can be inserted into a main program and called up when required.

library subroutine A tried and tested subroutine stored in a library, and which can be inserted into a user's program when required.

library track One track on a magnetic disk or tape used to store information about the contents (such as titles, format and index data).

LIFO (last in first out) A queue system that reads the last item stored, first. See also **FIFO.**

lifter A mechanical device that lifts magnetic tape away from the heads when rewinding the tape (to prevent wearing the heads and damage to the tape).

light conduit Fibre optics used to transmit light from one place to another rather than for the transmission of data.

light emitting diode (LED) A semiconductor diode that emits light when a current is applied (used in calculators and clock displays and as indicators).

light guide Fine strands of glass or plastic protected by a surrounding material, used for the transmission of light.

light pen A computer accessory in the shape of a pen that contains a light-sensitive device that can detect pixels on a video screen (often used with suitable software to draw graphics on a screen orposition a cursor).

light pipe see **light guide**

light-sensitive device A device (such as a phototransistor) which is sensitive to light, and produces a change in signal strength or resistance.

limited-distance modem A data transmission device with a very short range that sends pure digital data rather than a modulated carrier.

limiting resolution The maximum number of lines that make up a video picture.

line 1 A physical connection for data transmission (such as a cable between parts of a system or a telephone wire). See also **land line. 2** One trace by the electron picture beam on a screen or monitor. **3** A row of characters (printed on a page or displayed on a computer screen or printer). An **information line** is a line running across the screen which gives the user information about the program being executed or the file being edited. **4** A series of characters received as a single input by a computer. **5** One row of commands or arguments in a computer program.

linear function A mathematical expression where the input is not raised to a power above one and contains no multiplications other than by a constant. For example, the expression Y 10 + 5X - 3W is a linear function; the expression Y $(10 + 5X^2)$ is not a linear function.

linear integrated circuit An electronic device whose output varies linearly with its input over a restricted range — a device usually used to provide gain to an analog signal.

linear list A list that has no free space for new records within its structure.

linear program A computer program that contains no loops or branches.

linear programming A method of mathematically breaking down a problem so that it can be solved by computer.

linear search A search method which compares each item in a list with the search key until the correct entry is found (starting with the first item and working sequentially towards the end).

line blanking interval The period of time when the picture beam is not displayed, this is during line flyback.

line busy tone A signal indicating that a telephone link cannot be made since the intended receiver is busy.

line communications Signal transmission using a cable link or telegraph wire.

line control Special codes used to control a communications channel.

line driver A high-power circuit and amplifier used to send signals over a long distance line without too much loss of signal.

line editor A piece of software that allows the operator to modify one line of text from a file at a time.

line ending A character which shows that a line has ended, instructed by pressing the carriage return key.

line feed (LF) A control on a printer or computer terminal that moves the cursor down by one line.

line flyback The return of the electron beam from the end of one line to the beginning of the next.

line folding To move a section of a long line of text onto the next row.

line frequency The number of picture lines that are scanned per second.

line impedance The impedance of a communications line or cable (equipment should have a matching load to minimize power loss).

line input A command to receive all characters including punctuation entered up to a carriage return code.

line length The number of characters contained in a displayed line (on a computer screen this is normally 80 characters, on a printer often 132 characters).

line level The amplitude of a signal transmitted over a cable.

line load The number of messages transmitted over a line compared to the maximum capacity.

line number A number that refers to a line of program code in a computer program. The programming language will normally sort out the program into order according to line number.

line printer A device for printing draft quality information at high speeds, typical output is 200 to 3000 lines per minute. Line printers print a whole line at a time, running from right to left and left to right, and are usually dot matrix printers with not very high quality print. Compare these to page printers, which print a whole page at a time.

line spacing The distance between two rows of characters.

line speed The rate at which data is sent along a line.

lines per minute (LPM) The number of lines printed by a line printer per minute.

line switching A communications line and circuit established on demand and held until no longer required.

line transient A large voltage spike on a line.

link 1 Software routine that allows data transfer between incompatible programs. **2** A communications path or channel between two components or devices. **3** To join or interface two pieces of software or hardware.

linkage editing Combining separate programs together, and standardizing the calls or references within them.

linkage software Special software which links sections of program code with any library routines or other code.

link control procedure (LCP) The rules defining the transmission of data over a channel.

linked list A list of data in which each entry carries the address of the next consecutive entry.

linked subroutine A number of computer instructions in a program that can be called at any time, with control being returned on completion to the next instruction in the main program.

link files A command to merge together a list of separate files.

linking Merging of a number of small programs together to enable them to run as one unit.

linking loader A short software routine that merges sections of programs to allow them to be run as one.

link loss Attenuation of signals transmitted over a link.

link trials Testing computer programs so as to see if each module works in conjunction with the others.

LIPS (logical inferences per second) A standard for the measurement of processing power of an inference engine. One inference often requires thousands of computer instructions.

liquid crystal display (LCD) Liquid crystals that turn black when a voltage is applied, used in many watch, calculator and digital displays. LCDs do not generate light and so cannot be seen in the dark without an external light source (as opposed to LEDs).

LISP (list processing) A high-level language used mainly in processing lists of instructions or data and in artificial intelligence work.

listing paper see **continuous stationery**

list processing 1 Computation of a series of items of data such as adding or deleting or sorting or updating entries. **2 (LISP)** A high-level language used mainly in processing lists of instructions or data, and in artificial intelligence work.

literal 1 (An operand) computer instruction that contains the actual number or address to be used, rather than a label or its location. **2** Printing error when one character is replaced by another or when two characters are transposed.

literate A person who can read. Someone who is **computer-literate** is someone able to understand expressions relating to computers and how to use a computer.

liveware The operators and users of a computer system (as opposed to the hardware and software).

LLL see **low-level language**

load 1 A job or piece of work to be done. **2** To transfer a file or program from disk or tape to main memory. **3** To put a disk or tape into a computer, so that a program (stored on it) can be run.

load and run or **load and go** A computer program that is loaded into main memory and then starts to execute itself automatically.

loader A program which loads another file or program into computer memory. An **initial program loader (IPL)** is a short routine that loads the first section of a program, after which it continues the loading process itself.

loading The action of transferring a file or program from disk to memory.

load point start of a recording section in a reel of magnetic tape

load sharing The use of more than one computer in a network to even out the work load on each processor.

local 1 A variable or argument that is only used in a certain section of a computer program or structure. **2** A keyboard not working with a CPU, but being used as a stand-alone terminal.

local area network (LAN or **lan)** A network in which various terminals and equipment are all a short distance from one another (at a maximum distance of about 500m, for example in the same building) and can be interconnected by cables. LANs use cables or optical fibre links; WANs use modems, radio and other long distance transmission methods. A **local area network server** is a dedicated computer and backing storage facility used by terminals and operators of a LAN. Compare with **WAN.**

local declaration The assignment of a variable that is only valid in a section of a computer program or structure.

local memory High speed RAM that is used instead of a hardware device to store bit streams or patterns.

local mode The operating state of a computer terminal that does not receive messages.

local variable A variable which can only be accessed by certain routines in a certain section of a computer program. Compare **global variable.**

location A number or absolute address which specifies the point in memory where a data word can be found and accessed.

locking a file The action of preventing any further writing to a file

lockout Preventing a user sending messages over a network by continuously transmitting data.

lock up A faulty operating state of computer that cannot be recovered from without switching off the power. This can be caused by an infinite program loop or a deadly embrace.

log 1 A record of computer processing operations. **2** To record a series of actions.

logarithm A mathematical operation that gives the power a number must be raised to, to give the required number.

logarithmic graph A graph whose axes have a scale that is the logarithm of the linear measurement.

logging on or **logging off** The process of opening or ending operations with a system.

logic 1 The science which deals with thought and reasoning; **formal logic** deals with the treatment of form and structure, ignoring content. **2** The mathematical treatment of formal logic operations such as AND, OR, etc., and their transformation into various circuits. **3** A system for deducing results from binary data. **4** The components of a computer or digital system. See also **Boolean algebra.**

logical channel An electronic circuit between a terminal and a network node in a packet switching system that is able to carry out some simple logical operations on the data received.

logical chart A graphical representation of logic elements, steps and decisions and their interconnections.

logical comparison A logical function to see if two logic signals are the same. This is the same as the AND operation.

logical decision One of two paths chosen as a result of one of two possible answers to a question.

logical error A fault in a program design causing incorrect branching or operations.

logical expression A function made up from a series of logical operators such as AND and OR.

logical high A logic state equal to logic true or 1. This is usually represented by a positive voltage (in TTL circuits this would be 5 volts).

logical low A logical state equal to logic false or 0. This is usually represented by a zero voltage level.

logical operator A character or word that describes the logical action it will perform (the most common logical operators are AND, NOT, and OR).

logical record A unit of information ready for processing that is not necessarily the same as the original data item in storage, which might contain control data, etc.

logical shift Data movement to the left or right in a word, the bits falling outside the word boundary are discarded, the free positions are filled with zeros. Compare with **arithmetic shift.**

logic bomb A section of code that performs various unpleasant functions such as system crash when a number of conditions are true (logic bombs are installed by unpleasant hackers or very annoyed programmers).

logic card or **logic board** A printed circuit board containing binary logic gates rather than analog components.

logic circuit An electronic circuit made up of various logical gates such as AND, OR and EXOR.

logic element A gate or combination of logic gates.

logic flowchart A graphical representation of logic elements, steps and decisions and the interconnections.

logic gate An electronic circuit that applies a logical operator to an input signal and produces an output. See also **gate.**

logic level The voltage used to represent a particular logic state (this is often five volts for a one and zero volts for a zero).

logic map A graphical representation of states and conditions in a logic circuit.

logic operation A computer operation or procedure in which a decision is made.

logic-seeking A printer that can print the required information with the minimum head movement, detecting ends of lines, justification commands, etc.

logic state One out of two possible levels in a digital circuit, the levels being 1 and 0 or TRUE and FALSE.

logic state analyzer Test equipment that displays the logic states of a number of components or circuits.

logic symbol A graphical symbol used to represent a type of logic function

log in or **log on** To enter various identification data, such as a password, usually by means of a terminal, to the central computer before accessing a program or data (used as a means of making sure that only authorized users can access the computer system).

LOGO A high-level programming language used mainly for educational purposes, incorporating graphical commands that are easy to use.

logoff see **logging off**

log off or **log out** To enter a symbol or instruction at the end of a computing session to close all files and break the channel between the user's terminal and the main computer.

logon see **logging on**

long haul network A communications network between distant computers that usually uses the public telephone system.

long persistence phosphor A video screen coating that retains the displayed image for a period of time longer than the refresh rate, reducing flicker effects.

look ahead The action taken by some CPUs to fetch instructions and examine them before they are executed (to speed up operations).

look-up table or **LUT** A collection of stored results that can be accessed very rapidly by a program without the need to calculate each result whenever needed.

loop A procedure or series of instructions in a computer program that are performed again and again until a test shows that a specific condition has been met or until the program is completed.

loop body A main section of instructions within a loop that carry out the primary function rather than being used to enter or leave or setup the loop.

loop check A check that data has been correctly transmitted down a line by returning the same data to the transmitter.

loop counter A register that contains the number of times a loop has been repeated.

loop network A communications network that consists of a ring of cable joining all terminals.

looping program A computer program that runs continuously.

loop program A sequence of instructions that are repeated until a condition is met.

lower case Small characters (such as a, b, c, as opposed to upper case A, B, C).

low-level language (LLL) A programming language similar to assembler and in which each instruction has a single equivalent machine code instruction (the language is particular to one system or computer). Compare with **high-level language.**

low-order digit A digit in the position within a number that represents the lowest weighting of the number base. For example, the number 234156 has a low-order digit of 6.

low-priority work A task which is not particularly important (and which is usually carried out in the background).

low-resolution graphics or **low-res graphics** The ability to display character-sized graphic blocks or preset shapes on a screen rather than using individual pixels. Compare **high-resolution.**

low speed communications Data transmission at less than 2400 bits per second.

LPM see **lines per minute**

LQ see **letter quality**

LSB (least significant bit) A binary digit occupying the right hand position of a word and carrying the least power of two in the word, usually equal to two raised to zero 1.

LSD (least significant digit) A digit which occupies the right hand position in a number and so carries least power (equal to the number radix raised to zero 1).

LSI (large scale integration) A single integrated circuit which contains between 500 and 10,000 circuits.

luggable A personal computer that is just about portable and usually will not run off batteries (it is much heavier and less compact than a lap-top or true transportable machine).

LUT see **look-up table**

M

M (Mega-) 1 A prefix meaning one million. **2** A symbol that represents 1,048,576, used only in computer and electronic-related applications, equal to 2^{20} .

MAC (message authentication code) A special code transmitted at the same time as a message as proof of its authenticity.

machine A computer or system or processor made of various components connected together to provide a function or perform a task.

machine address A number or absolute address which specifies the point in memory where a data word can be found and accessed.

machine check A fault caused by equipment failure.

machine code or **machine language** A programming language that consists of commands in binary code that can be directly understood by the central processing unit without the need for translation. An instruction in **machine code format** is usually made up of 1, 2 or 3 bytes for the operand, data and address. It directly controls the CPU and is recognized without the need for translation.

machine cycle The minimum period of time taken by the CPU for the execution of an instruction.

machine dependent system A system which is not standardized or which cannot be used on hardware or software from a different manufacturer without modifications. **Machine independent software** can be run on any computer system, and a **machine independent language** can be translated and executed on any computer that has a suitable compiler.

machine equation A formula which an analog computer has been programmed to solve.

machine instruction An instruction which can be recognized by a machine and is part of its limited set of commands.

machine intelligence The design of computer programs and devices that attempt to imitate human intelligence and decision-making functions, providing basic reasoning and other human characteristics.

machine intimate software Software that operates and interacts closely with the hardware in a system rather than relying on standard operating system calls to the hardware. This is often the cause of incompatibility problems.

machine language 1 The way in which machine code is written. **2** See machine code.

machine language compile To generate a machine code program from a HLL program by translating and assembling each HLL instruction.

machine language programming The slowest and most complex method of programming a CPU, but the fastest in execution, achieved by entering directly into RAM or ROM the binary representation for the machine code instructions to be carried out, rather than using an assembler with assembly language programs or a compiler with high-level language programs.

machine-readable data Commands or data or text stored on a medium that can be directly input to the computer.

machine run The action of processing instructions in a program by a computer.

machine translation A computer system that is used to translate text and commands from one language and syntax to another.

machine word The number of bits of data operated on simultaneously by a CPU in one machine cycle, often 8, 16 or 32 bits.

macro A (short) routine or block of instructions which can later be identified and called by a single word or label.

macro assembler or **assembly program** An assembler program that is able to decode macro instructions.

macro call The use of a label in an assembly language program to indicate to an assembler that the macro routine is to be inserted at that point.

macro code or **macro command** One word that is used to represent a number of instructions, simplifying program writing.

macro definition A description in a program or the operating system, of the structure, function and instructions that make up a macro operation.

macroelement A number of data items treated as one element.

macro expansion A process in which a macro call is replaced with the instructions in the macro.

macro flowchart A graphical representation of the logical steps, stages and actions within a routine.

macro instruction One programming instruction that refers to a number of instructions within a routine or macro.

macro language A programming language that allows the programmer to define and use macro instructions.

macro programming Writing a program using macro instructions or defining macro instructions.

magnetic bubble memory A method of storing large amounts of binary data as small magnetized areas in the medium itself, made of certain pure materials. This method of data storage never really became popular due to high cost compared to new developments in disk storage.

magnetic cartridge or **cassette** A small box containing a reel of magnetic tape and a pick up reel.

magnetic cell A small piece of material whose magnetic field can be altered to represent the two states of binary data.

magnetic core An early main memory system for storing data in the first types of computer, each bit of data was stored in a magnetic cell.

magnetic disk A flat, circular piece of material coated with a substance, allowing signals and data to be stored magnetically. A **magnetic disk unit** is a peripheral made up of a disk drive and the necessary control electronics. See also **floppy disk, hard disk.**

magnetic drum A data storage peripheral that uses a coated cylinder to store data magnetically; these are not often used now.

magnetic encoding The way in which the binary data signals are coded and stored on a magnetic medium.

magnetic flux A measure of magnetic field strength per unit area.

magnetic head An electromagnetic component that converts electrical signals into a magnetic field, allowing them to be stored on a magnetic medium.

magnetic ink A type of printing ink that contains a magnetic material, used in **magnetic ink character recognition (MICR),** systems that identify characters by sensing the magnetic ink patterns (as used on bank cheques).

magnetic master An original version of a recorded tape or disk.

magnetic material or **medium** A substance that will retain a magnetic flux pattern after a magnetic field is removed. **Magnetic media,** such as disk, tape, etc., are used to store signals.

magnetic memory or **store** Storage that uses a medium that can store data bits as magnetic field changes.

magnetic recording Transferring an electrical signal onto a moving magnetic tape * disk by means of an magnetic field generated by a magnetic head.

magnetic screen A metal screen used to prevent stray magnetic fields affecting electronic components.

magnetic storm A disturbance in the earth's magnetic fields affecting radio and cable communications.

magnetic tape A narrow length of thin plastic coated with a magnetic material used to store signals magnetically. Magnetic tape is available on spools of between 200 and 800 metres. For use in cassette players or tape drives, it is also available in **magnetic tape cartridges** or **cassettes** small boxes containing a reel of magnetic tape and a pick up reel. Magnetic tape is magnetized by the read/write head. Tape is a storage medium which only allows serial access, that is, all the tape has to be read until the required location is found (as opposed to disk storage, which can be accessed randomly).

magnetic tape encoder A device that directly writes data entered at a keyboard onto magnetic tape.

magnetic tape reader A machine that can read signals stored on magnetic tape and convert them to an electrical form that can be understood by a computer.

magnetic tape recorder A device with a magnetic head, motor and circuitry to allow electrical signals to be recorded onto or played back from a magnetic tape.

magnetic thin film storage A high-speed, low-access time RAM device that uses a matrix of magnetic cells and a matrix of read/write heads to access them.

magnetic transfer To copy signals stored on one type of magnetic medium to another.

mag tape see **magnetic tape**

mail Electronic messages to and from users of a bulletin board or network. The electronic storage space with an address in which a user's incoming messages are stored is a **mailbox** or **mail box**. See also **E-mail.**

mail-merge A word-processing program which allows a standard form letter to be printed out to a series of different names and addresses.

main clock The clock signal that synchronizes all the components in a system.

mainframe (computer) A large-scale high power computer system that can handle high capacity memory and backing storage devices as well as a number of operators simultaneously. **Mainframe access** is via microcomputers.

main memory or **main storage** The fast access dynamic RAM whose locations can be directly and immediately addressed by the CPU.

main routine A section of instructions that make up the main part of a program (a program often consists of a main routine and several subroutines, which are called from the main routine).

maintenance 1 Keeping a machine in good working condition. **2** Tasks carried out in order to keep a system running, such as repairing faults, replacing components, etc.

maintenance contract An arrangement with a repair company that provides regular checks and special repair prices in the event of a fault.

maintenance routine A software diagnostic tool used by an engineer during preventative maintenance operations.

major cycle The minimum access time of a mechanical storage device.

male connector A plug with conducting pins that can be inserted into a female connector to provide an electrical connection.

malfunction routine A software routine used to find and help diagnose the cause of an error or fault.

man machine interface (MMI) Hardware and software designed to make it easier for users to communicate effectively with a machine.

man-made noise Electrical interference caused by machines or motors. Compare **galactic noise.**

management information system (MIS) A computer system that provides management staff with relevant, up-to-date information.

manipulation Moving or editing or changing text or data. A high-speed database management program will allow the manipulation of very large amounts of data.

mantissa The fractional part of a number. The mantissa of the number 45.897 is 0.897.

manual A document containing instructions about the operation of a system or piece of software.

manual data processing Sorting and processing information without the help of a computer.

manual entry or **manual input** The act of entering data into a computer, by an operator via a keyboard.

map A diagram representing the internal layout of a computer's memory or communications regions. A **memory map** is a diagram indicating the allocation of address ranges to various memory devices, such as RAM, ROM and memory-mapped input/output devices. When addresses have been allocated to a computer's input/output devices to allow them to be accessed as if they are a memory location they are said to be **memory-mapped.** See also **bit-map, bit-mapped.**

MAR (memory address register) A register within the CPU that contains the next location to be accessed.

marching display A display device that contains a buffer to show the last few characters entered.

marker A code inserted in a file or text to indicate a special section. A **word marker** indicates the start of a word in a variable word length machine.

mark block To put block markers at the beginning and end of a block of text.

mark hold A continuously transmitted mark signal that indicates there are no messages on the network. Thektimeiduringlwhich a mark signal is being carried out.

mark sense To print characters with conductive or magnetic ink so that they are then machine readable.

mark sense device or **reader** A device that reads data from special cards containing conductive or magnetic marks.

mark sensing card A preprinted card with spaces for mark sense characters.

mark space Two-state transmission code using a mark and a space (without a mark) as signals.

mask 1 An integrated circuit layout stencil that is used to define the pattern to be etched or doped onto a slice of semiconductor. **2** A pattern of binary digits used to select various bits from a binary word (a one in the mask retains that bit in the word).

maskable interrupt An interrupt which can be activated by using an interrupt mask. The opposite type is a **non-maskable interrupt (NMI),** which is a high priority interrupt signal that cannot be deactivated.

mask bit One bit (of a word) used to select the required bit from a word or string.

masked ROM A read-only memory device that is programmed during manufacture, by depositing metal onto selected regions dictated by the shape of a mask.

masking An operation used to select various bits in a word.

mask register A storage location in a computer that contains the pattern of bits used as a mask.

mass storage The storage and retrieval of large amounts of data. A **mass storage device** such as a hard disk is able to store large amounts of data, and a complete **mass storage system** can hold more than one million million bits of data.

master card The first punched card in a pack that provides information about the rest of the pack.

master clock A timing signal to which all components in a system are synchronized.

master computer A computer in a multiprocessor system that controls the other processors and allocates jobs, etc.

master control program (MCP) Software that controls the operations in a system.

master data Reference data which is stored in a master file.

master disk 1 A disk containing all the files for a task. **2** A disk containing the code for a computer's operating system that must be loaded before the system will operate.

master file A set of all the reference data required for an application, which is updated periodically.

master/master computer system A system in which each processor is a master, dedicated to one task. A system with a controlling master computer and a slave that takes commands from the master is called a **master/slave computer system.**

master program file A magnetic medium which contains all the programs required for an application.

master tape Magnetic tape which contains all the vital operating system routines, loaded once when the computer is switched on (by the initial program loader).

master terminal One terminal in a network that has priority over any other, used by the system manager to set up the system or carry out privileged commands.

match 1 To search through a database for a similar piece of information. **2** To set a register or electrical impedance equal to another.

mathematical model A representation of a system using mathematical ideas and formulae.

mathematical subroutines Library routines that carry out standard mathematical functions, such as square roots, logarithms, cosine, sine, etc.

maths chip or **maths coprocessor** A dedicated IC that can be added to a system to carry out mathematical functions far more rapidly than a standard CPU, speeding up the execution of a program.

matrix 1 An array of numbers or data items arranged in rows and columns. **2** The pattern of the dots that make up a character on a computer screen or dot-matrix or laser printer.

matrix rotation Swapping the rows with the columns in an array (equal to rotating by 90 degrees).

matrix printer or **dot-matrix printer** A printer in which the characters are made up by a series of dots printed close together, producing a page line by line; a dot-matrix printer can be used either for printing using a ribbon or for thermal or electrostatic printing.

maximum capacity The greatest amount of data that can be stored.

maximum transmission rate The greatest amount of data that can be transmitted every second.

maximum usable frequency The highest signal frequency which can be used in a circuit without distortion.

maximum users The greatest number of users that a system can support at any one time.

MB or **Mbyte (megabyte)** A measurement of a mass storage device equal to 1,048,576 bytes of storage (i.e. equal to 2^{20} bytes).

Mb (megabit) A measurement of units of data equal to 1,048,576 bits.

Mbps (mega bits per second) A measure of the number of million bits transmitted every second by a device.

Mbyte See **MB**

MFLOPS (mega floating point operations per second) A measurement of computing power and speed, equal to one million floating point operations per second.

MBR (memory buffer register) A register in a CPU that temporarily buffers all inputs and outputs.

MCP see **master control program**

MDR (memory data register) A register in a CPU that holds data before it is processed or moved to a memory location.

mean time between failures (MTBF) The average period of time during which a piece of equipment will operate between failures. Similar to **mean time to failure (MTF)** the average period of time during which a device will operate (usually continuously) before failing.

mean time to repair The average period of time required to repair a faulty piece of equipment.

medium scale integration (MSI) An integrated circuit with 10 to 500 components.

medium speed A data communication speed between 2400 and 9600 bits per second. Medium speed transmission describes the maximum rate of transfer for a normal voice grade channel.

meet A logical function whose output is true if both inputs are true.

mega-1 A prefix used in general terms, meaning one million. **2** A prefix meaning 1,048,576 (equal to 2^{20}) and used only in computing and electronic related applications.

megabit (Mb) A measurement of units of data equal to 1,048,576 bits. **Megabits per second (Mbps)** is the measure of the number of million bits transmitted every second.

megabyte (MB) A measurement of mass storage, equal to 1,048,576 bytes.

megaflops (MFLOPS) A measure of computing power and speed equal to one million floating point instructions per second.

memory A storage space in a computer system or medium that is capable of retaining data or instructions. **Magnetic memory** is storage that uses a medium that can store data bits as magnetic field changes. An example would be a floppy disk. **Main memory** is fast access RAM whose locations can be directly and immediately addressed by a CPU.

memory access time The time delay between requesting access to a location and being able to do so.

memory address register (MAR) A register within the CPU that contains the address of the next location to be accessed.

memory bank A number of smaller storage devices connected together to form one large area of memory.

memory board An add-in printed circuit board containing memory chips.

memory buffer register (MBR) A register in a CPU that temporarily buffers all inputs and outputs.

memory capacity The number of bits or bytes that can be stored within a memory device.

memory cell The smallest location that can be individually accessed. This may be a byte, a word or a bit.

memory chip An electronic component that is able to store binary data, usually as a charge or by changing the state of a semiconductor switch.

memory cycle The period of time from when the CPU reads or writes to a location and the action being performed.

memory data register (MDR) A register in a CPU which holds data before it is processed or moved to a memory location.

memory diagnostic Software routine that checks each memory location in main memory for faults.

memory dump A printout of all the contents of an area of memory.

memory edit To change (selectively) the contents of various memory locations.

memory hierarchy The different types of memory available in a system, depending on capacity and access time.

memory intensive Software that uses large amounts of RAM or disk storage during run-time, such as programs whose entire code has to be in main memory during execution.

memory management Software that is part of the operating system and controls and regulates the flow and position in memory of files and data.

memory map A diagram indicating the allocation of address ranges to various devices such as RAM, ROM and memory-mapped input/output devices.

memory-mapped device A device with addresses allocated to a computer's input or output devices to allow them to be accessed as if they were a memory location. For example, a **memory-mapped screen** has an address allocated to each pixel, allowing direct access to the screen by the CPU. A **memory-mapped I/O** is an I/O port which can be accessed as if it were a memory location within the CPU's normal address range.

memory page One section of main store which is divided into pages, which contains data or programs.

memory protect A feature on most storage systems to prevent the accidental overwriting of data.

memory-resident program A program that is held permanently in memory, and can be run at any time by hitting a key — rather than asking the operating system to execute it again.

memory switching system A system which communicates information, stores it in memory and then transmits it according to instructions.

memory workspace The amount of extra memory required by a program to store data used during execution.

menu A list of options or programs available to the user, shown on the screen. **Main menu** is the list of the primary options available. **Pull-down** or **pull-up menus** can be displayed on screen at any time by pressing an appropriate key, and are usually displayed over the material already on screen.

menu-driven software A program in which commands or options are selected from a menu by the operator.

menu selection Choosing commands from a list of options presented to the operator.

mercury delay line An old method of storing serial data as pulses in a length of mercury, the data was constantly read, regenerated and fed back into the input.

merge To combine two data files, but still retaining an overall order. **merge sort** is a software application in which files are sorted and merged into a new file. See also **mail-merge.**

message format Predetermined rules defining the coding, size and speed of transmitted messages.

message heading A section of a message that contains routing and destination information.

message numbering The identification of messages by allocating a number to each one.

message slot The number of bits that can hold a message which circulates around a ring network.

message switching Storing, arranging and making up batches of convenient sizes of data to allow for their economical transmission over a network.

metabit An extra, identifying bit for each data word.

metacompilation Compiling a program that will compile other programs when executed.

metalanguage A language which describes a programming language.

metal oxide semiconductor (MOS) A production and design method for a certain family of integrated circuits using patterns of metal conductors and oxide deposited onto a semiconductor.

metal oxide semiconductor field effect transistor (MOSFET) A high-powered and high-speed field effect transistor manufactured using MOS techniques.

MFLOPS see **mega floating point instructions per second**

MICR (magnetic ink character recognition) A system that identifies characters by sensing magnetic ink patterns (as used on bank cheques).

micro see **microcomputer**

microchip A circuit in which all the active and passive components are formed on one small piece of semiconductor, by means of etching and chemical processes.

microcircuit A complex integrated circuit.

microcode ALU control instructions implemented as hardwired software.

microcomputer or **micro** A complete small, cheap, low-power computer system based around a microprocessor chip and having limited memory capacity. A **single-board microcomputer** is a microcomputer whose components are all contained on a single printed circuit board.

microcomputer architecture The layout and interconnection of a microcomputer's internal hardware.

microcomputer backplane The main printed circuit board of a system, containing most of the components and connections for expansion boards, etc.

microcomputer bus The main data, address and control buses in a microcomputer.

microcomputer development kit A basic computer based around a new CPU chip that allows hardware and software designers to experiment with the new device.

microcontroller A small, self-contained microcomputer for use in dedicated control applications.

microcycle The unit of time (usually a multiple of the system clock period) used to give the execution time of instructions.

microdevice A very small device, such as a microprocessor.

microelectronics The design and manufacture of electronic circuits with integrated circuits and chips.

microfloppy A small size magnetic floppy disk (usually refers to 3.5 inch disks).

microinstruction One hardwired instruction (part of a microcode) that controls the actions of the ALU.

microprocessor The central processing unit elements, often contained on a single integrated circuit chip, which, when combined with other memory and I/O chips, will make up a microcomputer. A microprocessor's addressing capabilities (the highest address that a CPU can directly address, without special features) depend on the address word size — the bigger the word the greater the addressing capacity.

microprocessor architecture The layout of the basic parts within a CPU (I/O, ALU, etc.)

microprocessor chip An integrated circuit that contains all the elements of a central processing unit, connected with other memory and I/O chips to make a microcomputer.

microprocessor unit (MPU) A unit containing the main elements of a microprocessor.

microprogram A series of microinstructions that perform a certain task when executed.

microprogram counter A register that stores the address of the next microinstruction to be carried out. A microprogram counter is the same as a memory address register.

microprogram instruction set The complete set of basic microinstructions available in a CPU.

microprogram store A storage device used to hold a microprogram.

microsequence A series of microinstructions.

mid-user The operator who retrieves relevant information from a database for a customer or end user.

middleware System software that has been customized by a dealer for a particular user.

migration (of data) The moving of data between a high priority or on-line device to a low-priority or off-line device.

milk disk A disk used to transfer data from a small machine onto a larger computer, which provides greater processing power.

milking machine A portable machine which can accept data from different machines, then transfer it to another larger computer.

MIMD (multiple instruction stream - multiple data stream) The architecture of a parallel processor that uses a number of ALUs and memory devices in parallel to provide high speed processing.

minidisk A magnetic disk smaller than the 5.25 inch standard, usually referring to a 3.5 inch disk.

minifloppy A magnetic disk (usually refers to the 5.25 inch standard disk).

minicomputer or **mini** A small computer, with a greater range of instructions and processing power than a microcomputer, but not able to compete with the speed or data handling capacity of a mainframe computer.

minimal latency coding see **minimum access code**

minimal tree A tree whose nodes are organized in the optimum way, providing maximum efficiency.

minimum access code or **minimum delay code** A coding system that provides the fastest access and retrieval time for stored data items.

minimum weight routing A method of optimizing the transmission path of a message through a network.

minmax A method used in artificial intelligence to solve problems, by evaluating the "for" and "against" points for each option.

minuend The number from which another is subtracted.

MIPS (million instructions per second) A measure of computing power of a computer.

MIS see **management information system**

MISD (multiple instruction stream - single data stream) The architecture of a parallel computer that has a single ALU and data bus with a number of control units.

MMI (man machine interface) The hardware and software designed to make it easier for users to communicate effectively with a machine.

mnemonic A shortened form of a word or function that is helpful as a reminder (such as INCA for increment register A).

mode dispersion The loss of power in a light signal transmitted down an optic fibre due to dispersion from transmission paths that are not directly along the axis of the fibre.

modem or **MODEM (modulator/demodulator)** A device that allows data to be sent by telephone, by converting binary signals from a computer into analog sound signals which can be transmitted over a telephone line. The process of converting binary signals to analog is called **modulation.** When the signal is received, another modem reverses the process (called demodulation). Both modems must be working according to the same standards for the correct transmission of data.

modification loop Instructions within a loop that change other instructions or data within a program.

modifier A programming instruction that alters the normal action of a command.

modular A method of constructing hardware or software products by connecting several smaller blocks together to produce a customized product.

modular programming Programming small individually written sections of computer code that can be made to fit into a structured program and can be called up from a main program.

modularization Designing programs from a set of standard modules.

modulated signal A constant frequency and amplitude carrier signal that is used in a modulated form to transmit data. The signal to be transmitted, used to modulate a carrier, is a **modulating signal.**

modulation A process of varying a carrier's amplitude or frequency or phase according to an applied signal.

modulator/demodulator see **modem**

module 1 A small section of a large program that can if necessary function independently as a program in its own right. **2** A self-contained piece of hardware that can be connected with other modules to form a new system.

modulo arithmetic A branch of arithmetic that uses the remainder of one number when divided by another.

modulo-N Modulo arithmetic using base N.

modulo-N check An error detection test using the remainder from a modulo arithmetic operation on data.

modulus or **MOD** The remainder after the division of one number by another. For example, 15 modulus 7 is equal to 1; 15 modulus 6 is equal to 3.

momentary switch A switch that only conducts while it is being pressed.

monadic or **Boolean operator** A logical operator with only one operand.

monadic operation An operation that uses one operand to produce one result.

monitor A visual display unit used to display high quality text or graphics, generated by a computer. A **multi-scan** or **multi-sync monitor** has circuitry to lock onto the required scanning frequency for any type of graphics card. See also **VDU.**

monitor program A computer program that allows basic commands to be entered to operate a system (such as load a program, examine the state of devices, etc.) See also **operating system.**

monochrome monitor A computer monitor that displays text and graphics in black, white and shades of grey instead of colours.

monolithic IC An integrated circuit manufactured on a single crystal of semiconductor.

monomode fibre An optical fibre that only allows light to travel along its axis without any internal reflections, as the result of having a very fine core diameter. See also **mode**.

monoprogramming system A computer batch processing system that executes one program at a time. Compare with **multiprogramming system.**

monospacing A system of printing where each character occupies the same amount of space. This is usual on cheaper models of printer, as well as on typewriters (as opposed to proportional spacing).

monostable An electronic circuit that produces an output pulse for a predetermined period when it receives an input signal.

Monte Carlo method A statistical analysis technique.

MOS (metal oxide semiconductor) A production and design method for a certain family of integrated circuits using patterns of metal conductors and oxide deposited onto a semiconductor.

MOS memory A solid-state memory using MOSFETs to store binary data.

mosaic A display character used in videotext systems; it is made up of small dots.

MOSFET (metal oxide semiconductor field effect transistor) A high power and high speed field effect transistor manufactured using MOS techniques.

most significant bit or **msb** or **MSB** The bit in a word that represents the greatest value or weighting (usually the bit which is furthest to the left). The most significant bit in an eight bit binary word represents 128 in decimal notation.

most significant character or **most significant digit (MSD)** The digit at the far left of a number, that represents the greatest power of the base.

motherboard The main printed circuit board of a system, containing most of the components and connections for expansion boards, etc.

mouse A small hand-held input device moved on a flat surface to control the position of a cursor on the screen. Software which uses a mouse rather than a keyboard for input is said to be **mouse-driven.**

mouse driver A program which converts data from a mouse to a standard form that can be used by any software. This usually means converting data from the mouse into coordinates that describe its position.

M out of N code A coding system providing error detection, each valid character which is N bits long must contain M binary "one" bits.

movable head disk A magnetic disk head assembly that moves across the disk until the required track is reached.

move block A command which changes the place of a block of text identified by block markers.

movement file A file containing recent changes or transactions to records, which is then used to update a master file.

MPS see **microprocessor system**

MPU see **microprocessor unit**

ms (millisecond) one thousandth of a second

msb or **MSB (most significant bit)** A bit in a word that represents the greatest value or weight (usually the bit furthest to the left).

MSD see **most significant digit**

MSI see **medium scale integration**

MTBF (mean time between failures) The average period of time that a piece of equipment will operate between failures.

MTF (mean time to failure) The average period of time for which a device will operate (usually continuously) before failing.

multi-access system A computer system that allows several users to access one file or program at the same time. See also **multi-user.**

multi-address or **multi-address instruction** An instruction that contains more than one address (of data or locations or input/output).

multi-board computer A computer which has several integrated circuit boards connected to a motherboard.

multi-bus system A computer architecture that uses a high speed bus between CPU and main memory and a slower bus between CPU and other peripherals.

multidimensional array A number of arrays arranged in parallel, providing depth.

multidimensional language A programming language that can be represented in a number of ways.

multi-disk option A system that can have disk drives installed in a number of sizes.

multi-disk reader A device which can read from various sizes and formats of disk.

multidrop circuit A network allowing communications between a number of terminals and a central computer, but not directly between terminals.

multifunction card An add-on expansion board that provides many features to upgrade a computer. This usually includes more dynamic RAM, another serial and parallel port, etc.

multifunction workstation A workstation on which several tasks can be carried out, such as wordprocessing and graphics.

multilayer A printed circuit board that has several layers or interconnecting conduction tracks.

multilink system A system where there is more than one connection between two points.

multimode fibre An optical fibre that allows many different paths in addition to the direct straight path for light beams, causing pulse stretching and interference on reception of the signal.

multi-part stationery Continuous stationery with two or more sheets together, either with carbons between or carbonless.

multipass overlap A system of producing higher quality print from a dot matrix printer by repeating the line of characters but shifted slightly, so making the dots less noticeable.

multiphase program A program that requires more than one fetch operation before execution is complete.

multiple access see **multi-access**

multiple address code An instruction with more than one address for the operands, result and the location of the next instruction to be executed. See also **three-plus-one; four-plus-one address.**

multiple bus architecture A computer architecture that uses a high speed bus between CPU and main memory and a slower bus between CPU and other peripherals.

multiple instruction stream - multiple data stream (MIMD) The architecture of a parallel processor that uses a number of ALUs and memories in parallel to provide high speed processing.

multiple instruction stream - single data stream (MISD) The architecture of a parallel computer that has a single ALU and data bus with a number of control units.

multiple precision The use of more than one byte of data for number storage to increase possible precision.

multiplex To combine several messages in the same transmission medium. A bus used to carry address, data and control signals at different times is said to be **multiplexed.**

multiplexed analog components (MAC) A standard television broadcast signal format.

multiplexor (MUX) A circuit that combines a number of inputs into a smaller number of outputs. For example, a 4 to 1 multiplexor combines four inputs into a single output. Compare with **demultiplexor.**

multipoint A connection with several lines, attaching several terminals to a single line to a single computer.

multiprecision The use of more than one data word to represent numbers, increasing the range or precision possible.

multiprocessing system A system in which several processing units work together sharing the same memory.

multiprocessor A number of processing units acting together or separately but sharing the same area of memory. When each processor in a multiprocessor system deals with a section of one or more processes the result is **multiprocessor interleaving.**

multi-programming An operating system used to execute more than one program apparently simultaneously (each program being executed a little at a time).

multi-scan or **multi-sync monitor** A monitor which contains circuitry to lock onto the required scanning frequency of any type of graphics card. This means that different resolution graphics (which require different scanning frequencies) can be displayed.

multi statement line A line in a computer program that contains more than one instruction or statement.

multi-strike printer ribbon An inked ribbon in a printer that can be used more than once.

multi-tasking The ability of a computer system to run two or more programs at the same time.

multi-terminal system A system where several terminals are linked to a single CPU.

multithread A program design using more than one logical path through it, each path being concurrently executed.

multi-user system A computer system that can support more than one user at a time.

multi-window editor A program used for creating and editing a number of applications programs independently, each in a separate window on screen at the same time.

Murray code A code used for teleprinters that uses only 5 bits.

music chip An integrated circuit capable of generating musical sounds and tunes.

MUX (multiplexor) A circuit that combines a number of inputs into a smaller number of outputs. Compare **demultiplexor.**

N

n see **nano-**

n-channel metal oxide semiconductor Transistor design, with MOS techniques, that uses an n-type region for conduction.

N-key rollover A facility on a keyboard where each keystroke (up to a maximum of N) is registered in sequence even if they are struck very fast.

NAK see **negative acknowledgement**

name An ordinary word used to identify an address in machine language. A list of reserved words or commands in a language and the addresses in the computer that refer to them is a **name table** or **symbol table.**

NAND function A logical function whose output is false if all inputs are true, and true if any input is false. A **NAND gate** is the electronic circuit that provides a NAND function. The NAND function is equivalent to an AND function with a NOT function at the output. The output is 0 only if both inputs are 1; if one input is 1 and the other 0, or if both inputs are 0, then the output is 1.

nano- (n) An abbreviation meaning one thousand millionth or in the USA, one billionth; so a **nanosecond (ns)** is one thousand millionth of a second. A **nanocircuit** or **nanosecond circuit** is an electronic and logic circuit that can respond to impulses within nanoseconds.

narrative Explanatory notes or comments to help a user operate a program. A **narrative statement** sets variables and allocates storage at the start of a program.

native format First or basic format of data or a program.

natural binary coded decimal (NBCD) The representation of single decimal digits as a pattern of 4 bits.

natural language A language that is used or understood by humans.

NC (numerical control) A machine operated automatically by a computer; circuits controlled by a stored program or data.

NDR (non destructive readout) A display system that continues to display previous characters when new ones are displayed.

near letter-quality (NLQ) Printing by a dot-matrix printer that provides higher quality type, which is almost as good as a typewriter, by decreasing the spaces between the dots.

needle The tiny metal pin on a dot matrix printer which prints one of the dots when it is forced onto an inked ribbon which strikes the paper.

negate To reverse the sign of a number. For example, if 23.4 is negated, the result is -23.4.

negative acknowledgement (NAK) A signal sent by a receiver to indicate that data has been incorrectly or incompletely received.

negative feedback A loop around a circuit in which part of the output signal is subtracted from the input signal.

negative number A number which represents the number subtracted from zero, indicated by a minus sign in front of the number.

negative-true logic The use of a lower voltage level to represent binary 1 than for binary 0.

neither-nor function A logical function whose output is false if any input is true.

NEQ function (non-equivalence function) A logical function where the output is true if the inputs are not the same, otherwise the output is false. The electronic circuit which implements a NEQ function is a **NEQ gate.**

nest To insert a subroutine within a program or another routine or to use a routine that calls itself recursively. One loop inside another loop in the same program is a **nested loop. A macro called from within another macro is a nested macrocall.**

nesting level A number of subroutines within a subroutine.

nesting store A hardware stack (normally stacks are implemented with software).

network 1 Any system made up of a number of points or circuits that are interconnected in some way. In computing, this is usually a communications network which is a group of devices such as terminals and printers that are interconnected with a central computer allowing the rapid and simple transfer of data. For computer equipment, there are two main divisions of networks: the **local area network (LAN)** is a network where the various terminals and equipment are all within a short distance of one another (at a maximum distance of 500m, for example in the same building) and can be interconnected by cables; the **wide area network (WAN)** is a network where the various terminals are far apart and linked by radio or satellite. **2** To link points together in a network, for example, networking workstations rather than using them as standalone systems.

network analysis The study of messages, destinations and routes in a network with the aim of providing a better operation.

network architecture The method in which a network is constructed, such as layers in an OSI system.

network control program The software that regulates the flow of and channels for data transmitted in a network.

network controller A network user responsible for allocating disk space, answering queries and solving problems from other users of the same network.

network diagram A graphical representation describing the interconnections between points.

network hardware The physical links, computers and control equipment that make up a network.

networking hardware or **network hardware** The physical links, computers and control equipment that make up a network. Networking hardware allows a machine with a floppy disk drive to use another PC's hard disk when both machines are linked by a cable and are using networking software.

networking software or **network software** Software which is used to establish the link between a user's program and the network.

networking specialist A company or person who specializes in designing and setting up networks.

network layer ISO/OSI standard layer that decides on the routes to be used, the costs, etc. See also **layer.**

network management The organization, planning, running and upkeep of a network.

network processor A signal multiplexer controlled by a microprocessor in a network.

network redundancy Extra links between points allowing continued operation in the event of one failing.

network software Software which is used to establish the link between a user's program and the network.

network timing The signals that correctly synchronize the transmission of data.

neutral transmission A transmission system in which a voltage pulse and zero volts represent the binary digits 1 and 0.

new (command) A program command that clears main memory of the present program ready to accept a new program.

new line character A character that moves a cursor or printhead to the beginning of the next line. See also **carriage return (CR); linefeed (LF).**

next instruction register A register in a CPU that contains the location where the next instruction to be executed is stored. See also **register.**

nexus The connection point between units in a network.

nibble or **nybble** Half the length of a standard byte. A nibble is normally 4 bits, but can vary according to different micros or people.

nil pointer A pointer used to indicate the end of a chained list of items.

nine's complement The decimal complement (equivalent to the binary one's complement) formed by subtracting each digit in the number from nine. See also **ten's complement.**

n-level logic Logic gate design in which no more than n gates occur in a series.

NLQ see **near letter-quality**

NMI see **non-maskable interrupt**

NMOS see **N-channel metal oxide semiconductor**

no-address operation An instruction which does not require an address within it.

node An interconnection point in a structure or network. For example, a network may have fibre optic connections with nodes up to one kilometre apart.

noise A random signal present in addition to any wanted signal, caused by static, temperature, power supply, magnetic or electric fields and also from stars and the sun.

noise immunity The ability of a circuit to ignore or filter out or be protected from noise.

noisy mode A floating point arithmetic system, in which a digit other than a zero is deliberately added in the least significant position during the normalization of a floating point number. The digit added is called a **noisy digit.**

nomenclature A predefined system for assigning words and symbols to represent numbers or terms.

nonaligned Two devices that are not correctly positioned in relation to each other, which results in bad performance rating.

nonaligned read head A read head that is not in the same position on a magnetic medium as the write head was, producing a loss of signal quality.

non-arithmetic shift see **logical shift**

noncompatibility The situation of two or more pieces of hardware or software that cannot exchange data or use the same peripherals.

non-destructive cursor A cursor on a display that does not erase characters already displayed as it passes over them.

non-destructive readout (NDR) A display device that retains previous characters when displaying new characters.

non-destructive test A series of tests carried out on a piece of equipment without destroying it.

non-equivalence function (NEQ) A logical function where the output is true if the inputs are not the same, otherwise the output is false. The electronic circuit which implements a NEQ function is a **non-equivalence gate** or **NEQ gate.**

nonerasable storage A storage medium that cannot be erased and re-used.

non-impact printer A printer (like an ink-jet printer) where the character form does not hit a ribbon to press the ink onto the paper.

nonlinear An electronic circuit whose output does not change linearly in proportion to its input.

non-maskable interrupt (NMI) A high priority interrupt signal that cannot be blocked by software and overrides other commands.

non-operable instruction An instruction that does not carry out any function, but increments the program counter.

non-printing codes Codes that represent an action of the printer rather than a printed character. For example, in wordprocessing, the line width can be set using one of the non-printing codes, .LW, then the required number indicating the number of characters in the line.

non return to zero (NRZ) A signalling system in which a positive voltage represents one binary digit and a negative voltage the other; a representation of binary data in which the signal changes when the data changes state, and does not return to zero volts after each bit of data.

non-scrollable The part of the screen display which is always displayed (in a WP, the text can scroll whilst instructions, etc., are non-scrollable). See also **status line.**

non-volatile memory or **non-volatile store** or **storage** A storage medium or memory that retains data even when the power has been switched off. Disks (both hard and floppy) and tapes are non-volatile memory stores; solid-state memory, such as RAM chips, are volatile unless battery backed.

no op or **no operation instruction** A programming instruction which does nothing.

NOR function A logical function whose output is false if either input is true. An electric circuit or chip which performs a NOR function is a **NOR gate.** The output is 1 only if both inputs are 0; if the two inputs are different or if both are 1, the output is 0.

normalization routine A routine that normalizes a floating point number and adds extra (noisy) digits in the least significant position.

normalize 1 To convert data into a form which can be read by a particular computer system. **2** To convert characters into all capitals or into all lower case form. **3** To store and represent numbers in a pre-agreed form, usually to provide maximum precision.

normalized form A floating point number that has been normalized so that its mantissa is within a certain range.

normal range The expected range for a result or number, any outside this range are errors.

NOT function A logical inverse function where the output is true if the input is false. The electronic circuit or chip which performs a NOT function is a **NOT gate.** If the input is 1, the output is 0; if the input is 0, the output is 1.

NOT-AND A logical function equivalent to the NAND function.

notation A method of writing or representing numbers. Examples are: **binary notation** — base two numerical system using only the digits 0 and 1; **decimal notation** — number representation in base 10, using the digits 0-9; **hexadecimal notation** — number system using base 16 and the digits 0-9 and A-F; **infix notation** — mathematical syntax where operators are embedded inside operands (such as C - D or X + Y); **octal notation** — number system using base 8 and the digits 0-7; **postfix notation** — mathematical operations written in a logical way, so that the operator appears after the operands, this removes the need for brackets; **prefix notation** — mathematical operations written in a logical way, so that the operator appears before the operands, this removes the need for brackets.

notched see **edge notched card**

notice board A type of bulletin board on which messages to all users can be left.

n-plus-one address instruction An instruction made up of a number (n) of addresses and one other address that is the location of the next instruction.

npn transistor A bipolar transistor design using p-type semiconductor for the base and n-type for the collector and emitter. See also **transistor, bipolar**

NRZ see **non return to zero**

ns An abbreviation for nanosecond.

n-type material or **N-type material** or **n-type semiconductor** A semiconductor that has been doped with a substance which provides extra electrons in the material, giving it an overall negative charge compared to the intrinsic semiconductor. See also **npn transistor.**

null character A character which means nothing (usually code 0).

null instruction A program instruction that does nothing.

null list A list which contains nothing.

null modem An emulator circuit that allows two pieces of equipment that normally require modems to communicate, to be connected together over a short distance.

null set A set that only contains zeros.

null string A string that contains no characters.

number cruncher A dedicated processor used for high-speed calculations. Performing high-speed calculations involving very large numbers is called **number crunching.**

number range The set of allowable values.

numeral A character or symbol which represents a number. Usually either Arabic numerals (figures written 1, 2, 3, 4, etc.) or Roman numerals (figures written I, II, III, IV, etc.).

numerical control (NC) or **computer numerical control (CNC)** The automatic operation of a machine by a computer or of circuits by stored data.

numeric array An array containing numbers.

numeric character A letter used in some notations to represent numbers (for example in hex the letters A-F are numeric characters).

numeric keypad or **numberic pad** A set of ten keys with figures, included in most computer keyboards as a separate group, used for entering large amounts of data in numeric form.

numeric operand An operand that only operates on numerals.

numeric punch A punched hole in rows 0-9 of a punched card.

nybble or **nibble** Half the length of a standard byte. A nybble is normally 4 bits, but can vary according to different micros.

O

OA see **office automation**

object 1 A variable used in an expert system within a reasoning operation. **2** Data in a statement which is to be operated on by the operator. See also **argument, operand.**

object or **object-orientated architecture** A structure where all files, outputs, etc., in a system are represented as objects.

object code Binary code which directly operates a central processing unit (a program code after it has been translated, compiled or assembled into machine code).

object computer The computer system for which a program has been written and compiled.

object deck Punched cards that contain a program.

object language The language of a program after it has been translated. Compare with **source language.**

object program A computer program in object code form, produced by a compiler or assembler.

OCCAM A computer programming language, used in large multiprocessor * multi-user systems. This is the development language for transputer systems.

OCP (order code processor) (In a multiprocessor system) a processor which decides and performs the arithmetic and logical operations according to the program code.

OCR 1 (optical character reader) A device which scans printed or written characters, recognizes them, and converts them into machine-readable form for processing in a computer. **2 (optical character recognition)** A process that allows printed or written characters to be recognized optically and converted into machine-readable code that can be input into a computer, using an optical character reader. Some character fonts have been specially designed to be easily read using an OCR reader. These are the **OCR fonts.** There are two OCR fonts in common use: OCR-A, which is easy for scanners to read, and OCR-B, which is easier for people to read than the OCR-A font.

octal (notation) The number notation using base 8, with digits 0 to 7 (the octal digits). In octal, decimal 9 is octal 11.

octal scale The power of eight associated with each digit position in a number.

octet A group of eight bits treated as one unit; word made up of eight bits. See also **byte.**

odd-even check A method of checking that transmitted binary data has not been corrupted.

odd parity (check) An error checking system in which any series of bits transmitted must have an odd number of binary ones.

OEM (original equipment manufacturer) A company which produces equipment using basic parts made by other manufacturers, and customizes the product for a particular application.

office automation (OA) The use of machines and computers to carry out normal office tasks.

office computer A small computer (sometimes with a hard disk and several terminals) suitable for office use.

office of the future The design of an office that is completely coordinated by a computer. See also **paperless office.**

off-line 1 A processor or printer or terminal that is not connected to a network or central computer (usually temporarily). **Off-line printing** and **off-line processing** use a printer or processing device not under the control of a central computer. **2** A peripheral connected to a network, but not available for use.

offset A quantity added to a number or address to give a final number. The value to be added to a base address to provide a final indexed address is the **offset value** or **offset word.**

ohm The unit of measurement of electrical resistance.

O.K. A message sometimes used as a prompt in place of "ready" in some systems.

omission factor The number of relevant documents that were missed in a search.

OMR 1 (optical mark reader) A device that can recognize marks or lines on a special form (such as on an order form or a reply to a questionnaire) and that inputs them into a computer. **2 (optical mark recognition)** A process that allows certain marks or lines on special forms (such as on an order form or a reply to a questionnaire) to be recognized by an optical mark reader, and input into a computer.

on-board (A feature or circuit) which is contained on a motherboard or main PCB.

on chip A circuit constructed on a chip.

one address computer A CPU structure whose machine code only uses one address at a time.

one address instruction An instruction made up of an operator and one address.

one element A logical function that produces a true output if any input is true.

one for one A programming language, usually assembler, that produces one machine code instruction for each instruction or command word in the language. Compilers and interpreters are usually used for translating high-level languages which use more than one machine code instruction for each high-level instruction.

one-level address A storage address that directly, without any modification, accesses a location or device.

one-level code A binary code which directly operates the CPU, using only absolute addresses and values (this is the final form of a program after a compiler or assembler pass).

one-level store The organization of storage in which each different type of storage device is treated as if it were the same.

one-level subroutine A subroutine which does not call another subroutine during its execution.

one's complement The inverse of a binary number. For example, the one's complement of 10011 is 01100. See also **complement; two's complement.**

one-pass assembler An assembler that translates the source code in one action.

one-plus-one address An address format that provides the location of one register and the location of the next instruction.

one to zero ratio The ratio between the amplitude of a binary one and zero output.

onion skin architecture The design of a computer system in layers, according to function or priority, for example, a kernel at the centre, an operating system, a low-level language and then the user's program.

onion skin language A database manipulation language that can process hierarchical data structures.

on-line A terminal or device connected to and under the control of a central processor.

on-line database An interactive search, retrieve and update of database records, with a terminal that is on-line.

on-line information retrieval A system that allows an operator of an on-line terminal to access, search and display data held in a main computer.

on-line processing Processing by devices connected to and under the control of the central computer (the user remains in contact with the central computer while processing).

on-line storage Data storage equipment that is directly controlled by a computer.

on-line system A computer system that allows users who are on-line to transmit and receive information.

on-line transaction processing An interactive processing in which a user enters commands and data on a terminal which is linked to a central computer, with results being displayed on the screen.

on-screen Information that is displayed on a computer screen rather than printed out.

on the fly To examine and modify data during a program run without stopping the run.

O/P or **o/p** see **output**

op code (operation code) The part of the machine code instruction that defines the action to be performed.

open A command to prepare a file before reading or writing actions can occur. It is impossible to access data unless the file is open or has been opened.

open access A system in which many workstations are available for anyone to use.

open code Extra instructions required in a program that mainly uses macroinstructions.

open-ended program A program designed to allow future expansion and easy modification.

open reel Magnetic tape on a reel that is not enclosed in a cartridge or cassette.

open routine A routine which can be inserted into a larger routine or program without using a call instruction.

open subroutine Code for a subroutine which is copied into memory whenever a call instruction is found, rather than executing a jump to the subroutine's address.

open system A system which is constructed in such a way that different operating systems can work together.

Open System Interconnection (OSI) A standardized ISO network which is constructed in layered form, with each layer having a specific task, allowing different systems to communicate if they conform to the standard. See also **ISO/OSI layers, international.**

operand Data (in a computer instruction) which is to be operated on by the operator. For example, in the instruction ADD 74, the operator ADD will add the operand 74 to the accumulator.

operand field Space allocated for an operand in a program instruction. See also **argument, machine-code instruction.**

operating code (op code) The part of the machine code instruction that defines the action to be performed.

operating console A terminal in an interactive system which sends and receives information.

operating instructions Commands and instructions used to operate a computer.

operating system (OS) Software that controls the basic, low-level hardware operations, and file management, without the user having to operate it (the operating system is usually supplied with the computer as part of the bundled software or in ROM).

operating time The total time required to carry out a task.

operational information Information about the normal operations of a system.

operation code (op code) The part of a machine-code instruction that defines the action to be performed.

operation cycle The section of the machine cycle during which the instruction is executed. See also **fetch-execute cycle, machine cycle.**

operation decoder The hardware that converts a machine-code instruction (in binary form) into actions.

operation field The part of an assembly language statement that contains the mnemonic or symbol for the op code.

operation priority The sequence in which the operations within a statement are carried out. This is usually defined by the language and compiler used.

operation register A register that contains the op code during its execution.

operations manual see **instruction manual**

operation time The period of time that an operation requires for its operation cycle.

operation trial A series of tests to check programs and data preparation.

operator 1 A person who makes a machine or process work; a person who operates a computer. **2** A character or symbol or word that defines a function or operation. For example, x is the multiplication operator.

operator's console The input and output device used by an operator to control a computer (usually consisting of a keyboard and VDU).

operator precedence The order in which a number of mathematical operations will be carried out.

operator procedure A set of actions that an operator has to carry out to work a machine or process.

op register A register that contains the operating code for the instruction that is being executed.

optic fibre see **optical fibre**

optical bar reader or **bar code reader** or **optical wand** An optical device that reads data from a bar code.

optical character reader (OCR) A device which scans printed or written characters, recognizes them, and converts them into machine-readable code for processing in a computer. The process that allows printed or written characters to be recognized optically and converted into machine-readable code that can be input into a computer, using an optical character reader is **optical character recognition,** which is also abbreviated to **OCR.**

optical communication system A communication system using fibre optics.

optical data link A connection between two devices to allow the transmission of data using light signals (either line-of-sight or optic fibre).

optical disk A disk that contains binary data in the form of small holes in the surface which are read with a laser beam. Also called WORM (write once, read many times, for computers) which can be programmed once, or compact disk (CD) and video disk which are programmed at manufacture.

optical fibre A fine strand of glass or plastic protected by a surrounding material, that is used for the convenient transmission of light signals.

optical font or **OCR font** A character design that can be easily read using an OCR reader.

optical mark reader (OMR) A device that can recognize marks or lines on a special forms (such as on an order form or a reply to a questionnaire) and convert them into a form a computer can process. The process of doing this is **optical mark recognition,** also abbreviated to **OMR.**

optical memory Optical disks used as a backing storage medium.

optical scanner Equipment that converts an image into electrical signals which can be stored in and displayed on a computer.

optical storage Data storage using mediums such as optical disk, etc.

optical transmission The use of fibre optic cables, laser beams and other light sources to carry data, in the form of pulses of light.

optical wand see **optical bar reader**

optimizer A program which adapts another program to run more efficiently. A program that has been passed through an optimizer to remove any inefficient code or statements is an **optimized code.**

optimum code or **minimum access code** or **minimum delay code** A coding system that provides the fastest access and retrieval time for stored data items.

option A choice or action which can be chosen from a range. Options are usually displayed along the top or bottom of the screen, or are described in the menus.

optoelectrical Which converts light to electrical signals or electrical signals into light.

optoelectronics Electronic components that can generate or detect light, such as phototransistors, light-emitting diodes.

OR function A logical function that produces a true output if any input is true. The electronic implementation of the OR function is by an **OR gate.** The result of the OR function will be 1 if either or both inputs is 1; if both inputs are 0, then the result is 0.

order code see **operation code**

order code processor (OCP) (In a multiprocessor system) a processor which decodes and performs the arithmetic and logical operations according to the program code.

ordered list A list of data items which has been sorted into an order.

origin 1 The position on a display screen to which all coordinates are referenced, usually the top left hand corner of the screen. 2 The location in memory at which the first instruction of a program is stored. See also **indexed.**

original equipment manufacturer (OEM) A company which produces equipment using basic parts made by other manufacturers, and customizes the product for a particular application.

orthogonal An instruction made up of independent parameters or parts.

OS (operating system) Software that controls the basic, low-level hardware operations, and file management, without the user having to operate it (the operating system is usually supplied with the computer as part of the bundled software in ROM).

OSI see **open system interconnection, ISO/OSI**

out of range (A number or quantity) that is outside the limits of a system.

outage The time during which a system is not operational.

outlet A connection or point in a circuit or network where a signal or data can be accessed.

output (o/p or O/P) 1 Information or data that is transferred from a CPU or the main memory to another device such as a monitor or printer or secondary storage device. 2 The action of transferring the information or data from store to a user, from a computer to a monitor or printer.

output area or **block** A section of memory that contains data to be transferred to an output device.

output bound or **limited** A processor that cannot function at normal speed because of a slower peripheral.

output buffer register A temporary store for data that is waiting to be output.

output device A device (such as a monitor or printer) which allows information to be displayed.

output file A set of records that have been completely processed according to various parameters.

output formatter 1 Software used to format data or programs (and output them) so that they are compatible with another sort of storage medium. 2 The part of a word processor program that formats text according to embedded commands.

output mode A computer mode in which data is moved from internal storage * the CPU to external devices.

output register A register that stores data to be output until the receiver is ready or the channel is free.

output stream A communications channel carrying data output to a peripheral.

output port A circuit and connector that allow a computer to output or transmit data to other devices or machines.

overflow or **OV 1** A mathematical result that is greater than the limits of the computer's number storage system. **2** A situation in a network when the number of transmissions is greater than the line capacity and are transferred by another route.

overflow bit or **flag** or **indicator** A single bit in a word that is set to one (1) if a mathematical overflow has occurred.

overflow check Examining an overflow flag to see if an overflow has occurred

overhead Extra code that has to be included in a program for language, operating system or organizational requirements. For example, the line numbers in a BASIC program are an overhead.

overhead bit A single bit used for error detection in a transmission.

overlap Two things where one covers part of the other or two sections of data that are placed on top of each other. Multipass overlap is a system of producing higher quality print from a dot matrix printer by repeating the line of characters but shifted slightly, so making the dots less noticeable (used to produce NLQ print).

overlay 1 (For a keyboard) a strip of paper that is placed above keys on a keyboard to indicate their function. **2** (In programming) a program that is larger than the main memory capacity of a computer, and is loaded into memory in small sections as and when required, so that main memory only contains the sections it requires to run a program. Compare with **virtual memory management.**

overlay manager System software that manages (during run-time) the loading and execution of sections of a program when they are required.

overlay region The area of main memory that can be used by the overlay manager to store the current section of the program being run.

overlay segments The short sections of a long program that can be loaded into memory when required and executed.

overlay network Two communications networks that have some common interconnections.

overpunching Altering data on a paper tape by punching additional holes.

overstrike To print on top of an existing character to produce a new one.

overwrite To write data to a location (memory or tape or disk) and, in doing so, to destroy any data already contained in that location.

P

P-code The intermediate code produced by a compiler that is ready for an interpreter to process, usually from PASCAL programs.

pack 1 A number of punched cards or magnetic disks. **2** To store a quantity of data in a reduced form, often by representing several characters of data with one stored character.

package (software package) A set of computer programs and manuals that cover all aspects of a particular task (such as payroll, stock control, invoicing, etc.)

packed decimal A way of storing decimal digits in a small space, by using only four bits for each digit.

packed format Two binary coded decimal digits stored within one computer word or byte (usually achieved by removing the check or parity bit).

packet A group of bits of uniform size which can be transmitted as a group, using a packet switched network.

packet assembler/disassembler (PAD) A dedicated computer that converts serial data from asynchronous terminals to a form that can be transmitted along a packet switched (synchronous) network; a remote terminal may be connected to a PAD device through which it accesses the host computer.

packet switched data service or **packet switched network (PSN)** A service which transmits data in packets of a set length.

packet switching A method of sending messages or data in uniform-sized packets, and processing and routing packets rather than bit streams.

packing density The amount of bits of data which can be stored in a unit area of a disk or tape.

packing routine A program which packs data into a small storage area.

PAD = PACKET ASSEMBLER/DISASSEMBLER

pad character An extra character added to a string or packet or file until it is a required size.

padding Material (characters or digits) added to fill out a string or packet until it is the right length.

paddle A computer peripheral consisting of a knob or device which is turned to move a cursor or pointer on the screen.

page 1 A section of main store, which contains data or programs. A page is an area of memory used by a virtual memory management system. **2** One section of a main program which can be loaded into main memory when required. **3** To divide the computer backing store into sections to allow long programs to be executed in a small main memory.

page addressing Main memory which has been split into blocks, with a unique address allocated to each block of memory which can then be called up and accessed individually, when required.

page boundary A point where one page ends and the next starts.

page description language (PDL) Software that controls a printer's actions to print a page of text to a particular format according to a user's instructions.

page display A monitor that can display an entire page as it will appear when printed out.

page length The number of lines that make up the length of a page (in word-processing).

pages per minute (ppm) A measurement of the speed of a printer as the number of pages of text printed every minute.

page printer A printer which composes one page of text and then prints it rapidly.

page protection Software controls to ensure that pages are not overwritten by accident or copied into a reserved section of memory.

page table A list of all the pages and their locations within main memory, used by the operating system when accessing a page.

paging A virtual memory technique that splits main memory into small blocks (pages) which are allocated an address and which can be called up when required. A virtual memory management system stores data as pages in memory to provide an apparently larger capacity main memory by storing unused pages in backing store, copying them into main memory only when required.

paging algorithm A formula by which the memory management allocates memory to pages, also covering the transfer from backing storage to main memory in the most efficient way.

paired registers Two basic word size registers used together as one large word size register (often used for storing address words). Many 8-bit CPUs uses a paired register to provide a 16-bit address register.

palette The range of colours which can be used (on a printer or computer display).

panel A flat section of a casing with control knobs or sockets. On most computers, there is a back panel with connectors for power, terminals, printers, etc. There is also a control panel with indicators and switches which allows an operator to monitor and control the actions of a computer or peripheral, and a front panel with the control switches and status indicators.

paper-fed device A device which is activated when paper is introduced into it.

paper feed A slot into which paper is introduced (in a printer).

paperless office An electronic office or office which uses computers and other electronic devices for office tasks and is said to avoid the use of paper.

paper tape A long strip of paper on which data can be recorded, usually in the form of punched holes.

paper tape feed The method by which paper tape is passed into a machine.

paper tape punch A device which punches holes in paper tape to carry data.

paper tape reader A device which accepts punched paper tape and converts the punched information stored on it into signals which a computer can process.

paper throw The rapid vertical movement of paper in a printer.

paper tray A container used to hold paper to be fed into a printer.

parallel 1 (Of a computer system) in which two or more processors operate simultaneously on one or more items of data. **2** Two or more bits of a word transmitted over separate lines at the same time.

parallel access Data transfer between two devices with a number of bits (usually one byte wide) being sent simultaneously.

parallel adder A number of adders joined together in parallel, allowing several digits to be added at once.

parallel computer A computer with one or more logic or arithmetic units, allowing parallel processing.

parallel connection A transmission link that handles parallel data. An average transmission rate is 60,000 bps through parallel connection.

parallel data transmission The transmission of a number of data bits of data simultaneously along a number of data lines.

parallel input/output (PIO) Data input or output from a computer in a parallel form.

parallel input/output chip A dedicated integrated circuit that performs all handshaking, buffering, etc., needed when transferring parallel data to and from a CPU.

parallel input/parallel output (PIPO) A device that can accept and transmit data in a parallel form.

parallel input/serial output (PISO) A device that can accept parallel data and transmit serial data.

parallel interface or **port** A circuit and connector that allows parallel data to be received or transmitted.

parallel operation A number of processes carried out simultaneously on a number of inputs.

parallel port see **parallel interface**

parallel priority system A number of peripherals connected in parallel to one bus; if they require attention, they send their address and an interrupt signal, which is then processed by the computer according to device priority.

parallel printer A printer that accepts character data in parallel form.

parallel processing A computer operating on several tasks simultaneously.

parallel running To run an old and a new computer system together to allow the new system to be checked before it becomes the only system used.

parallel search storage Data retrieval from storage that uses part of the data other than an address to locate the data.

parallel transfer Data transfer between two devices with a number of bits (usually one byte wide) being sent simultaneously.

parallel transmission A number of data lines carrying all the bits of a data word simultaneously.

parameter The information which defines the limits or actions of something, such as a variable or routine or program. The X parameter defines the number of characters displayed across a screen.

parameter-driven software Software whose main functions can be modified and tailored to a user's needs by a number of variables.

parameterization An action of setting parameters for software.

parameter testing A program to examine the parameters and set up the system or program accordingly.

parameter word A data word that contains information defining the limits or actions of a routine or program.

parametric subroutine A subroutine that uses parameters to define its limits or actions.

parity bit An extra bit added to a data word as a parity checking device.

parity check A method of checking that there are no errors and that transmitted binary data has not been corrupted. This is usually either an **even parity check** which is an error checking system in which any series of bits transmitted must have an even number of binary ones, or an **odd parity check** which is an error checking system in which any series of bits transmitted must have an odd number of binary ones.

parity flag An indicator that shows if data has passed a parity check or if data has odd or even parity.

parity interrupt An interrupt signal from an error checking routine that indicates that received data has failed a parity check and is corrupt.

parity track One track on magnetic or paper tape that carries the parity bit.

parsing An operation (by a compiler or interpretor) to break down high-level language code into its element parts when translating into machine code.

partial carry A temporary storage of all carries generated by parallel adders rather than a direct transfer.

partial RAM RAM chip in which only a certain area of the chip functions correctly, usually in newly released chips; partial RAMs can be used by employing more than one to make up the capacity of one fully functional chip.

partition 1 A section of computer memory set aside as memory for a foreground or background task. 2 To divide a large file or block into several smaller units which can be accessed and handled more easily.

partitioned file One file made up of several smaller sequential files, each part can be accessed individually by the control program.

PASCAL A high-level structured programming language used both on micros and for teaching programming.

pass 1 A single operation. **2** The execution of a loop, once; the action of moving the whole length of a magnetic tape over the read/write heads.

password A word or series of characters which identifies a user so that he can access a system. The user has to key in the password before being able to access the database.

patch A temporary correction made to a program; a small correction made to software by the user, on the instructions of the software publisher.

path A possible route or sequence of events or instructions within the execution of a program.

PC 1 (personal computer) A low cost microcomputer intended mainly for home and light business use. A computer is **PC compatible** if it is compatible with another common make (usually the IBM PC) **2** see **printed circuit (board), program counter**

PCB see **printed circuit board**

PCM (plug-compatible manufacturer) A company that produces add-on boards which are compatible with another manufacturer's computer.

PCU (peripheral control unit) A device that converts input and output signals and instructions to a form that a peripheral device will understand.

PDL see **page description language, program design language**

peek A BASIC computer instruction that allows the user to read the contents of a memory location. Using the instruction PEEK 1452 will allow the user to examine the contents of memory location 1452.

pel see **pixel**

pen recorder A peripheral which moves a pen over paper according to an input (a value or coordinate). This is used in plotting graphics.

perforated tape Paper tape on which data can be recorded in the form of punched holes. The machine that punches holes in a paper tape is a **perforator.**

peripheral 1 An item of hardware (such as terminal, printer, monitor, etc.) which is attached to a main computer system. **2** Any device that allows communication between a system and the device itself, but is not directly operated by the system. For example, peripherals such as disk drives or printers allow data transfer and are controlled by a system, but contain independent circuits for their operation.

peripheral control unit (PCU) A device that converts the input/output signals and instructions from a computer to a form and protocol which the peripheral will understand.

peripheral driver A program or routine used to interface, manage and control an input/output device or peripheral.

peripheral equipment 1 External devices that are used with a computer, such as printers or scanners. **2** Communications equipment external to a central processor that provides extra features.

peripheral interface adapter (PIA) A circuit that allows a computer to communicate with a peripheral by providing serial and parallel ports and other handshaking signals required to interface the peripheral.

peripheral-limited A CPU that cannot execute instructions at normal speed because of a slow peripheral.

peripheral memory The storage capacity available in a peripheral.

peripheral processing units (PPU) A device used for input, output or storage which is controlled by the CPU.

peripheral software driver A small routine or section of a program that can be called by the user, allowing the user to access and control a peripheral easily.

peripheral transfer The movement of data between a CPU and peripheral.

peripheral unit 1 An item of hardware (such as terminal, printer, monitor, etc.) which is attached to a main computer system. **2** Any device that allows communication between a system and the device itself, but is not operated only by the system.

permanent dynamic memory A storage medium which retains data even when power is removed.

permanent error An error in a system which cannot be mended.

permanent file A data file that is stored in a backing storage device such as a disk drive.

permanent memory Computer memory that retains data even when power is removed. See also **non-volatile memory.**

persistence The length of time that a CRT will continue to display an image after the picture beam has stopped tracing it on the screen.

personal computer (PC) A low-cost microcomputer intended mainly for home and light business use.

personal identification device (PID) A device (such as a card) connected or inserted into a system to identify or provide authorization for a user.

personal identification number (PIN) A unique sequence of digits that identifies a user to provide authorization to access a system (often used on automatic cash dispensers or with a PID or password to enter a system).

PERT (Program Evaluation and Review Technique) definition of tasks or jobs and the time each requires, arranged in order to achieve a goal

petal printer see **daisy wheel printer**

phantom ROM A duplicate area of read-only memory that is accessed by a special code.

phased change-over A new device that is gradually introduced as the old one is used less and less.

phosphor A substance that produces light when excited by some form of energy, usually an electron beam, used for the coating inside a cathode ray tube (the **phosphor coating**). The individual dots of red, green and blue phosphor on a colour CRT screen are called **phosphor dots.**

phosphor efficiency A measure of the amount of light produced in ratio to the energy received from an electron beam.

photodigital memory Computer memory system that uses a laser to write data onto a piece of film which can then be read many times but not written to again. These are also called WORM (Write Once Read Many times memory).

physical database The organization and structure of a stored database.

physical layer The ISO/OSI defined network layer that defines rules for bit rate, power and medium for signal transmission.

physical record 1 The maximum unit of data that can be transmitted in a single operation. **2** All the information, including control data for one record stored in a computer system.

PIA (peripheral interface adapter) A circuit that allows a computer to communicate with a peripheral by providing serial and parallel ports and other handshaking signals required to interface the peripheral.

pico- (p) A prefix representing one million millionth of a unit. So a **picosecond (ps)** is one million millionth of a second.

picture beam A moving electron beam in a monitor that produces an image on the screen by illuminating the phosphor coating and by varying its intensity according to the received signal.

picture element or pixel The smallest single unit or point on a display whose colour or brightness can be controlled.

PID (personal identification device) A device (such as a card) connected or inserted into a system to identify or provide authorization for a user.

pie chart A diagram in which ratios are shown as slices of a circle.

piggyback To connect two integrated circuits in parallel, one top of the other to save space. **Piggyback entry** is unauthorized access to a computer system by using an authorized user's password or terminal.

PILOT A computer programming language that uses a text-based format and is mainly used in computer-aided learning.

PIN (personal identification number) A unique sequence of digits that identifies the user.

pin One of several short pieces of wire attached to an integrated circuit package that allows the IC to be connected to a circuit board.

pinchwheel A small rubber wheel in a tape machine that holds the tape in place and prevents flutter.

pin cushion distortion Optical distortion (due to a faulty monitor) in which objects are seen with stretched corners due to lens aberration.

pinfeed see **tractor feed**

PIO see **parallel input/output, PIPO, PISO**

pipeline 1 A **pipeline computer** is a CPU or ALU that is constructed in blocks and executes instructions in steps, each block dealing with one part of the instruction, so speeding up program execution. **2** To schedule inputs to arrive at the microprocessor when nothing else is happening, so increasing apparent speed. **3** To begin processing of a second instruction while still processing the present one to increase speed of execution of a program.

pipelining 1 A method of scheduling inputs to arrive at the microprocessor when nothing else is happening, so increasing apparent speed. **2** Beginning the processing of a second instruction while still processing the present one to increase speed of execution of a program.

PIPO see **parallel input/parallel output**

pirate 1 A person who copies a patented invention or a copyright work and sells it. **2** To manufacture copies of an original copyrighted work illegally. The items most frequently pirated are programs on magnetic disks and tapes which are relatively simple to copy.

PISO see **parallel input/serial output**

pixel or **picture element** The smallest single unit or point of a display whose colour or brightness can be controlled. In high resolution display systems the colour or brightness of a single pixel can be controlled; in low resolution systems a group of pixels are controlled at the same time.

PL/1 (programming language/1) A high level programming language mainly used in commercial and scientific work on large computers, containing features of ALGOL, COBOL and FORTRAN.

PLA (programmable logic array) An integrated circuit that can be permanently programmed to perform logic operations on data. A PLA consists of a large matrix of paths between input and output pins, with logic gates and a fusible link at each connection point which can be broken or left to conduct when programming to define a function from input to output.

plaintext Text or information that has been encrypted or coded.

PLAN A low-level programming language.

planner Software that allows appointments and important meetings to be recorded and arranged in the most efficient way.

plasma display or **gas plasma display** A display screen using the electroluminescing properties of certain gases to display text. This is a modern, thin display usually used in small portable computers.

plastic bubble keyboard A keyboard whose keys are small bubbles in a plastic sheet over a contact which when pressed completes a circuit.

These are very solid and cheap keyboards but are not ideal for rapid typing.

play back To read data or a signal from a recording medium.

playback head A transducer that reads signals recorded on a storage medium and usually converts them to an electrical signal.

player missile graphics see **sprites**

PLD see **programmable logic device**

plex database A database structure in which data items can be linked together.

plex structure A network structure or data structure in which each node is connected to all the others.

PL/M (programming language for microprocessors) A high-level programming language derived from PL/1 for use on microprocessors.

plot To draw an image (especially a graph) based on information supplied as a series of coordinates.

plotting mode The ability of some word-processors to produce graphs by printing a number of closely spaced characters rather than individual pixels (this results in a broad low-resolution line).

plotter A computer peripheral that draws straight lines between two coordinates. Plotters are used for graph and diagram plotting and can plot curved lines as a number of short straight lines. A **printer-plotter** is a high-resolution printer that is able to mimic a plotter and produce low-resolution plots.

plotter driver Dedicated software that converts simple instructions issued by a user into complex control instructions to direct the plotter.

plotter pen The instrument used in a plotter to draw lines on the paper as it moves over it according to the instructions received from a computer.

plug A connector with protruding pins that is inserted into a socket to provide an electrical connection. Equipment which is manufactured to operate with another system when connected to it by a connector or cable is said to be **plug-compatible.**

plug-in unit A small electronic circuit that can be simply plugged into a system to increase its power or capabilities.

pointer 1 A variable in a computer program that contains the address to a data item or instruction. **2** A graphical symbol used to indicate the position of a cursor on a computer display.

pointer file A file of pointers referring to large amounts of stored data.

point-of-sale (POS) A place in a shop where goods are paid for. This now incorporates **electronic point-of-sale (EPOS):** a system that uses a computer terminal at a point-of-sale site for electronic fund transfer or stock control as well as product pricing, etc. **Point-of-sale terminal** or **POS terminal** is a computer terminal at a point-of-sale, used to provide detailed product information and connected to a central computer to give immediate stock control information.

point to point A communications network where every point is connected to every other. This provides rapid reliable transmissions but is very expensive and wasteful in cabling.

poke A computer instruction that modifies an entry in a memory by writing a number to an address in memory. For example, POKE 1423,74 will write the data 74 into location 1423.

POL see **problem-orientated language**

polar coordinates A system of defining positions as an angle and distance from the origin. Compare with **Cartesian coordinates.**

polarized plug A plug which has a feature (usually a peg or a special shape) so that it can only be inserted into a socket in one way. In the same way, a **polarized edge connector** has a hole or key to prevent it being plugged in the wrong way round.

polar signal A signal that uses positive and negative voltage levels.

Polish notation see **reverse**

poll To determine the state of a peripheral in a network.

polled interrupt An interrupt that is noticed by polling a device rather than waiting for the device to interrupt the CPU.

polling A system of communication between a controlling computer and a number of networked terminals; the computer checks each terminal in turn to see if it is ready to receive or transmit data, and takes the required action. The polling system differs from other communications systems in that the computer asks the terminals to transmit or receive, not the other way round.

polling characters A special sequence of characters for each terminal to be polled; when a terminal recognises its sequence, it responds.

polling interval A period of time between two polling operations.

polling list The order in which terminals are to be polled by a computer.

polling overhead The amount of time spent by a computer in calling and checking each terminal in a network.

polynomial code An error detection system that uses a set of mathematical rules applied to the message before it is transmitted and again when it is received to reproduce the original message.

POP An instruction to a computer to read and remove the last piece of data from a stack.

POP 2 A high level programming language used for list processing applications.

pop-down menu or **pop-up menu** A menu that can be displayed on the screen at any time by pressing the appropriate key, usually displayed over material already on the screen.

port A socket or physical connection allowing data transfer between a computer's internal communications channel and another external device. A **parallel port** is a circuit and connector that allows parallel data to be received or transmitted, while a **printer port** is an output port of a computer to which a printer is connected to receive character data (either serial or parallel).

portable 1 A compact self-contained computer that can be carried around and used either with a battery pack or mains power supply. **2** Any hardware or software or data files that can used on a range of different computers. **Portable software** or **portable programs** can be run on several different computer systems.

portability The extent to which software or hardware can be used on several systems.

port selector A switch that allows the user to choose which peripheral a computer is connected to via its output port.

port sharing A device that is placed between one I/O port and a number of peripherals, allowing the computer access to all of them.

POS (point-of-sale) A place in a shop where goods are paid for. Compare with **EPOS (electronic point-of-sale)**, which is a system that uses a computer terminal at a point-of-sale site for electronic fund transfer or stock control as well as product pricing, etc.

positioning time The amount of time required to access data stored in a disk drive or tape machine, including all mechanical movements of the read head and arm.

positive display A screen where the text and graphics are shown as black on a white background to imitate a printed page.

positive logic A logic system in which a logical one is represented by a positive voltage level, and a logical zero represented by a zero or negative voltage level.

positive response A communication signal that indicates correct reception of a message.

positive terminal A connection to a power supply source that is at a higher electrical potential than ground and supplies current to a component.

post To enter data into a record in a file.

postbyte In a program instruction, the data byte following the op code that defines the register to be used.

postfix notation Mathematical operations written in a logical way, so that the operator appears after the operands, this removes the need for brackets. For example, normal notation is (x-y) + z, but using postfix notation this becomes xy - z+. This is often referred to as **reverse Polish notation.**

post-formatted text Text which is arranged at printing time rather than on screen.

post mortem The examination of a computer program or piece of hardware after it has failed to try to find out why the failure took place.

postprocessor 1 A microprocessor that handles semi-processed data from another device. **2** A program that processes data from another program, which has already been processed.

potential difference The voltage difference between two points in a circuit.

power A mathematical term describing the number of times a number is to be multiplied by itself. For example, 5 to the power 2 is equal to 25. The power number is written as small figures in superscript: 10^5 ("ten to the power five").

power dump To remove all electrical power from a computer.

power failure The stoppage of the electrical power supply (for a long or very short period of time) which will cause electrical equipment to stop working or malfunction, unless they are battery-backed.

power loss The amount of power lost (in transmission or due to connection equipment).

power off Switching off or disconnecting an electrical device from its power supply.

power on An indication that electrical power is being supplied to a piece of electrical equipment.

power-on reset The automatic reset of a CPU to a known initial state immediately after power is applied (some CPUs will not automatically start with clear registers, etc., but might contain garbage).

power pack A self-contained box that will provide a voltage and current supply for a circuit.

power supply or **power supply unit (PSU)** An electrical circuit that provides certain direct current voltage and current levels from an alternating current source for use in other electrical circuits; a PSU will regulate, smooth and reduce the mains voltage level for use in low power electronic circuits.

power up To switch on or apply a voltage to a electrical device.

ppm see **pages per minute**

pre-allocation The execution of a process which does not begin until all memory and peripheral requirements are free for use.

precedence The computational rules defining the order in which mathematical operations are calculated (usually multiplications are done first, then divisions, additions, and subtractions last).

precision Great accuracy. The **precision of a number** is the number of digits in a number. Many CPUs as well as compilers offer increased mathematical precision using either **double precision**: operations using two data words to store a number, providing greater precision, or **multiple precision**: using more than one byte of data for number storage to increase possible precision.

precompiled code Code that is output from a compiler, ready to be executed.

predicate A function or statement used in rule-based programs such as expert systems.

pre-edit To change text before it is run through a machine to make sure it is compatible.

pre-fetch Instructions that are read and stored in a short, temporary queue with a CPU that contains the next few instructions to be processed, increasing the speed of execution.

prefix 1 A code or instruction or character at the beginning of a message or instruction. **2** A word attached to the beginning of another word to give it a special meaning.

prefix notation Mathematical operations written in a logical way, so that the operator appears before the operands, this removes the need for brackets.

preformatted text Text which has been formatted already.

preprocess To carry out initial organization and simple processing of data. Many compilers have two stages; one to preprocess (operations such as parsing and organization) the source code, the second to convert it into machine code.

preprocessor 1 Software that partly processes or prepares data before it is compiled or translated. **2** A small computer that carries out some initial processing of raw data before passing it to the main computer.

preprogrammed chip A chip which has been programmed in the factory to perform one function.

presentation layer The ISO/OSI standard network layer that agrees on formats, codes and requests for start and end of a connection. See also **ISO/OSI, layer.**

prestore To store data in memory before it is processed.

presumptive address An initial address in a program, used as a reference for future addressing operations.

presumptive instruction An unmodified program instruction which is processed to obtain the instruction to be executed.

preventive maintenance Regular checks on equipment to correct and repair any small faults before they cause a major problem. A preventive maintenance contract is a useful safeguard against major breakdowns of a system.

preview To display text or graphics on a screen as it will appear when it is printed out. Many new wordprocessors allow a WYSIWYG-style preview of what the finished printed page will look like before it is printed. A **previewer** is a feature that allows a user to see on screen what a page will look like when it will be printed.

primary key A unique identifying word that selects one entry from a database.

primary memory or **store** or **main memory** 1 A small, fast-access area of internal memory of a computer system (whose main memory is slower secondary storage) which stores the program currently being used. 2 The main internal memory of a computer system.

primary station The single station in a data network that can select a path and transmit; the primary station status is temporary and is transferred from one station to another.

prime A number that can only be divided by itself and by one. For example, the number seven is a prime.

prime attribute The most important feature or design of a system.

primer A manual or simple instruction book with instructions and examples to show how a new program or system operates.

print control character A special character sent to a printer that directs it to perform an action or function (such as change font), rather than print a character.

printed circuit or **printed circuit board (PCB)** A flat insulating material that has conducting tracks of metal printed or etched onto its surface which complete a circuit when components are mounted on it.

printer A device that converts input data words into a printed readable form.

printer buffer A temporary store for character data waiting to be printed (used to free the computer before the printing is completed making the operation faster).

printer control characters Embedded command characters in a text which transmit printing commands to a printer.

printer driver A short piece of dedicated software that converts and formats users' commands ready for a printer.

printer-plotter A high resolution printer that is able to operate as a low resolution plotter.

printer port An output port of a computer to which a printer is connected to receive character data (either parallel or serial).

printer quality The standard of printed text from a particular printer (high resolution dot-matrix printers produce near letter-quality text, daisy-wheel printers produce letter-quality text).

printer ribbon A roll of inked material which passes between a printhead and the paper.

print format The way in which text is arranged when printed out, according to embedded codes, etc. The print format is used to set the margins, headers, page lengths, etc.

print hammer A moving arm in a daisy-wheel printer that presses the metal character form onto the printer ribbon leaving a mark on the paper.

printhead 1 The row of needles in a dot-matrix printer that produce characters as a series of dots. 2 The metal form of a character in a daisy-wheel printer that is pressed onto an inked ribbon to print the character on paper.

print life The number of characters a component can print before needing to be replaced. A printhead can have a print life of over 400 million characters.

print modifiers Codes within a document that cause a printer to change mode, such as from bold to italic.

print out Using a printer to print information stored in a computer. The printed copy of information stored in a computer is a **printout.**

print pause Temporarily stopping a printer while printing (for instance, to change paper).

print spooling The automatic printing of a number of different documents in a queue at the normal speed of the printer, while the computer is doing some other task.

printwheel A daisy-wheel or a wheel made up of a number of arms, with a character shape at the end of each arm, used in a daisy-wheel printer.

priority The importance of a device or software routine in a computer system. The operating system will have priority over the application when disk space is allocated; a disk drive is more important than a printer, so it has a higher priority.

priority interrupt A signal to a computer that takes precedence over any other task. A list of peripherals and their priority when they send an interrupt signal (used instead of a hardware priority schedule) is the **priority interrupt table.** See also **interrupt, non-maskable interrupt.**

priority sequence The order in which various devices that have sent an interrupt signal are processed, according to their importance or urgency; a disk drive will usually come before a printer in a priority sequence.

priority scheduler A system that organizes tasks into correct processing priority (to improve performance).

privacy The right of an individual to limit the extent of and control access to the data about him. **Privacy of data** is a rule that data is secret and must not be accessed by users who have not been authorized. **Privacy of information** is a rule that unauthorized users cannot obtain data about private individuals from databases or that each individual has the right to know what information is being held about him or her on a database.

privacy transformation The encryption of messages or data to ensure that it remains private.

private address space A memory address range that is reserved for a single user, not for public access.

privilege The status of a user; referring to the type of program he can run and the resources he can use. The systems manager will have a privileged status so he can access any file on the system.

privileged account A computer account that allows the user access to special programs or access to sensitive system data. For example, the systems manager can access anyone else's account from his privileged account.

privileged instructions Computer commands which can only be executed via a privileged account, such as delete another account or set up a new user or examine passwords.

problem-orientated language (POL) A high-level programming language that allows certain problems to be expressed easily.

problem diagnosis Finding the cause of a fault or error, and the method of repairing it.

procedure 1 A small section of computer instruction code that provides a frequently used function and can be called upon from a main program. To sort files into alphabetic order, you can call a procedure from the main program by the instruction SORT. **2** A method or route used when solving a problem, such as a procedure to retrieve lost files.

procedure-orientated language A high-level programming language that allows procedures to be programmed easily.

procedural language A high-level programming language in which the programmer enters the actions required to achieve the result wanted.

process 1 A number of tasks that must be carried out to achieve a goal. **2** To carry out a number of tasks to produce a result (such as sorting data or finding the solution to a problem).

process-bound program A program that spends more time executing instructions and using the CPU than in I/O operations.

process chart A diagram that shows each step of the computer procedures needed in a system.

process control The automatic control of a process by a computer. A dedicated computer that controls and manages a process is a **process control computer**. A **process control system** is a system offering complete input and output modules, a CPU with memory and a program (usually stored in ROM) and control and feedback devices such as A/D and D/A converters that completely monitors, manages and regulates a process.

processor A hardware or software device that is able to manipulate or modify data according to instructions. Two examples of hardware and software processors are: **the central processing unit** which is a hardware device that allows a computer to manipulate and modify data; **a compiler** is a software language processor that translates data and instructions in one language into another form.

processor controlled keying Data entry by an operator which is prompted and controlled by a computer.

processor interrupt To send an interrupt signal to a processor requesting attention, that will usually cause it to stop what it is doing and attend to the calling device.

processor-limited (An operation or execution time) that is set by the speed of the processor rather than a peripheral.

processor status word (PSW) A data word which contains a number of status bits, such as carry flag, zero flag and overflow flag.

program 1 A complete set of instructions in some programming language which direct a computer to carry out a particular task. **2** To write or prepare a set of instructions which direct a computer to perform a certain task.

program address counter A register in a CPU that contains the location of the next instruction to be processed.

program branch One or more paths within a program that can be followed after a conditional statement.

program cards Punched cards that contain the instructions that make up a program.

program coding sheet A specially preprinted form on which computer instructions can be written, simplifying program writing.

program compatibility The ability of two pieces of software to function correctly together.

program compilation The translation of an encoded source program into machine code.

program counter (PC) or **instruction address register (IAR)** A register in a CPU that contains the location of the next instruction to be processed. See also **instruction address register; sequence control register.**

program crash The unexpected failure of a program due to a programming error or a hardware fault.

program design language (PDL) A programming language used to design the structure of a program.

program development All the operations involved in creating a computer program from first ideas to initial writing, debugging and the final product.

program development system All the hardware and software needed for program development on a system.

program documentation A set of instruction notes, examples and tips on how to use a program. See also **manual.**

program editor Software that allows the user to alter, delete and add instructions to a program file.

program execution Instructing a processor to execute in sequence the instructions in a program.

program file A file containing a program rather than data.

program flowchart A diagram that graphically describes the various steps in a program.

program generator Software that allows users to write complex programs using a few simple instructions.

program instruction A single word or expression that represents one operation (in a high level program each program instruction can consist of a number of low level machine code instructions).

program library A collection of useful procedures and programs which can be used for various purposes and included into new software.

program line One row of commands or arguments in a computer program. The **program line number** refers to a line of program code in a computer program.

program listing A list of the set of instructions that make up a program (program listings are displayed in an ordered manner, BASIC listings by line number, assembly listings by memory location; they do not necessarily represent the order in which the program will be executed, since there could be jumps or subroutines).

programmable A device that can accept and store instructions then execute them. A very small computer, which can be held in the hand, used for inputting information when a larger terminal is not available (as by a salesman on a call) is called a **hand-held programmable.**

programmable logic array (PLA) or **programmable logic device (PLD)** An integrated circuit that can be permanently programmed to perform logic operations on data using a matrix of links between input and output pins. Programmable logic arrays are usually used to replace a number of separate logic gates, so reducing space and cost.

programmable interrupt controller A circuit or chip which can be programmed to ignore certain interrupts, accept only high priority interrupts and select the priority of interrupts.

programmable key A special key on a computer terminal keyboard that can be programmed to produce a special character or to carry out various functions.

programmable memory (PROM) An electronic device in which data can be stored. See also **EAROM; EEPROM; EPROM; ROM.**

programmable read only memory (PROM) A memory integrated circuit that can be programmed with data by a user (some PROMs provide permanent storage, others such as EPROMs are erasable).

program maintenance The actions of keeping a program free of errors and up to date.

programmed halt An instruction within a program that when executed, halts the processor. To restart the CPU a reset action is required.

programmer 1 A person who is capable of designing and writing a working program. **2** A device that allows data to be written into a programmable read only memory.

programming in logic see **PROLOG**

programming language Software that allows a user to write a series of instructions to define a particular task, which will then be translated to a form that is understood by the computer. Programming languages are grouped into different levels: the **high-level languages** such as BASIC and PASCAL are easy to understand and use, but offer slow execution time since each instruction is made up of a number of machine code instructions; **low-level languages** such as assembler, are more complex to read and program in but offer faster execution time.

programming standards The rules to which programs must conform to produce compatible code.

program name A unique identification name assigned to a stored program file.

program origin The address at which the first instruction of a program is stored.

program relocation Moving a stored program from one area of memory to another.

program register A register in a CPU that contains an instruction during decoding and execution operations.

program report generator Software that allows users to create reports from files, databases and other stored data.

program run Executing (in correct order) the instructions in a program.

program segment A section of a main program that can be executed in its own right, without the rest of the main program being required.

program specification A document that contains details of all the functions and abilities of a computer program.

program stack A section of memory reserved for storing temporary system or program data.

program statement A high-level program instruction that is made up of a number of machine code instructions.

program step One operation within a program, usually a single instruction.

program storage The section of main memory in which programs (rather than operating system or data) can be stored.

program structure The way in which sections of program code are interlinked and operate.

program testing Testing a new program with test data to ensure that it functions correctly.

program verification A number of tests and checks performed to ensure that a program functions correctly.

PROLOG (programming in logic) A high-level programming language using logical operations for artificial intelligence and data retrieval applications.

PROM (programmable read-only memory) A read-only memory which can be programmed by the user (as opposed to ROM, which is programmed by the manufacturer).

PROM burner or **programmer** An electronic device used to program a PROM.

prompt A message or character displayed to remind the user that an input is expected. Many systems use the prompt READY to indicate that the system is available to receive instructions. The Yes/No prompt (Y/N on the screen), indicates that the user has to decide whether to continue with the operation or not.

propagated error One error in a process that has affected later operations.

propagating error An error that occurs in one place or operation and affects another operation or process.

propagation delay The time taken for a signal to travel through a circuit; time taken for an output to appear in a logic gate after the input is applied.

protected location A memory location that cannot be altered or cannot be accessed without authorization.

protected storage A section of memory that cannot be altered.

protocol Pre-agreed signals, codes and rules to be used for data exchange between systems.

protocol standards A number of standards laid down to allow data exchange between any computer systems conforming to the standard.

prototype The first working model of a device or program, which is then tested and adapted to improve it.

pseudo-code English sentence structures, used to describe program instructions which are translated at a later date into machine code.

pseudo-instruction A label (in an assembly language program) that represents a number of instructions.

pseudo-operation An command in an assembler program that controls the assembler rather than producing machine code.

pseudo-random A generated sequence that appears random but is repeated over a long period.

pseudo-random number generator Hardware or software that produces pseudo-random numbers.

PSU (power supply unit) An electrical circuit that provides certain direct current voltage and current levels from an alternating current source to other electrical circuits. A PSU will regulate, smooth and step down a higher voltage supply for use in small electronic equipment.

PSW see **processor status word**

PTR see **paper tape reader**

public data network Data transmission service for the public.

public domain (PD) Documents or texts or programs that have no copyright and can be copied by anyone.

public key cipher system A cipher that uses a public key to encrypt messages and a secret key to decrypt them (conventional cipher systems use one secret key to encrypt and decrypt messages). See also **cipher, key.**

pull-down or **pull-up menu** A menu that can be displayed on screen at any time by pressing an appropriate key, usually displayed over the material already on screen.

pulse 1 A short rush of electricity; short period of a voltage level. **2** To apply a short-duration voltage level to a circuit. An electric pulse can be used to transmit information, as the binary digits 0 and 1 correspond to 'no pulse' and 'pulse' (the voltage level used to distinguish the binary digits 0 and 1, is often zero and 5 or 12 volts, with the pulse width depending on transmission rate).

punch card or **punched card** A small piece of card which contains holes which represent various instructions or data.

punched card reader A device that transforms data on a punched card to a form that can be recognized by a computer.

punched (paper) tape A strip of paper tape that contains holes to represent data.

pure code Program code that does not modify itself during execution.

purge To remove unnecessary or out-of-date data from a file.

push-down list or **stack** A temporary storage queue system where the last item added is at the top of the list. See also **LIFO.**

push instruction or **operation** A computer instruction that stores data on a LIFO list or stack.

push-up list or **stack** A temporary storage queue system where the last item added is at the bottom of the list. See also **FIFO.**

Q

QBE see **query by example**

QISAM (queued indexed sequential access method) An indexed sequential file that is read item by item into a buffer.

QSAM (queued sequential access method) A queue of blocks that are waiting to be processed, retrieved using a sequential access method.

QL see **query language**

quadruplex Four signals combined into a single one.

quality The way in which the output from a printer is measured: either draft or letter quality. High-resolution dot-matrix printers produce near-letter quality, daisy-wheel printers produce letter-quality text.

quantifier A sign or symbol which indicates the quantity or range of a predicate.

quantize To convert an analog signal into a numerical representation. An input signal is quantized by an analog to digital converter.

quantizing noise Noise present in a signal due to inaccuracies in the quantizing process.

quantizer A device used to convert an analog input signal to a numerical form, that can be processed by a computer.

quantization The conversion of an analog signal to a numerical representation.

quantization error An error in converting an analog signal into a numerical form due to limited accuracy or rapidly changing signal. See also **A/D**.

quartz (crystal) clock A small slice of quartz crystal which vibrates at a certain frequency when an electrical voltage is supplied, used as a very accurate clock signal for computers and other high precision timing applications.

quasi-instruction A label (in an assembly program) that represents a number of instructions.

query by example (QBE) A way of finding information in a database by stating the items that are to be found.

query facility A program (usually a database or retrieval system) that allows the user to ask questions and receive answers or access certain information according to the query.

query language (QL) A language in a database management system, that allows a database to be searched and queried easily.

query processing Processing queries, either by extracting information from a database or by translating query commands from a query language.

queue A list of data or tasks that are waiting to be processed; a series of documents (such as orders, application forms) which are dealt with in order. In a multitasking operating system, there will be a **file queue** (a number of files temporarily stored in order before being processed) and a **job queue** containing a number of tasks arranged in order waiting to be processed in a batch system.

queued indexed sequential access method (QISAM) An indexed sequential file that is read item by item into a buffer.

queue discipline The method used as the queue structure, either LIFO or FIFO.

queued sequential access method (QSAM) A queue of blocks that are waiting to be processed, retrieved using a sequential access method.

queue management or **queue manager** Software which orders tasks to be processed

quicksort A very rapid file sorting and ordering method.

quiescent The state of a process or circuit or device when no input signal is applied.

quintet A byte made up of five bits.

quit To leave a system or a program; to log off from a system.

quotient The result of one number divided by another. When two numbers are divided, the answer is made up of a quotient and a remainder (the fractional part), 16 divided by 4 is equal to a quotient of 4 and zero remainder, 16 divided by 5 is equal to a quotient of 3 and a remainder of 1.

QWERTY keyboard An English language keyboard for a typewriter or computer, where the letters on the top line are Q-W-E-R-T-Y. Compare **AZERTY.**

R

R & D see **research and development**

R & D department The department in a company that investigates new products, discoveries and techniques.

race An error condition in a digital circuit, in which the state or output of the circuit is very dependent on the exact timing between the input signals (faulty output is due to unequal propagation delays on the separate input signals at a gate).

rack A metal supporting frame for electronic circuit boards and peripheral devices such as disk drives. A **rack mounted system** is one which consists of removable circuit boards in a supporting frame.

radial transfer Data transfer between two peripherals or programs that are on different layers of a structured system (such as an ISO/OSI system).

radix The value of the base of the number system being used. For example, hexadecimal numbers have a radix of 16.

radix complement see **ten's, two's complement**

radix notation Numbers represented to a certain radix. See also **base notation.**

radix point A dot which indicates the division between a whole unit and its fractional parts.

ragged left, ragged right Printed text with a flush right-hand margin and uneven left-hand margin or with a flush left-hand margin and uneven right-hand margin. Unjustified text, with a ragged right margin, is simply called **ragged text.**

RAM (random access memory) A memory device that allows access to any location in any order, without having to access the rest first. RAM is usually one of two forms, either **dynamic RAM,** the most common form of RAM integrated circuits, which use capacititive charge to retain data but which must be refreshed (read from and rewritten to) every few thousandths of a second; or **static RAM** which are RAM integrated circuits that do not have to be refreshed but cannot store as much data per chip as dynamic RAM. Dynamic RAM uses a capacitor to store a bit of data (as a charge), and needs to have each location refreshed from time to time to retain the data. It is very fast and can contain more data per unit area than static RAM which uses a latch to store the state of a bit; static RAM has the advantage of not requiring to be refreshed to retain its data, and will keep data for as long as power is supplied. **Partial RAM** is a RAM chip in which only a certain area of the chip functions correctly, usually in newly released chips (partial RAM's can be used by employing more than one to make up the capacity of one fully functional chip). Compare **sequential access memory.**

RAM chip An integrated circuit which stores (binary) data, allowing random access.

RAM disk A section of dynamic RAM that is made to look like and behave as a high-speed disk drive (using special software).

RAM loader A routine that will transfer a program from external backing store into RAM.

RAM refresh Electronic signals used to update the contents of dynamic RAM chips every few thousandths of a second, involving reading and rewriting the contents, needed to retain data.

RAM refresh rate The number of times every second that the data in a dynamic RAM chip has to be read and rewritten.

random access The direct acces or ability to access immediately memory locations in any order. Disk drives are random access, magnetic tape is sequential access memory.

random access device A device whose access time to retrieve data is not dependent on the location or type of data.

random access files A file in which each item or record can be immediately accessed by its address, without searching through the rest of the file, and is not dependent on the previous location.

random access memory (RAM) Memory that allows access to any location in any order, usually in the form of integrated circuits.

random access storage A storage medium that allows access to any location in any order.

random number A number whose value cannot be predicted.

random number generator A program which generates random numbers (used in lotteries, games, etc.)

random process A system whose output cannot be related to its input or internal structure.

random processing Processing of data in the order required rather than the order in which it is stored.

range left To move text to align it to the left margin; to move the contents of a word to the left edge.

rank To sort data into an order, usually according to size or importance.

rapid access A device whose access time is very short.

rapid access memory or **fast access memory (FAM)** Storage locations that can be read from or written to very quickly.

raster A system of scanning the whole of a CRT screen with a picture beam by sweeping across it horizontally, moving down one pixel or line at a time.

raster graphics Graphics in which the picture is built up in lines across the screen or page.

raster image processor A circuit which translates software instructions into an image or complete page which is then printed by the printer.

raster scan One sweep of the picture beam horizontally across the front of a CRT screen.

rated throughput The maximum throughput of a device that will still meet original specifications.

rational number A number that can be written as the ratio of two whole numbers. For example, 24 over 7 is a rational number; 0.333 can be written as the rational number 1/3.

raw data 1 Pieces of information that have not yet been input into a computer system. 2 Data in a database which has to be processed to provide information to the user.

reactive mode A computer operating mode in which each entry by the user causes something to happen but does not provide an immediate response. Compare with **interactive; batch.**

read back check A system to ensure that data was correctly received, in which the transmitted data is sent back and checked against the original for any errors.

read cycle The period of time between address data being sent to a storage device and the data being returned.

reader A device that reads data stored on one medium and converts it into another form.

read head A transducer that reads signals stored on a magnetic medium and converts them back to their original electrical form.

read-in or **read in** To transfer data from an external source to main memory.

read only A device or circuit whose stored data cannot be changed.

read only memory (ROM) A memory device that has had data written into it at the time of manufacture, and now its contents can only be read.

readout A display of data. A **readout device** is one that allows information (numbers or characters) to be displayed.

read rate The number of bytes or bits that a reader can read in a certain time.

read/write channel A channel that can carry signals travelling in two directions.

read/write cycle A sequence of events used to retrieve and store data.

read/write head A transducer that can read or write data from the surface of a magnetic storage medium, such as a floppy disk.

read/write memory A storage medium that can be written to and read from. Compare with **read only.**

ready state A communications line or device that is waiting to accept data.

real memory The actual physical memory that can be addressed by a CPU. Compare with **virtual memory.**

real number (In computing) a number that is represented with a fractional part (sometimes refers to numbers represented in a floating-point form).

real time Actions or processing time that is of the same order of magnitude as the problem to be solved (i.e. the processing time is within the same time as the problem to be solved, so that the result can influence the source of the data). For example, an aircraft navigation system needs to be able to process the position of the plane in real time and take suitable action before it hits another.

real-time clock A clock in a computer that provides the correct time of day. Compare **relative-time clock.**

real-time input Data input to a system as it happens or is required.

real-time multi-tasking A system that is executing several real-time tasks simultaneously without slowing the execution of any of the processes.

real-time processing A processing operation that takes a time of the same order of magnitude as the problem to be solved.

real-time simulation A computer model of a process where each simulated process is executed in a similar time to the real process.

real-time system A system whose processing time is within that of the problem, so that it can influence the source of the data. In a real-time system, as you move the joystick left, the image on the screen moves left. If there is a pause for processing it is not a true real-time system.

reboot To reload an operating system during a computing session. See also **boot.**

recall To bring back text or files from a backing store device; to bring back text or files from store for editing.

receive only A computer terminal that can only accept and display data but not transmit.

receiver register A temporary storage register for data inputs, before processing.

recode To code a program which has been coded for one system, so that it will work with the instruction set of another system's CPU.

recognition A process that allows something to be recognized, such as letters on a printed text or bars on bar codes, etc.

recognition logic The software that incorporates logical functions, as used in OCR systems, AI, etc.

recompile To compile a source program again, usually after changes or debugging.

reconfigure To alter the structure of data in a system.

reconfiguration Altering the structure of data in a system. See also **configure, set up.**

reconstitute To return a file to a previous state, usually to restore a file after a crash or corruption.

record count The number of records within a stored file.

recorder Equipment able to transfer input signals onto a storage medium, such as disk or tape.

record format or **layout** The organization and length of separate fields in a record.

record gap see **block gap**

record head or **write head** A transducer that converts an electrical signal into a magnetic field to write the data onto a magnetic medium.

recording density The number of bits of data that can be stored in a unit area on a magnetic disk or tape.

record length The quantity of data in a record.

records manager A program which maintains records and can access and process them to provide information.

records management A program which maintains records and can access and process them to provide information.

recoverable error An error type that allows program execution to be continued after it has occurred.

recovery 1 Getting back files which have been lost. **2** Returning to normal operating after a fault. **Recovery procedure** is the processes required to return a system to normal operation after an error.

rectify 1 To correct something or to make something right. **2** To remove the positive or negative sections of a signal so that it is unipolar. An electronic circuit that converts an alternating current supply into a direct current supply is a **rectifier.**

recursion or **recursive routine** A subroutine in a program that calls itself during execution.

recursive call A subroutine that calls itself when it is run.

redefine To change the function or value assigned to a variable or object. If an operator **redefines a key** the function of that programmable key is changed: for example, a key can be redefined to display only the figure five when pressed.

red, green, blue (RGB) A high-definition monitor system that uses three separate input signals controlling red, green and blue colour picture beams. There are three colour guns producing red, green and blue beams acting on groups of three phosphor dots at each pixel location.

redraw The action of drawing again. This is a feature often found in DTP and CAD programs, that will re-draw the screen if a lot of changes have been made.

reduce To convert raw data into a more compact form which can then be easily processed.

reduced instruction set computer (RISC) A CPU design whose instruction set contains a small number of simple fast-executing instructions, that makes program writing more complex, but increases speed. Compare with **WISC.**

redundant 1 (Data) that can be removed without losing any information. **2** An extra piece of equipment kept ready for a task in case of faults.

redundant character A character added to a block of characters for error detection or protocol purposes, and carries no information.

redundant code A check bit or data added to a block of data for error detection purposes, and carries no information.

redundancy Providing extra components in a system in case there is a breakdown.

redundancy checking A check made on received data to ensure they have their correct redundant codes and so detect any errors.

reel A circular holder round which a tape is rolled. The **pick-up reel** is the empty reel used to store tape as it is played from a full reel. A **reel to reel recorder** uses tape held on one reel and feeds it to a pick-up reel.

re-entrant program or **code** or **routine** One program or code shared by many users in a multi-user system (it can be interrupted or called again by another user before it has finished its previous run, and returns to the point at which it was interrupted when it has finished that run).

re-entry Calling a routine from within that routine; running a program from within that program.

re-entry point The point in a program or routine where it is re-entered.

reference address An initial address in a program used as an origin or base for others.

reference file A master file (of data) which is kept so that it can be referred to.

reference instruction A command that provides access to sorted or stored data.

reference list A list of routines or instructions and their location within a program.

reference table A list of ordered items.

reference time A point in time that is used as an origin for further timings * measurements.

reflected code A coding system in which the binary representation of decimal numbers changes by only one bit at a time from one number to the next.

reflective disk A video disk that contains data recorded as small holes etched into its surface. The data can be read using a reflected laser beam.

reformat To format a disk that already contains data. Reformatting destroys all the data on a disk. See also **format.**

refresh 1 To update regularly the contents of dynamic RAM by reading and rewriting stored data to ensure data is retained. This operation has to be performed every few thousandths of a second; the actual RAM refresh rate is dependent upon the speed of the RAM chip. Normally extra circuitry is required to generate the refresh signals, but some self-refreshing RAM chips contain built-in circuitry to generate refresh signals, allowing data to be retained when the power is off, using a battery backup. **2 (Screen refresh)** To update regularly the images on a CRT screen by scanning each pixel with a picture beam to make sure the image is still visible.

refresh rate 1 The number of times per second the contents of a dynamic RAM chip must be refreshed. **2** The number of times per second that the image on a CRT is redrawn.

regenerate A feature of many CAD and DTP programs that will completly recalculate every line and point within a drawing after a number of changes have been made.

regenerative memory A storage medium whose contents need to be regularly refreshed to retain its contents. Dynamic RAM is regenerative memory — it needs to be refreshed every 250ns; a CRT display can be thought of as regenerative memory, as it requires regular refresh picture scans to prevent flicker.

regenerative reading A reading operation that automatically regenerates and rewrites the data back into memory.

regional breakpoint A breakpoint that can be inserted anywhere within a program that is being debugged. See also **breakpoint, debugging.**

register 1 A special location within a CPU (usually one or two words wide) that is used to hold data and addresses to be processed in a machine code operation. **2** A reserved memory location used for special storage purposes.

register addressing An instruction whose address field contains the register in which the operand is stored.

register file A number of registers used for temporary storage.

register length The size (in bits) of a register. In a small micro, the data register is usually eight bits wide, and an address register is sixteen bits wide; in newer personal computers the data register is usually sixteen or twenty-four bits wide.

register map A display of the contents of all the registers.

regulate To control a process (usually using sensors and a feedback mechanism).

regulated power supply A constant, controlled voltage or current source whose output will not vary with input supply variation. A regulated power supply is required for all computers where components cannot withstand voltage variations.

rehyphenation Changing the hyphenation of words in a text after it has been put into a new page format or line width.

rejection error An error by a scanner which cannot read a character and so leaves a blank.

relational database A set of data in which all the items are related.

relational operator or **logical operator** A symbol that compares two items.

relative address A location specified in relation to a reference address.

relative coding Writing a program using relative address instructions.

relative coordinates Positional information given in relation to a reference point.

relative data Data that gives new coordinate information relative to previous coordinates.

relative error The difference between a number and its correct value (caused by rounding off).

relative-time clock Regular pulses (from a chip or circuit) that allow software in a computer to calculate the real time.

release A version of a product which is put on the market.

relocate To move data from one area of storage to another. Many programs are self-relocating: that is they can be loaded into any part of memory which will modify the addresses depending on the program origin address.

relocatable program A computer program that can be loaded into and executed from any area of memory.

relocation constant A quantity added to all addresses to move them to another section of memory, (equal to the new base address).

REM (remark) A statement in a BASIC program that is ignored by the interpreter, allowing the programmer to write explanatory notes.

remainder A number equal to the dividend minus the product of the quotient and divider. For example, 7 divided by 3 is equal to 2 remainder 1. Compare with **quotient.**

remedial maintenance Maintenance to repair faults which have developed in a system.

remote console or **device** An input/output device located away from the computer (sending data to it by line or modem).

remote job entry (RJE) A batch processing system where instructions are transmitted to the computer from a remote terminal.

remote station A communications station that can be controlled by a central computer.

remote terminal A computer terminal connected to a distant computer system.

rename (REN) An instruction to give a new name to a file.

renumber A feature of some computer languages that allows the programmer to allocate new values to all or some of a program's line numbers (this, obviously, is only available for languages that use line numbers, such as BASIC). See also **line number.**

repaginate To change the lengths of pages of text before they are printed.

repeat counter A register that holds the number of times a routine or task has been repeated.

repeat key A key on a keyboard which repeats the character when pressed.

repeating group A pattern of data that is duplicated in a bit stream.

reperforator A machine that punches paper tape according to received signals.

reperforator transmitter A reperforator and a punched tape transmitter connected together.

repertoire The range of functions of a device or software.

repetitive letter A form letter or standard letter into which the details of each addressee (such as name and address) are inserted.

replace Instruction to a computer to find a certain item of data and put another in its place. See also **search and replace.**

replication 1 Extra components in a system in case there is a breakdown * fault in one. **2** Copying a record or data to another location.

report generator Software that allows data from database files to be merged with a document (in the form of graphs or tables) to provide a complete report.

report program generator (RPG) A programming language used mainly on personal computers for the preparation of business reports, allowing data in files, databases, etc., to be included.

reprogram To alter a program so that it can be run on another type of computer.

request to send signal (RTS) A signal sent by a transmitter to a receiver asking if the receiver is ready to accept data (used in the RS232C serial connection).

re-route To send (data or signals) by a different route through a network.

rerun point The place within a program from where to start a running again after a crash or halt.

res see **resolution**

rescue dump Data saved on disk automatically when a computer fault occurs (it describes the state of the system at that time, used to help in debugging).

research and development (R & D) The investigation of new products, discoveries and techniques.

reserved sector An area of disk space that is used only for control data storage.

reserved word A word or phrase used as an identifier in a programming language (it performs a particular operation or instruction and so cannot be used for other uses by the programmer or user).

reset To return a system to its initial state, to allow a program or process to be started again. There are two types of reset: **hard reset** is an electrical signal that usually returns the system to its initial. state when it was switched on, requiring a reboot; **soft reset** is an instruction that terminates any current program execution and returns it to its initial state, and the user to the monitor or BIOS. A hard reset is similar to soft reset but with a few important differences: it is a switch that directly signals the CPU, while soft reset signals the operating system; hard reset clears all memory contents, a soft reset does not affect memory contents; hard reset should always reset the system, a soft reset does not always work (if for example, the operating system has been upset, a soft reset will not work).

reset button or **key** A switch that allows a program to be terminated and reset manually.

resident data or **resident program** Data or program that is always in a computer.

resident software or **memory-resident software** A program that is held permanently in memory (whilst the machine is on).

resolution The number of pixels that a screen or printer can display per unit area. The resolution of most personal computer screens is not much more than 70 dpi (dots per inch).

resource allocation Dividing available resources in a system between jobs. This is usually undertaken by the operating system.

resource sharing The use of one resource in a network or system by several users.

response frame A page in a videotext system that allows a user to enter data.

response time 1 The time which passes between the user starting an action by pressing a key and the result appearing on the screen. **2** The speed with which a system responds to a stimulus.

restore To put back into an earlier state.

restrict To keep something within a certain limit; to allow only certain people to access information.

resume To restart the program from the point where it was left, without changing any data.

retrieval The process of searching, locating and recovering information from a file or storage device. This usually refers to information retrieval: locating quantities of data stored in a database and producing information from the data.

retrofit A device or accessory added to a system to upgrade it.

retrospective parallel running Running a new computer system with old data to check if it is accurate.

retrospective search A search of documents on a certain subject since a certain date.

return An instruction that causes program execution to return to the main program from a subroutine.

return address 1 The address to be returned to after a called routine finishes. **2** The key on a keyboard used to indicate that all the required data has been entered. **3** (**carriage return**) An indication of an end of line (in printing).

reverse characters Characters which are displayed in the opposite way to other characters for emphasis (as black on white or white on black, when other characters are the opposite).

reverse interrupt A signal sent by a receiver to request the termination of transmissions.

reverse polarity A situation where the positive and negative terminals have been confused, resulting in the equipment not functioning.

reverse Polish notation (RPN) A mathematical operations written in a logical way, so that the operator appears after the numbers to be acted upon, this removes the need for brackets. In reverse Polish notation three plus four, minus two is written as 3 4 + 2 - 5; normal notation: (x-y) + z, but using RPN: xy - z+. The same as **postfix notation.**

reverse video A screen display mode where white and black are reversed (colours are complemented).

revert command A command in text that returns a formatted page to its original state.

revise To update or correct a version of a document or file.

rewind To return a tape or film or counter to its starting point. For example, the tape rewinds onto the spool automatically.

RGB (red, green, blue) A high-definition colour monitor system that uses three separate input signals controlling red, green and blue colour picture beams. There are three colour guns producing red, green and blue beams acting on groups of three phosphor dots at each pixel location.

RI see **ring indicator**

ribbon cable A number of insulated conductors arranged next to each other forming a flat cable.

right justify To align text to the right margin so that the text is straight.

right justification Aligning the text and spacing characters within a line so that the right margin is straight.

right shift To move a section of data one bit to the right. See also **logical shift, arithmetic shift.**

ring A data list whose last entry points back to the first entry.

ring (data) network A type of network where each terminal is connected one after the other in a circle. See also **chained list.**

ring back system A remote computer system in which a user attempting to access it phones once, allows it to ring a number of times, disconnects, waits a moment, then redials (usually in a bulletin board system).

ring indicator (RI) A signal from a line answering device that it has detected a call to the DTE and has answered by going into an off-hook state.

ring shift Data movement to the left or right in a word, the bits falling outside the word boundary are discarded, the free positions are filled with zeros.

RISC (reduced instruction set computer) CPU design whose instruction set contains a small number of simple fast-executing instructions, that makes program writing more complex, but increases speed. See also **WISC.**

rise time The time taken for a voltage to increase its amplitude (from 10 to 90 per cent or zero to RMS value of its final amplitude).

RJE (remote job entry) A batch processing system in which instructions are transmitted to the computer from a remote terminal.

RMS (root mean square) A measure of the amplitude of a signal (equal to the square root of the mean value of the signal). **RMS line current** is the root mean square of the electrical current on a line.

RO (receive only) A computer terminal that can only accept and display data, not transmit.

robot A device which can be programmed to carry out certain manufacturing tasks which are similar to tasks carried out by people.

robotics The study of artificial intelligence, programming and building involved with robot construction.

robustness 1 The strength of a system's casing and its ability to be knocked or dropped without harm. 2 A system's ability to continue functioning even with errors or faults during a program execution.

rogue indicator A special code used only for control applications such as an end of file marker.

rogue value or **terminator** An item in a list of data, which shows that the list is terminated.

roll in/roll out The transfer of one process (in a multiprogramming system) from storage to processor then back once it has had its allocated processing time.

rollback Reloading software after an error in which the master software has been corrupted.

roll-in To transfer data from backing store into main memory.

roll-out To save the contents of main memory onto backing store.

rollover A keyboard with a small temporary buffer so that it can still transmit correct data when several keys are pressed at once.

roll scroll Displayed text that moves up or down the computer screen one line at a time.

ROM (read only memory) A memory device that has had data written into it at the time of manufacture, and now its contents can only be read. Software which is stored in ROM is called **romware.**

ROM cartridge Software that is stored in a ROM device which is mounted in a cartridge that can be easily plugged into a computer.

roman An ordinary typeface, neither italic nor bold.

Roman numerals The figures written I, II, III, IV, etc. (as opposed to Arabic numerals such as 1, 2, 3, 4, etc.).

root mean square (RMS) A measure of the amplitude of a signal (equal to the square root of the mean value of the signal).

rotation The amount by which an object has been rotated. This is normally applied to bit rotation or a rotate operation, in which a pattern of bits are shifted in a word to the left or right, the old last bit moving to the new first bit position.

round robin A way of organizing the use of a computer by several users, so that each uses it for a time and then they pass it on the next in turn.

rounding characters Making a displayed character more pleasant to look at (within the limits of pixel size) by making sharp corners and edges smooth.

route A path taken by a message between a transmitter and receiver in a network.

routing Determining a suitable route for a message through a network.

routing overheads The actions that have to be taken when routing messages.

routing page A videotext page describing the routes to other pages.

routine A number of instructions that perform a particular task, but are not a complete program; they are included as part of a program. For example, the RETURN instruction at the end of a routine sends control back to the main program. Routines are usually called from a main program to perform a task, control is then returned to the part of the main program from which the routine was called once that task is complete.

row 1 A line of printed or displayed characters. 2 Horizontal line on a punched card. 3 A horizontal set of data elements in an array or matrix.

RPG see **report program generator**

RS-232C An EIA approved standard used in serial data transmission, covering voltage and control signals. The RS-232C standard is the normal serial interface found on most PCs and terminals, and usually uses a 9 or 25 pin connector. The RS-232C has now been superceeded by the RS-423 and RS-422 interface standards, similar to the RS-232, but allowing higher transmission rates.

RSA cipher system The Rivest, Shamir and Adleman public key cipher system.

RS-flip-flop (reset-set flip-flop) An electronic bistable device whose output can be changed according to the Reset and Set inputs. See also **flip-flop.**

RTE see **real time execution**

RTL see **resistor-transistor logic**

RTS see **request to send signal**

rubber banding see **elastic banding**

rule A description of the required outcome to a certain input, used within an expert system to produce an 'intelligent' output to information that is input. In a **rule-based system** artifical Intelligence software applies the rules and knowledge defined by experts in a particular field to a user's data in order to solve a problem.

run The execution by a computer of a set of instructions or programs or procedures. A program run involves executing (in correct order) the instructions in a program.

run around To fit text around an image on a printed page. This is a feature of the more powerful DTP systems available.

runaway The uncontrolled operation of a device or computer (due to a malfunction or error).

run in To operate a system at a lower capacity for a time in case of any faults.

run indicator An indicator bit or LED that shows that a computer is currently executing a program.

run-time or **run-duration** 1 The period of a time a program takes to run. **2** The time during which a computer is executing a program. **2** An operation carried out only when a program is running.

run-time error A fault that is only detected when a program is run or error made while a program is running. See also **execution error.**

run-time system Software that is required in main storage while a program is running (to execute instructions to peripherals, etc.)

R/W see **read/write**

R/W cycle (read/write cycle) The sequence of events that are involved during the process of retrieving or storing data.

R/W head (read/write head) An electromagnetic device that allows data to be read from or written to a storage medium.

RX see **receive, receiver**

S

S100 bus or **S-100 bus** An IEEE-696 standard bus, a popular 8 and 16 bit microcomputer bus using 100 lines and a 100-pin connector. See also **bus.**

SAFE (signature analysis using functional analysis) A signature validation technique, used to authenticate and identify a user by their signature.

safety net Software or hardware device that protects the system or files from excessive damage in the event of a system crash.

salami technique A computer fraud technique involving many separate small transactions that are difficult to detect and trace.

SAM (serial access memory) A storage device where a particular data item can only be accessed by reading through all the previous items in the list (as opposed to random access). Magnetic tape is a form of SAM; you have to go through the whole tape to access one item, while disks provide random access to stored data.

sample and hold circuit A circuit that freezes an analog input signal long enough for an A/D converter to produce a stable output. This is normally just a few thousandths of a second, but if the input signal were not frozen, the A/D convertor would produce a varying output.

sampling interval The time period between two consecutive samples.

sampling rate The number of measurements of a signal recorded every second. See also **analog/digital conversion, quantize.**

sampler 1 An electronic circuit that takes a number of samples of a signal and stores them for future analysis. **2** An electronic circuit used to record audio signals in digital form and store them to allow future playback. If the sampling is on a music signal and the sampling frequency is great enough, digitally stored signals sound like the original analog signal. For analog signals, a sampling rate of at least two times the greatest frequency is required to provide adequate detail.

sans serif A typeface whose letters have no serifs.

sapphire A blue-coloured precious stone used as a substrate for certain chips.

SAR (store address register) A register within the CPU that contains the address of the next location to be accessed.

satellite computer A smaller computer doing various tasks under the control of a main computer. A **satellite terminal** is a computer terminal that is outside the main network. In a network the floppy disk units are called "satellites" and the hard disk unit the "server". In a star network each satellite is linked individually to a central server.

save To store data or a program on an auxiliary storage device. Don't forget to save files before switching off.

save area An area of temporary storage within a computer's main memory, used for registers and control data.

SBC (single board computer) A computer whose main components such as processor, input/output and memory are all contained on one PCB.

scalar A variable that has a single value assigned to it. A scalar has a single magnitude value, a vector has two or more positional values.

scan 1 To examine an image or object or list of items to obtain data. **2** To convert an image or picture into a form that can be displayed on a computer. This is normally achieved by using a number of photelectric devices and converting their output using an A/D convertor. **3** One sweep of the picture beam horizontally across the front of the CRT screen.

scan area The section of an image that can be read by a scanner.

scan length The number of items in a file or list that are examined in a scan.

scanner A device that scans. This is either an **image scanner** (an input device that converts documents or drawings or photographs into digitized machine-readable form) or an **optical scanner** (a piece of equipment that converts an image into electrical signals which can be stored in and displayed on a computer).

scanner memory The area of memory that is allocated to store images which have been scanned.

scanning The action of examining and producing data from the shape of an object or drawing. **Automatic scanning** or **auto-baud sensing** uses a circuit that can automatically sense and select the correct baud rate for a line. A modem with auto-baud scanning can automatically sense which baud rate to operate on and switches automatically to that baud rate.

scanning device A device that allows micrographic images to be selected rapidly from a reel of film.

scanning error An error introduced while scanning an image.

scanning line The path traced out on a CRT screen by the picture beam as it moves across the screen.

scanning rate The time taken to scan across one line of a CRT image.

scanning resolution The ability of a scanner to distinguish between small points (A usual resolution is 300 dots per inch).

scanning software A dedicated program that controls a scanner and allows certain operations (rotate or edit or store, etc.) to be performed on a scanned image.

scatter graph Individual points or values plotted on a two axis graph. Compare this with the more usual line graph, in which lines are drawn between the individual points plotted.

scavenging Searching through and accessing database material without permission.

schedule The order in which tasks are to be done or order in which CPU time will be allocated to processes in a multi-user system.

scheduler A program which organizes use of a CPU or of peripherals which are shared by several users.

scheduling A method of working which allows several users to share the use of a CPU.

schema A graphical description of a process or database structure.

SCR see **sequence control register**

scramble To code speech or data which is transmitted in such a way that it cannot be understood unless it is decoded.

scrambler 1 A device that codes a data stream into a pseudorandom form before transmission to eliminate any series of one's or zero's or alternate one's and zero's that would cause synchronization problems at the receiver and produce unwanted harmonics. **2** A device that codes speech or other signals prior to transmission so that someone who is listening in without authorization cannot understand what is being transmitted (the scrambled signals are de-scrambled on reception to provide the original signals).

scratch file or **work file** A temporary work area which is only used for current work or calculations.

scratchpad A workspace or area of high speed memory that is used for temporary storage of data currently in use.

screen A display device capable of showing a quantity of information, such as a CRT or VDU. See also **readout.**

screen border The margin around text on a screen in which no text can displayed.

screen buffer A temporary storage area for characters or graphics before they are displayed.

screen dump Outputting the text or graphics displayed on a screen to a printer.

screen editor or **text editor** Software that allows the user to edit text on-screen, with one complete screen of information being displayed at a time.

screen grab Digitizing a single frame from a display or television.

screen memory (In a memory-mapped screen) the area of memory that represents the whole screen, usually with one byte representing one or a number of pixels.

scroll To move displayed text vertically up or down the screen, one line or pixel at a time. **Smooth scroll** is when the text is moved up a screen pixel by pixel rather than line by line, which gives a smoother movement.

scrub To wipe or delete or erase information off a disk or remove data from store.

SCSI see **small computer system interface**

SD see **single density (disk)**

SDI see **selective dissemination of information**

SDLC see **synchronous data link control**

SDR (store data register) A register in a CPU which holds data before it is processed or moved to memory location.

search The process of looking for and identifying a character or word or section of data in a document or file.

search key 1 A word or phrase that is to be found in a text. **2** A chosen field and other data used to select various records in a database.

search and replace A feature found on some word-processing programs that allows the user to find certain words or phrases, then replace them with another word or phrase.

searching storage A method of data retrieval that uses part of the data rather than an address to locate the data.

search memory A method of data retrieval that uses part of the data rather than an address to locate the data.

second generation computer A computer which used transistors instead of valves.

second-level addressing An instruction that contains the address at which the operand is stored.

secondary channel A second channel that carries control information which is transmitted at the same time as data.

secondary storage Any data storage medium (such as magnetic tape or floppy disk) that is not the main, high-speed computer storage (RAM). This type of storage is usually of a higher capacity, lower cost and slower access time than main memory.

section A part of a main program that can be executed in its own right, without the rest of the main program being required.

sector 1 The smallest area on a magnetic disk that can be addressed by a computer. 2 To divide a disk into a series of sectors. The disk is divided into many tracks, each of which is then divided into a number of sectors which can hold a certain number of bits. A disk is said to be **soft-sectored** when sectors are described by an address and start code data written onto it when the disk is formatted. See also **FORMAT**

sector formatting Dividing a disk into a series of addressable sectors (a table of their addresses is also formed, allowing each sector to be accessed).

sectoring hole A hole in the edge of a disk to indicate where the first sector is located.

secured file A file that is protected against accidental writing or deletion or against unauthorized access.

secure system A computer system that cannot be accessed without the correct authorization code or password.

security backup A copy of a disk or tape or file kept in a safe place in case the working copy is lost or damaged.

security check The identification of authorized users (by a password) before granting access.

seek area A section of memory that is to be searched for a particular item of data or a word.

seek time The time taken by a read/write head to find the right track on a disk.

segment 1 A section of a main program that can be executed in its own right, without the rest of the main program being required. 2 To divide a long program into shorter sections which can then be called up when required. See also **overlay.**

select To find and retrieve specific information from a database.

selectable An option or device which can be selected. Many add-in boards allow their options to be selected using combinations of wire jumpers.

selectable attributes The functions or attributes of a device which can be chosen by the user.

selective dump A display or printout of a selected area of memory.

selective sort Sorting a section of data items into order.

self-checking code A character coding system that can detect an error or bad character but not correct it.

self-checking system A system that carries out diagnostic tests on itself, usually at switch on.

self-correcting codes A character coding system that can detect and correct an error or bad character.

self-diagnostic A computer that runs a series of diagnostic programs, usually when it is switched on, to ensure that it is all working correctly; often memory, peripherals and disk drives are tested.

self-documenting program A computer program that provides the user with operating instructions as it runs.

self-learning An expert system that adds each new piece of information or rule to its database, improving its knowledge, expertise and performance as it is used.

self-refreshing RAM A dynamic RAM chip that has built-in circuitry to generate refresh signals, allowing data to be retained when the power is off, using battery back-up.

self-relocating program A program that can be loaded into any part of memory, and will modify its addresses depending on the program origin address.

self-resetting or **self-restoring loop** A loop that returns any locations or registers accessed during its execution to the state they were in.

semantics (In computing) the meanings of words or symbols used in programs. A **semantic error** is an error due to use of an incorrect symbol within a program instruction.

semaphore The coordination of two jobs and appropriate handshaking to prevent lock-outs or other problems when both require a peripheral or function.

semicompiled An object code program converted from a source code program, but not containing the code for functions from libraries, etc., that were used in the source code.

semiconductor A material that has conductive properties between those of a conductor (such as a metal) and an insulator. Semiconductor material (such as silicon) is used as a base for manufacturing integrated circuits and other solid-state components, usually by depositing various types of doping substances on or into its surface.

semiconductor device An electronic component that is constructed on a small piece of semiconductor (the components on the device are constructed using patterns of insulator or conductor or semiconductor material whose properties have been changed by doping).

semiconductor memory An electronic component that is capable of storing logical states using capacitors (dynamic memory) or latches and bistables (static memory), constructed as a semiconductor device to store bits of data.

semiconductor or **solid-state laser** A piece of semiconductor bar that has a polished end, and a semi-silvered mirror, generating pulses of photons that reflect inside the bar until they have enough power to leave via the semi-silvered end.

semi-processed data Raw data which has had some processing carried out, such as sorting, recording, error detection, etc.

send-only device A device such as a terminal which cannot receive data, only transmit it.

sense To examine the state of a device or electronic component.

sense recovery time The time that a RAM takes to switch from read to write mode.

sense switch A switch on a computer front panel whose state can by examined by the computer.

sensor An electronic device that produces an output dependent upon the condition or physical state of a process. See also **transducer.**

sentinel 1 A marker or pointer to a special section of data. **2** A flag that reports the status of a register after a mathematical or logical operation.

separated graphics Displayed characters that do not take up the whole of a character matrix, resulting in spaces between them.

separator A symbol used to distinguish parts of an instruction line in a program, such as command and argument. This is often a comma or semicolon. See also **delimiter.**

septet A word made up of seven bits.

sequence A number of items or data arranged as a logical, ordered list.

sequence check A check carried out to ensure that sorted data is in the correct order.

sequence control register (SCR) or **sequence counter** or **sequence register** or **instruction address register** A CPU register that contains the address of the next instruction to be processed.

sequencer The section within a bit-slice microprocessor that contains the next microprogram address.

sequential access A method of retrieving data from a storage device by starting at the beginning of the medium (such as tape) and reading each record until the required data is found. A tape storage system uses sequential access, since the tape has to be played through until the section required is found. The access time of sequential access storage is dependent on the position in the file of the data, compared with random access that has the same access time for any piece of data in a list. Random access is available on disks.

sequential access storage A storage medium in which the data is accessed sequentially.

sequential batch processing Completing one job in a batch before the next can be started.

sequential computer A type of computer, for which each instruction must be completed before the next is started, and so cannot handle parallel processing.

sequential file or **serial file** A stored file whose records are accessed sequentially.

sequential logic A logical circuit whose output depends on the logic state of the previous inputs. Compare with **combinational circuit.**

sequential operation A central processor in which operations are executed one after the other.

sequential processing Data or instructions processed sequentially, in the same order as they are accessed. See also **indexed.**

sequential search A search method in which each item in a list (starting at the beginning) is checked until the required one is found.

serial Data or instructions ordered sequentially (one after the other) and not in parallel.

serial access A method of retrieving data from a storage device by starting at the beginning of the medium (such as tape) and reading each record until the required data is found. A tape storage system uses serial access, since the tape has to be played through until the section required is found. The access time of serial access storage is dependent on the position in the file of the data, compared with random access that has the same access time for any piece of data in a list. Random access is available on disks.

serial-access memory (SAM) A storage method in which a particular data item can only be accessed by reading all the previous items in the list (as opposed to random access).

serial computer A computer system that has a single ALU and carries out instructions one at a time. See also **sequential computer.**

serial data transmission The transmission of the separate bits that make up data words, one at a time down a single line.

serial input/output (SIO) see **serial transmission**

serial input/parallel output (SIPO) or **serial to parallel converter** A device that can accept serial data and convert it to and transmit parallel data.

serial input/serial output (SISO) see **serial transmission**

serial interface or **port** A circuit that converts parallel data in a computer to and from a serial form that allows serial data to be transmitted and received from other equipment (the most common form is the RS232C interface).

serial memory A memory device in which data is stored sequentially, only allowing sequential access.

serial printer A printer that prints characters one at a time. Compare with **page printer.**

serial processing Data or instructions that are processed sequentially, in the same order as they are retrieved.

serial to parallel converter An electronic device that converts data from a serial form to a parallel form.

serial transmission or **serial input/output** Data transmitted one bit at a time (this is the normal method of transmission over long distances, since although slower it uses fewer lines and so is cheaper than parallel transmission).

serif A small decorative line attached to parts of characters in certain typefaces. **Sans serif** typefaces, for example Helvetica, do not have serifs.

server A dedicated computer or peripheral that provides a function to a network. In a PC-based network, this is usually called a **file server** (a small microcomputer and large backing storage device that is used for the management and storage of users' files in a network). In a local area network, there is a **LAN server** (a dedicated computer and backing storage used by terminals and operators in a LAN). In a network the hard disk machine is called the 'server' and the floppy disk units the 'satellites'. In a star network each satellite is linked individually to a central server.

service bit A transmitted bit that is used for control purposes rather than data.

service contract An agreement that an engineer will service equipment if it goes wrong.

service program A useful program that is used for routine activities such as file searching, copying, sorting, debugging, etc.

session key A cipher key that is only valid (and so can only be used for) a particular session.

session layer The layer in the ISO/OSI standard model that makes the connection/disconnection between transmitter and receiver.

sexadecimal see **hexadecimal**

sextet A word that is made up of six bits.

shadow memory or **page** Duplicate memory locations accessed by a special code.

shadow page table A conversion table that lists real memory locations with their equivalent shadow memory locations. See also **virtual.**

shannon A measure of the information content of a transmission.

Shannon's Law A law defining the maximum information carrying capacity of a transmission line. Shannon's Law is defined as $B \lg(1 + S/N)$ where B is the Bandwidth, lg is logarithm to the base two and S/N is Signal to Noise ratio.

shared access A computer or peripheral used by more than one person or system. See also **time-sharing system, multi-user.**

shared bus One bus used (usually) for address and data transfer between the CPU and a peripheral.

shared file A stored file that can be accessed by more than one user or system.

shared logic system One computer and backing storage device used by a number of people in a network for an application.

shared memory An area of memory that can be accessed by more than one CPU.

shared resources system A system in which one peripheral or backing storage device or other resource is used by a number of users.

shareware Software that is available free for people to try, but if kept and used further, the user is expected to pay a fee to the writer (often confused with public domain software which is completely free).

sheet feed A paper feed system that puts single sheets of paper into a printer, one at a time. A **sheet feed attachment** is a separate device which can be attached to a printer to allow single sheets of paper to be fed in automatically.

shell sort An algorithm that is used for sorting data items, in which items can be moved more than one position per sort action.

shield 1 A metal screen connected to earth, that prevents harmful voltages or interference reaching sensitive electronic equipment. **2** To protect a signal or device from external interference or harmful voltages.

shielded cable A cable that is made up of a conductive core surrounded by an insulator, then a conductive layer to protect the transmitted signal against interference.

shift 1 To move a bit or word of data left or right by a certain amount (usually one bit). **2** To press a key on a keyboard to change from one character set to another, allowing other characters (such as capitals) to be used.

shift character A transmitted character code that indicates that the following code is to be shifted.

shift code A method of increasing total possible bit combinations by using a number of bits to indicate the following code is to be shifted (so that it represents another code).

shift instruction A computer command to shift the contents of a register to the left or right.

shift key A key on a keyboard that switches secondary functions for keys, such as another character set, by changing the output to upper case.

shift left The left arithmetic shift of data in a word (the number is doubled for each left shift). For example, 0110 left-shifted once is 1100.

shift register An area of temporary storage into which data can be shifted.

shift right The right arithmetic shift of data in a word (the number is halved for each right shift).

short haul modem A modem used to transmit data over short distances (often within a building), usually without using a carrier.

short-circuited Two points (in a circuit) that are electrically connected, usually accidentally.

shut down To switch off and stop the functions of a machine or system.

shut-off mechanism A device which stops a process in case of fault. Most hard disks have an automatic shut-off mechanism to pull the head back from the read position when the power is turned off.

shutter A device on a camera which opens and shuts rapidly allowing light from an object to fall on the film.

sign The polarity of a number or signal (whether it is positive or negative).

signal 1 A (generated) analog or digital waveform used to carry information. **2** A short message used to carry control codes.

signal conditioning Converting or translating a signal into a form that is accepted by a device.

signal distance The number of bit positions with different contents in two data words. See also **HAMMING**

signal element The smallest basic unit used when transmitting digital data.

sign and magnitude or **signed magnitude** A number representation in which the most significant bit indicates the sign of the number, the rest of the bits its value.

sign and modulus A way of representing numbers, where a single bit shows if the number is positive or negative (usually 0 = positive, 1 = negative).

signature A special authentication code, such as a password, which a user gives prior to access to a system or prior to the execution of a task; it is used to prove identity.

sign bit or **sign indicator** A single bit that indicates if a binary number is positive or negative (usually 0 = positive, 1 = negative).

sign digit One digit that indicates if a number is positive or negative.

signed field A storage field which can contain a number and a sign bit.

sign off To logoff a system.

sign on To logon to a system.

sign position A digit or bit position that contains the sign bit or digit.

silicon An element with semiconductor properties, used in crystal form as a base for integrated circuit manufacture. Silicon is used in the electronics industry as a base material for integrated circuits. It is grown as a long crystal which is then sliced into wafers before being etched or treated, producing several hundred chips per wafer. Other materials, such as germanium or gallium arsenide, are also used as a base for ICs.

silicon chip A small piece of silicon in and on the surface of which a complete circuit or logic function has been produced (by depositing other substances or by doping).

silicon disk or **RAM disk** A section of RAM that is made to look and behave like a high speed disk drive.

silicon gate A type of MOS transistor gate that uses doped silicon regions instead of a metal oxide to provide the function. See also **MOS, gate.**

silicon on sapphire (SOS) A manufacturing technique that allows MOS devices to be constructed onto a sapphire substrate for high speed operation.

Silicon Glen An area of Scotland where many Scottish information technology companies are based.

silicon transistor A microelectronic transistor manufactured on a silicon semiconductor base.

Silicon Valley An area of California where many US semiconductor device manufacturers are based (also used to refer to the Thames Valley).

silicon wafer A thin slice of a pure silicon crystal, usually around 4 inches in diameter on which integrated circuits are produced (these are then cut out of the wafer to produce individual chips).

SIMD see **single instruction stream multiple data stream**

simplex Data transmission in only one direction at a time. The opposite is **duplex.**

simulate To copy the behaviour of an event, a system or a device with another.

simulator A device that simulates another system. These are normally financial forecasting tools, or games (for instance a flight simulator program on a PC — which allows a user to pilot a simulated plane, showing a realistic control panel and moving scenes, either as training programme or computer game).

simulation An operation in which a computer is made to imitate a real life situation or a machine, and shows how something works or will work in the future.

simultaneity In which the CPU and the I/O sections of a computer can handle different data or tasks at the same time.

simultaneous processing Two or more processes executed at the same time.

simultaneous transmission The transmission of data or control codes in two directions at the same time. Same as **duplex.**

single address code or **instruction** A machine code instruction that contains one operator and one address.

single address message A message with just one single destination.

single board computer (SBC) A micro or mini computer whose components are all contained on a single printed circuit board.

single function software An applications program that can only be used for one kind of task. Some applications programs are 'integrated'; that is they can perform a number of tasks such as wordprocessor, speadsheet and database.

single instruction stream multiple data stream (SIMD) The architecture of a parallel computer that has a number of ALUs and data buses with one control unit.

single instruction stream single data stream (SISD) The architecture of a serial computer, that has one ALU and data bus, with one control unit.

single key response A program that requires the user to hit only one key (Return does not have to pressed) to select an option.

single length precision A number stored within one word. Compare with **double length, multiple length.**

single length working Using numbers that are stored within a single word.

single line display A small screen which displays a single line of characters at a time.

single operand instruction see **single address instruction**

single operation A communications system that allows data to travel in only one direction at a time (controlled by codes S/O = send only, R/O = receive only, S/R = send or receive) See also **simplex.**

single pass operation Software that produces the required result or carries out a task after one run.

single pole A switch that connects two points.

single sheet feed A device attached to a printer that allows single sheets of paper to be used instead of continuous stationery.

single-sided disk A floppy disk that can only be used to store data on one side, because of the way it is manufactured or formatted.

single step To execute a program one instruction at a time. This is usually carried out when trying to debug a program: the programmer uses a debugging program that will display the results of a program as it is executed one instruction at a time, allowing him to see when and where errors occur.

single-user system A computer system which can only be used by a single user at a time (as opposed to a multi-user system).

sink 1 The receiving end of a communications line. **2** A **heat sink** is a metal device used to conduct heat away from an electronic component to prevent damage.

SIO see **serial input/output**

SIPO see **serial input/parallel output**

SISD see **single instruction stream single data stream**

SISO see **serial input/serial output**

sixteen-bit (A microcomputer system or CPU) that handles data in sixteen bit words, providing much faster operation than older eight bit systems.

skeletal code A program which is not complete, with the basic structure coded.

skip To ignore an instruction in a sequence of instructions. **High-speed skip** is the rapid vertical movement of paper through a printer, ignoring the normal line advance.

skip capability A feature of certain word-processors that allows the user to jump backwards or forwards by a quantity of text in a document.

skip instruction A null computer command which directs the CPU to the next instruction.

slashed zero A printed or written sign (0) to distinguish a zero from the letter O.

slave A remote secondary computer or terminal whose tasks are assigned and controlled by a central computer.

slave cache or **store** A section of high-speed memory which stores data that the CPU can access quickly.

slave processor A dedicated processor that is controlled by a master processor.

slave terminal A terminal controlled by a main computer or terminal.

sleep A system that is waiting for a signal (log-on) before doing anything. See also **wake-up.**

slot or **expansion slot** An expansion connector available on a computer's backplane or motherboard, into which an expansion board can be plugged.

SLSI see **super large scale integration**

small scale integration (SSI) An integrated circuit with 1 to 10 components.

smart card A plastic card with a memory and microprocessor embedded in it, so that it can be used for direct money transfer or for identification of the user.

smart terminal or **intelligent terminal** A computer terminal that is able to process information. The opposite is a **dumb terminal.**

smog or **electronic smog** Excessive stray electromagnetic fields and static electricity generated by large numbers of electronic equipment (this can damage equipment and a person's health).

SNA see **systems network architecture**

snapshot 1 To record all the states of a computer at a particular instant, useful at a later time to recover from a system crash. **2** Storing in main memory the contents of a screen full of information at an instant.

snapshot dump A printout of all the registers and a section of memory at a particular instant, used when debugging a program.

SNOBOL (string orientated symbolic language) A high-level programming language that uses string processing methods.

soak To run a program or device continuously for a period of time to make sure it functions correctly.

soft data Data that is not permanently stored in hardware (it usually refers to data stored on magnetic medium).

soft copy Text displayed or listed on screen (as opposed to hard copy on paper).

soft error A random error caused by software or data errors (this type of error is very difficult to trace and identify since it only appears under certain conditions). Compare with **hard error.**

soft-fail A system that is still partly operational even after a part of the system has failed.

soft hyphen A hyphen which is inserted when a word is split at the end of a line on screen, but is not present when the word is written normally.

soft keys Keys, whose function or the character which they print when pressed can be changed by the user or by means of a program.

soft keyboard A keyboard on which the functions of the keys can be changed by programs.

soft-reset An instruction that terminates any program execution and returns the user to the monitor program or BIOS. Compare with **hard reset.**

soft-sectored disk A disk in which the sectors are described by an address and start code data written onto it when the disk is formatted.

soft zone An area of text to the left of the right margin in a wordprocessed document, where, if a word does not fit completely, a hyphen is automatically inserted.

software Any program or group of programs which instructs the hardware on how it should perform, including operating systems, word processors and applications programs.

software compatible A computer that will load and run programs written for another computer.

software development The various stages and processes required to produce working programs from an initial idea.

software documentation Information, notes and diagrams that describe the function, use and operation of a piece of software.

software engineer A person who can write working software to fit an application.

software engineering A field of study covering all software-related subjects.

software house A company which develops and sells computer programs.

software interrupt A high priority interrupt signal generated by a program, requesting a chance to use the central processor.

software library A number of specially written routines, stored in a library file which can be inserted (by a programmer) into a program, saving time and effort.

software licence An agreement between a user and a software house, giving details of the rights of the user to use or copy the software.

software life cycle A period of time when a piece of software exists, from its initial design to the moment when it becomes out of date.

software maintenance Carrying out updates and modifications to a software package to make sure the program is up to date.

software manual see **software documentation**

software package A complete set of programs (and the manual) that allow a certain task to be performed.

software quality assurance (SQA) Making sure that software will perform as intended.

software reliability The ability of a piece of software to perform the task required correctly.

software specification Detailed information about a piece of software's abilities, functions and methods.

software system All the programs required for one or more tasks.

software tool A program used in the development of other programs. This could be a special editor, debugger or compiler.

solderless Not using solder to make an electrical connection; (a board, such as a breadboard) which does not need solder to connect the components.

solid error An error that is always present when certain equipment is used.

solid font printer A printer which uses a whole character shape to print in one movement, such as a daisy wheel printer.

solid-state device An electronic device that operates by using the effects of electrical or magnetic signals in a solid semiconductor material. A **solid-state memory device** is a solid-state device which acts as memory (usually in the form of RAM or ROM chips).

son file The latest working version of a file. Compare with **father file, grandfather file.**

sort To put data into order, according to a system, on the instructions of the user (for example, sorting addresses into alphabetical order or orders according to account numbers). A **shell sort** is an algorithm for sorting data items, in which items can be moved more than position per sort action. A **sort/merge** program allows new files to be sorted and then merged in correct order into existing files.

sortkey or **sort field** A field in a stored file that is used to sort the file. For example, the orders were sorted according to dates by assigning the date field as the sortkey.

SOS see **silicon on sapphire**

source code An original program code written by a programmer which cannot be directly executed by a computer, but has to be translated into an object code program by a compiler or interpreter.

source deck or **pack** A set of punched cards that contain the source code for a program.

source file A program written in source language, which is then converted to machine code by a compiler.

source language Any programming language in which a program is originally written before it is compiled or translated.

source listing 1 A listing of a text in its original form. **2** A listing of a source program.

source program A program, prior to translation, written in a programming language by a programmer.

SP see **stack pointer**

space bar A long bar at the bottom of a keyboard, which inserts a space into the text when pressed.

space character A character code that prints a space. The ASCII code is 32.

span The set of allowed values between a maximum and minimum.

spark printer A thermal printer which produces characters on thermal paper by electric sparks.

sparse array A data matrix structure containing mainly zero or null entries.

spec see **specification**

special character A character which is not a normal one in a certain font (such as a certain accent or symbol).

specification Detailed information about what is to be supplied or about a job to be done.

specific address A storage address that directly, without any modification, accesses a location or device.

specific code A binary code which directly operates the central processing unit, using only absolute addresses and values.

specific coding Program code that has been written so that it only uses absolute addresses and values.

specificity The ratio of non-relevant entries not retrieved to the total number of non-relevant entries contained in a file, database or library.

speech chip An integrated circuit that generates sounds (usually phonemes) which when played together make a sound like human speech.

speech recognition Analysing spoken words in such a way that a computer can recognize spoken words and commands.

speech synthesis The production of spoken words by a speech synthesizer.

speech synthesizer A device which takes data from a computer and outputs it as spoken words. This is done in one of two ways; either by using a digital to analog converter to produce speech from previously captured and converted speech, or by using a dedicated speech chip.

speed of loop A method of benchmarking a computer by measuring the number of loops executed in a certain time.

spellcheck A feature of some word-processors that allows the spelling of a text to be corrected by comparing it with a dictionary held in the computer.

spike A very short duration voltage pulse. Electronic components are very vulnerable to voltage spikes, and are often damaged by them.

spillage A situation when too much data is being processed and cannot be contained in a buffer, so it overflows and is lost.

split screen A program that allows more than one text file to appear on the screen at the same time (such as the text being worked on and another text from memory for comparison).

spool A reel on to which a tape or printer ribbon is wound.

spooler or **spooling device** A device which holds a tape and which receives information from a disk for storage.

spooling Transferring data to a disk from which it can be printed at the normal speed of the printer, leaving the computer available to do something else.

spreadsheet A program which allows numbers and formulae to be entered into interlinked cells, so that if one number changes, the effects on all the formulae can be seen at once can be seen. Spreadsheets are used for detailed tabulations, allowing various mathemtatical operations such as additions or percentages to be performed automatically.

sprite An object which moves round the screen in computer graphics.

sprocket or **sprocket wheel** A wheel with teeth round it which fit into holes along the edge of continuous stationery or punched tape. This works a **sprocket feed,** where the printer pulls the paper by turning sprocket wheels which fit into a series of holes (**sprocket holes**) along each edge of the sheet. See also **tractor feed.**

spur A connection point into a network.

SPX see **simplex**

SS see **single-sided**

SSD see **single-sided disk**

SSI see **small scale integration**

stable state The state of a system when no external signals are applied.

stack A temporary storage (within a central processing unit) for data, registers or tasks where items are added and retrieved from the same end of the list. See also **LIFO.**

stack job processor Storing a number of jobs to be processed in a stack and automatically executing the next one after the current one has been completed.

stack pointer (SP) An address register containing the location of the most recently stored item of data or the location of the next item of data to be retrieved.

stand-alone system A system that can operate independently of a master or central processor.

stand-alone terminal A computer terminal with a processor and memory which can be directly connected to a modem, without being a member of a network or cluster.

standard document or **standard form** or **standard paragraph** or **standard text** A printed document or form or paragraph which is used many times (with different names and addresses often inserted, as in a form letter).

standard function A feature which is included as normal in a computer system.

standard interface An interface between two or more systems that conforms to pre-defined standards.

standard letter A letter which is sent without any change to the main text, but is personalised by inserting the name and address of each of the different people to whom it is sent.

standard subroutine A routine which carries out an often used function, such as keyboard input or screen display.

standards converter A device to convert received signals conforming to one standard into a different standard.

standby equipment Secondary system (identical to the main system), to be used if the main system breaks down.

star network A network of several machines where each terminal or floppy disk unit or satellite is linked individually to a central hard disk machine or server. Compare **bus network, ring network.**

star program A perfect program that runs first time with no errors or bugs.

start bit or **element** A bit transmitted in asynchronous communications to indicate the start of a character.

start of header A transmitted code indicating the start of header (address or destination) information for a message which follows it.

start of text (SOT or **STX)** A transmitted code indicating the end of control or address information and the start of the message.

statement 1 An expression used to convey an instruction or define a process. **2** An instruction in a source language which is translated into several machine code instructions.

state-of-the-art Feature of very modern technology or something which is technically as advanced as possible.

static 1 Data which does not change with time. **2** A system that is not dynamic.

static dump A printout of the state of a system when it has finished a process.

static memory Non-volatile memory that does not require refreshing.

static RAM RAM which retains data for as long as the power supply is on, and where the data does not have to be refreshed. Static RAM uses bistable devices such as flip-flops to store data; these take up more space on a chip than the capacititive storage method of dynamic RAM but do not require refreshing. Compare with **dynamic ram.**

static subroutine A subroutine that uses no variables apart from the operand addresses.

station A point in a network or communications system that contains devices to control the input and output of messages, allowing it to be used as a sink or source. A **secondary station** is a station that is receiving data.

status bit A single bit in a word used to provide information about the state or result of an operation.

status line A line at the top or bottom of a screen which gives information about the task currently being worked on (number of lines, number of columns, filename, time, etc.).

status poll A signal from a computer requesting information on the current status of a terminal.

status register A register containing information on the status of a peripheral device.

steady state A circuit or device or program state in which no action is occurring but which can accept an input.

stochastic model A mathematical representation of a system that includes the effects of random actions.

stop and wait protocol A communications protocol in which the transmitter waits for a signal from the receiver that the message was correctly received before transmitting further data.

stop bit or **stop element** A transmitted bit used in asynchronous communications to indicate the end of a character.

stop code An instruction that temporarily stops a process to allow the user to enter data.

stop instruction A computer programming instruction that stops a program being executed.

stop list A list of words that are not to be used or are not significant for a file or library search.

stop time The time taken for a spinning disk to come to a stop after it is no longer powered.

storage A memory device or part of the computer system in which data or programs are kept for further use. This can be split into various groups: **auxiliary storage** (any data storage medium, such as magnetic tape or disk, that is not the main, high speed memory); **dynamic storage** or **memory** (memory that requires its contents to be updated regularly); **external storage** (a storage device which is located outside the main computer system but which can be accessed by the CPU); **intermediate storage** (temporary area of memory for items that are currently being processed); **mass storage system** (data storage that can hold more than one million million bits of data); **primary storage** (small fast-access internal memory of a system which contains the program currently being executed, or main internal memory of a system); **secondary storage** (any data storage medium, such as magnetic tape* floppy disk, that is not the main, high-speed computer storage).

storage allocation The way in which memory is allocated for different uses, such as programs, variables, data, etc.

storage capacity The amount of space available for the storage of data.

storage density A number of bits that can be recorded per unit area of storage medium.

storage device Any electronic or magnetic device that can store data and then allow it to be retrieved when required.

storage media The various materials which are able to store data.

storage tube A special CRT used for computer graphics that retains an image on screen without the need for refresh actions.

store 1 A memory device or part of the computer system in which data or programs are kept for further use. **2** To save data, which can then be used again as necessary.

store address register (SAR) A register in a CPU that contains the address of the next location to be accessed.

store data register (SDR) A register in a CPU which holds data before it is proceesed or moved to a memory location.

stored program A computer program that is stored in memory. If it is stored in dynamic RAM it will be lost when the machine is switched off, but if stored on disk or tape (i.e., in backing store) it will be permanently retained.

straight-line coding A program written to avoid the use of loops and branches, providing a faster execution time.

streamer or **tape streamer** or **streaming tape drive** A device containing a continuous loop of tape, used as backing storage.

string Any series of consecutive alphanumeric characters or words that are manipulated and treated as a single unit by the computer.

string area A section of memory in which strings of alphanumeric characters are stored.

string concatenation Linking a series of strings together.

string length The number of characters contained in a string.

string name An identification label assigned to a string. This is a feature of only certain programming languages.

string orientated symbolic language (SNOBOL) A high-level programming language that uses string processing methods.

string variable A variable used in a computer language that can contain alphanumeric characters as well as numbers.

structured programming The well-ordered and logical technique of assembling programs.

stylus A pen-like device that is used in computer graphics systems to dictate the cursor position on the screen.

stylus printer see **dot matrix printer**

subaddress A peripheral identification code, used to access one peripheral (this is then followed by address data to access a location within the peripheral's memory).

subdirectory A directory of disk or tape contents contained within another or the main directory.

subprogram 1 A subroutine within a program. 2 A program called up by a main program.

subroutine A section of a program which performs a required function and that can be called upon at any time from inside the main program. Subroutines are either closed or open: a **closed** or **linked subroutine** is made up of a number of computer instructions in a program that can be called at any time, with control being returned on completion to the next instruction after the call; an **open subroutine** consists of code for a subroutine which is copied into the relevant part of the program whenever the compiler finds a call instruction. A **static subroutine** uses no variables apart from the operand addresses.

subroutine call A programming instruction that directs control to a subroutine. When a subroutine is called (by a call instruction) it returns to the main program with a return instruction.

subscript A small character which is printed below the line of other characters. See also **superscript.**

subset A small set of data items which forms part of another larger set.

substitute character A character that is displayed if a received character is not recognized.

substitution error An error made by an optical character recognition system which mistakes one character or letter for another.

substitution table A list of characters or codes that are to be inserted in the place of selected received codes.

substrate The base material on which an integrated circuit is constructed. See also **integrated circuit.**

subsystem One small part of a large system.

subtrahend (In a subtraction operation) the number to be subtracted from the minuend.

suffix notation Mathematical operations written in a logical way, so that the symbol appears after the numbers to be acted upon. See also **postfix notation.**

suite of programs A group of programs which run one after the other, used for a particular task.

summation check An error detection check performed by adding together the characters received and comparing with the required total.

supercomputer A very powerful mainframe computer used for high speed mathematical tasks.

super large scale integration (SLSI) An integrated circuit with more than 100,000 components.

supervisor The section of a computer operating system that regulates the use of peripherals and the operations undertaken by the CPU.

supervisory program or **executive program** The master program in a computer system that controls the execution of other programs.

supervisory signal 1 A signal that indicates if a circuit is busy. 2 A signal that provides an indication of the state of a device.

support chip A dedicated IC that works with a CPU, and carries out an additional function or a standard function very rapidly, so speeding up the processing time.

surge A sudden increase in electrical power in a system, due to a fault or noise or component failure. Power surges can burn out circuits before the user has time to disconnect the system; a /Z/ surge protector fitted between the computer and the electric socket will help prevent damage as it will cut off the power supply to sensitive equipment if it detects a possible dangerous power surge.

swap To stop using one program, put it into store temporarily, then run another program, and when that is finished, return to the first one.

swim Computer graphics that move slightly due to a faulty display unit.

switch 1 The point in a computer program where control can be passed to one of a number of choices. 2 A mechanical or solid state device that can electrically connect or isolate two or more lines.

symbol table or **library** A list of labels or names in a compiler or assembler, which relate to their addresses in the machine code program.

symbolic address An address represented by a symbol or name.

symbolic code or **instruction** An instruction that is in mnemonic form rather than a binary number.

symbolic debugging A debugger that allows symbolic representation of variables or locations.

symbolic language 1 Any computer language where locations are represented by names. 2 Any language used to write source code.

symbolic name The name used as a label for a variable or location.

symbolic programming Writing a program in a source language.

symmetric difference A logical function whose output is true if either of two inputs is true, and false if both inputs are the same.

sync see **synchronization**

sync bit A bit transmitted to enable devices to synchronize themselves correctly.

sync pulses Pulses transmitted to make sure that the receiver is synchronized with the transmitter.

synchronization The action of synchronizing two or more devices.

synchronize To make sure that two or more devices or processes are coordinated in time or action.

synchronous Two or more devices or processes which run in sync with something else (such as a main clock).

synchronous computer A computer in which each action can only take place when a timing pulse arrives.

synchronous data link control (SDLC) The protocol and rules used to define the way in which synchronous data is transmitted or received.

synchronous data network A communications network in which all the actions throughout the network are controlled by a single timing signal.

synchronous detection A method of obtaining the signal from an amplitude modulation carrier.

synchronous idle character A character transmitted by a DTE to ensure correct synchronization when no other character is being transmitted.

synchronous network A network in which all the links are synchronized with a single timing signal.

synchronous system A system in which all devices are synchronized to a main clock signal.

synchronous transmission The transmission of data from one device to another, where both devices are controlled by the same clock, and the transmitted data is synchronized with the clock signal.

syntactic error A programming error caused by a program statement which does not correctly follow the syntax of the language.

syntax The grammatical rules that apply to a programming language.

syntax analysis A stage during compilation where statements are checked to see if they obey the rules of syntax.

synthesizer A device which generates something (signals or sound or speech). A **speech synthesizer** generates sounds which are similar to the human voice.

synthetic address A location used by a program that has been produced by instructions within the program.

synthetic language A programming language in which the source program is written.

sysgen see **system generation**

system Any group of hardware or software or peripherals, etc., which work together. A **computer system** is the central processor with storage and associated peripherals making up a working computer. A **secure system** is one which cannot be accessed without correct authorization.

system check Running diagnostic routines on a system to ensure that there are no problems or faults.

system control panel The main computer system control switches and status indicators.

system crash A situation in which the operating system stops working and has to be restarted.

system design Identifying and investigating possible solutions to a problem, and constructing the most appropriate system to solve it.

system diagnostics The tests, features and messages that help find hardware or software faults.

system disk A disk which holds the system software.

system firmware The basic operating system functions and routines in a ROM device.

system flowchart A diagram that shows each step of the computer procedures needed in a system.

system generation or **sysgen** The process of producing an optimum operating system for a particular task.

system library Stored files that hold the various parts of a computer's operating system.

system log A record of computer processor operations. This can help identify the cause and help in the recovery of a system crash.

systems analysis 1 Analysing a process or system to see if it could be more efficiently carried out by a computer. **2** Examining an existing system with the aim of improving or replacing it. The person who undertakes systems analysis is a **systems analyst.**

system security Measures, such as password, priority protection, authorization codes, etc., designed to stop browsing and hackers.

systems program or **systems software** Programs which control the way in which a computer system works. They are written by **systems programmers.**

T

tab To tabulate or to arrange text in columns with the cursor automatically running from one column to the next in keyboarding. The movement of the cursor in a word-processing program from one tab stop to the next is called **tabbing.**

tab memory The ability of a editing program (usually a word-processor) to store details about various tab settings.

tab rack or **ruler line** A graduated scale, displayed on the screen, showing the position of tabulation columns.

tab stops Preset points along a line, where the printing head or cursor will stop for each tabulation command.

table lookup Using one known value to select one entry in a table, providing a secondary value.

tabulate To arrange text in columns, with the cursor moving to each new column automatically as the text is keyboarded.

tabulation 1 Arranging a table of figures. 2 Moving a printing head or cursor a preset distance along a line.

tabulation markers Symbols displayed to indicate the position of tabulation stops.

tabulation stops see **tab stops**

tabulator A part of a typewriter or word-processor which automatically sets words or figures into columns.

tactile keyboard A keyboard that provides some indication that a key has been pressed, such as a beep.

tag 1 One section of a computer instruction. 2 An identifying character attached to a file or item (of data).

tail 1 Data recognized as the end of a list of data. 2 A control code used to signal the end of a message.

take-up reel The reel onto which magnetic tape is collected.

tape (mag tape or **magnetic tape)** A narrow length of thin plastic coated with a magnetic material used to store signals magnetically. Magnetic tape is available on spools of between 200 and 800 metres. For use in cassette players or tape drives, it is also available in **tape cartridges** or **cassettes** which are small boxes containing a reel of magnetic tape and a pick up reel. Tape is magnetized by the read/write head. It is a storage medium which only allows serial access, that is, all the tape has to be read until the required location is found (as opposed to disk storage, which can be accessed randomly).

tape back-up To use magnetic tape as a medium for storing back-ups from faster main or secondary storage (such as RAM or hard disk).

tape cartridge A cassette box containing magnetic tape on a reel.

tape drive A mechanism which controls magnetic tape movement over the tape heads.

tape head A transducer that can read and write signals onto the surface of magnetic tape.

tape header Identification information at the beginning of a tape.

tape streamer A continuous loop of magnetic tape used for backing storage.

tape to card converter A device that reads data from magnetic tape and stores it on punched cards.

tape trailer Identification information at the beginning of a magnetic or paper tape.

tape transport The method by which the tape in a magnetic tape recorder is moved smoothly from reel to reel over the magnetic heads.

target computer The computer on which software is to be run (but not necessarily written on, e.g. using a cross-assembler).

target language The language into which a program will be translated from its source language.

target program An object program or computer program in object code form, produced by a compiler.

task management System software that controls the use and allocation of resources to programs.

task queue A temporary storage of jobs waiting to be processed.

TDS (transaction-driven system) A computer system that will normally run batch processing tasks until interrupted by a new transaction, at which point it allocates resources to the new transaction.

telebanking A system by which an account holder can carry out transactions with his bank via a terminal and communications network.

telematics The interaction of all data processing and communications devices (computers, networks, etc.)

telemetry Sending data from remote measuring devices over a telecommunications link.

telephone as a data carrier Using a modem to send binary data as sound signals over a telephone line.

teleprinter A device that is capable of sending and receiving data from a distant point by means of a telegraphic circuit, and printing out the message on a printer.

teleprinter interface A terminal interface or hardware and software combination required to control the functions of a terminal.

teleprinter roll The roll of paper onto which messages are printed.

teleprocessing (TP) Processing of data at a distance (as on a central computer from outside terminals).

teleshopping The use of a telephone-based data service such as viewdata to o order products from a shop.

telesoftware (TSW) Software which is received from a viewdata or teletext service.

teletext A method of transmitting text and information with a normal television signal, usually as a serial bit stream that can be displayed using a special decoder.

teletypewriter A keyboard and printer attached to a computer system which can input data either direct or by making punched paper tape which is then used to drive the printer.

template (In text processing) a section of standard text (such as a standard letter or invoice) into which specific details (company address or prices or quantities) can be added. See also **standard letter, form letter.**

template command A command that allows functions or other commands to be easily set. For example, a template paragraph command enables the user to specify the number of spaces by which each paragraph should be indented.

temporary register A register (within a CPU) which is used for temporary storage of the results of an ALU operation.

ten's complement The result formed by adding one to the nine's complement of a decimal number.

terminal 1 A device, usually made up of a display unit and a keyboard, which allows entry and display of information when on-line to a central computer system. Basically, there are two types of terminal: the dumb and the intelligent. A **dumb terminal** has no processing facilities. An **intelligent terminal** or **smart terminal** contains a CPU and memory, allowing basic data processing to be carried out, usually with the facility to allow the user to program it independently of the host computer. **2** An electrical connection point. **3** A point in a network where a message can be transmitted or received.

terminal area The part of a printer circuit board at which an electrical connection can be made normally using edge connectors.

terminal character set The range of characters available for a particular type of terminal, these might include graphics or specially customized characters.

terminal controller A hardware device or integrated circuit that controls a terminal including data communications and display.

terminal identity A unique code transmitted by a viewdata terminal to provide identification and authorization of a user.

terminal interface The hardware and software combination required to control the functions of a terminal from a computer.

terminal junky (TJ) Slang term for a person (a hacker) who is obsessed with computers.

terminal keyboard A standard QWERTY or special keyboard allowing input at a terminal.

terminator or **rogue value** An item in a list of data, which indicates the end of a list.

ternary A number system with three possible states.

test 1 An action carried out on a device or program to establish whether it is working correctly, and if not, which component or instruction is not working. **2** To carry out an examination of a device or program to see if it is working correctly.

test bed A software environment used to test programs.

test data Prepared data and operations with known results used to allow a new program to be tested.

test equipment Special equipment which tests hardware or software.

test run A program run with test data to ensure that the software is working correctly.

text Alphanumeric characters that convey information.

text compression The reducing the space required by a section of text, by using one code to represent more than one character, by removing spaces and punctuation marks, etc.

text-editing facilities (In a word-processing system) functions that allow the user to add, delete, move, insert and correct sections of text. The software that provides the user with text-editing facilities is called a **text editor**.

text file A stored file (usually on magnetic disk or tape) on a computer that contains text rather than digits or data.

text formatter A program that arranges a text file according to preset rules, such as line width and page size.

text manipulation Facilities within a program allowing text to be edited, changed, inserted and deleted.

text processing Word-processing or using a computer to keyboard, edit and output text, in the forms of letters, labels, etc.

text retrieval An information retrieval system that allows the user to examine complete documents rather than just a reference to one.

text screen An area of computer screen that has been set up to display text.

text-to-speech converter An electronic device that uses a speech synthesizer to produce the spoken equivalent of a piece of text that has been entered.

thermal paper Special paper whose coating turns black when heated, allowing characters to be printed by using a matrix of small heating elements.

thermal printer A type of printer where the character is formed on thermal paper with a printhead containing a matrix of small heating elements. This type of printer is very quiet in operation since the printing head does not strike the paper.

thimble printer A computer printer using a printing head similar to a daisy wheel but shaped like a thimble.

thin film memory High-speed access RAM device using a matrix of magnetic cells and a matrix of read/write heads to access them.

thin window A single line display window on a screen.

third generation computers The first computers to be contructed using integrated circuits instead of transistors.

third party A company which supplies items or services for a system sold by one party (the seller) to another (the buyer). A third party might supply computer maintenance or customized programs, etc.

thirty-two bit system A microcomputer system or CPU that is capable of processing data in thirty-two bit words.

thrashing A computer program design fault that results in the CPU wasting time moving pages of data between main memory and backing store.

thread A program that consists of many independent smaller sections or beads. A **threaded file** is one in which an entry will contain data and an address to the next entry that has the same data content. This allows rapid retrieval of all identical records. **Threaded language** is a programming language that allows many small sections of code to be written and then used by a main program. A **threaded tree** is a structure in which each node contains a pointer to other nodes.

three-address instruction An instruction which contains the addresses of two operands and the location where the result is to be stored.

three-dimensional or **3D** An image which has three dimensions (width, breadth and depth), and therefore gives the impression of being solid.

three state logic A logic gate or integrated circuit that has three possible output states rather than the usual two: logic high, logic low and high impedance.

throughput The rate of production by a machine or system, measured as total useful information processed in a set period of time.

tilt and swivel (monitor stand) A monitor which is mounted on a pivot so that it can be moved to point in the most convenient direction for the operator.

time Period expressed in hours, minutes, seconds, etc. Examples are: **addition time** — the time an adder takes to carry out an addition operation; **cycle time** — the time between start and stop of an operation, especially between addressing a memory location and receiving the data; **real time** — actions or processing time that is of the same order of magnitude as the problem to be solved (i.e. the processing time is within the same time as the problem to be solved, so that the result can influence the source of the data); **response time** — firstly, time which passes between the user starting an action (by pressing a key) and the result appearing on the screen, and secondly, the speed with which a system responds to a stimulus.

time division multiple access A time division multiplexing system that allocates time slots to various users according to demand.

time division multiplexing (TDM) A multiplexing system that allows a number of signals to be transmitted down a single line by sending a sample of the first signal for a short period, then the second, and so on.

timeout 1 An automatic logoff procedure carried out if no data is entered on an on-line terminal. **2** The period of time reserved for an operation.

timer A device which records the time taken for an operation to be completed.

time-sharing A computer system that allows several independent users to use it or be on-line at the same time. In a time-sharing system, each user appears to be using the computer all the time, when in fact each is using the CPU for a short time slice only; the CPU processes one user for a short time and then moves on to the next.

time slice The amount of time allowed for a single task in a time-sharing system or in multiprogramming; the period of time allocated for a user or program or job within a multitasking system.

time slot A period of time that contains an amount of data about one signal in a time division multiplexing system.

timing loop A computer program loop that is repeated a number of times to produce a certain time delay.

timing master A clock signal that synchronizes all the components in a system.

title An identification name given to a file or program or disk.

toggle To switch between two states.

token An internal name or code which replaces a reserved word or program statement in a high-level language.

token ring network A network in which a device can transmit data by taking one free token which circulates and inserting the message after it. A **control token** is the special sequence of bits transmitted over a LAN to provide control actions.

toner (Powdered or liquid) ink used in a laser printer. It is contained in a sealed container, the **toner cartridge,** which can be easily replaced in a laser printer, or alternatively the toner can be added by hand.

toolkit A series of functions which help a programmer write or debug programs.

tools A set of utility programs (backup, format, etc.) in a computer system.

top down programming or **structured programming** A method of writing programs where a complete system is divided into simple blocks or tasks, each block unit is written and tested before proceeding with the next one.

top-of-stack The newest data item added to a stack.

topology The way in which the various elements in a network are interconnected. **Network topology** normally describes the layout of machines in a network (such as a star network or a ring network or a bus network) which will determine what cabling and interfaces are needed and what possibilities the network can offer.

touch screen A computer display that has a grid of infrared transmitters and receivers positioned on either side of the screen. These are used to control the cursor position (when a user wants to make a selection or move the cursor, he points to the screen, breaking two of the beams, which gives the position of his finger).

TP see **teleprocessing, transaction processing**

TPI see **tracks per inch**

trace A method of verifying that a program is functioning correctly, in which the current status and contents of the registers and variables used are displayed after each instruction step.

trace program A diagnostic program that executes a program that is being debugged, one instruction at a time, displaying the states and registers.

track One of a series of thin concentric rings on a magnetic disk or thin lines on a tape, which the read/write head accesses and along which the data is stored in separate sectors. The first track on a tape is along the edge and the tape may have up to nine different tracks on it, while a disk has many concentric tracks around the central hub; the track and sector addresses are set up during formatting. The number of concentric data tracks on a disk surface per inch is measured as **tracks per inch (TPI)**.

trackball A device used to move a cursor on-screen, which is controlled by turning a ball contained in a case.

tractor feed A method of feeding paper into a printer, where sprocket wheels on the printer connect with the sprocket holes on either edge of the paper to pull the paper through.

traffic A term covering all the messages and other signals processed by a system.

traffic analysis The study of the times, types and quantities of messages and signals being processed by a system.

traffic density The number of messages and data transmitted over a network or system in a period of time.

traffic intensity The ratio of messages entering a queue against those leaving the queue within a certain time.

trailer The final byte of a file containing control or file characteristics.

trailer record The last record in a file containing control or file characteristics.

transaction One single action which affects a database (a sale, a change of address, a new customer, etc.).

transaction-driven system (TDS) A computer system that will normally run batch processing tasks until interrupted by a new transaction, at which point it allocates resources to the transaction.

transaction file or **change file** or **detail file** or **movement file** A file containing recent changes or transactions to records which is then used to update a master file.

transaction processing (TP) An interactive processing system in which a user enters commands and data on a terminal which is linked to a central computer, with the results being displayed on-screen.

transaction record or **change record** A record containing new data which is to be used to update a master record.

transceiver A transmitter and receiver or device which can both transmit and receive signals (such as a terminal or modem).

transcribe To copy data from one backing storage unit or medium to another. The action of transcribing data is **transcription.**

transducer An electronic device which converts signals in one form into signals in another. A **pressure transducer** converts physical pressure signals into electrical signals.

transfer To change command or control. **Conditional transfer** is the programming instruction that provides a jump to a section of a program if a certain condition is met. **Radial transfer** is the transfer of data between two peripherals or programs that are on different layers of a structured system (such as an OSI/ISO system)

transfer check A check that a data transfer is correct according to a set of rules

transfer command An instruction that directs processor control from one part of a program to another. See also **jump, call.**

transfer control When a branch or jump instruction within a program is executed, control is transferred to another point in the program.

transfer rate The speed at which data is transferred from backing store to main memory.

transfer time The time taken to transfer data between devices or locations.

transformational rules A set of rules that are applied to data that is to be transformed into coded form.

transformer A device which changes the voltage or current amplitude of an AC signal. A transformer consists of two electrically insulated coils of wire; the AC signal in one induces a similar signal in the other which can be a different amplitude according to the ratio of the turns in the coils of wire.

transient A state or signal which is present for a short period of time. A **line transient** or **voltage transient** is a spike of voltage that is caused by a time delay in two devices switching or noise on the line. A **power transient** is any very short duration voltage pulse or spike.

transient area A section of memory for user programs and data.

transient error A temporary error which occurs for a short period of time.

transient suppressor A device which suppresses voltage transients.

transistor An electronic semiconductor device which can control the current flow in a circuit. There are two main types of transistors: bipolar and unipolar: a **bipolar (junction) transistor (BJT)** is constructed of three layers of alternating types of doped semiconductor (p-n-p or n-p-n); each layer has a terminal labelled emitter, base and collector; usually the base controls the current flow between emitter and collector. A **bipolar** or **field effect transistor (FET)** is a device that can act as a variable current flow control (an external signal varies the resistance of the device and current flow by changing the width of a conducting channel by means of a field). It has three terminals: source, gate and drain.

transistor-resistor logic (TRL) Early logic gate design method using bipolar transistors and resistors.

transistor-transistor logic (TTL) The most common family of logic gates and high-speed transistor circuit design, in which the bipolar transistors are directly connected (usually collector to base) to provide the logic function

transition point The point in a program or system where a transition occurs.

translate To convert data from one form into another.

translation tables or **conversion tables** Lookup tables or collection of stored results that can be accessed very rapidly by a process without the need to calculate each result when needed.

translator (program) A program that translates a high level language program into another language (usually machine code). See also **interpreter, compiler.**

transmit To send information from one device to another, using any medium, such as radio, cable, wire link, etc.

transmission The action of sending signals from one device to another. This can be **neutral transmission** in which a voltage pulse and zero volts represent the binary digits 1 and 0, or **parallel transmission** in which a number of data lines carry all the bits of a data word simultaneously, or **serial transmission** where data is transmitted one bit at a time (this is the normal method of transmission over longer distances, since although slower, it uses fewer lines and so is cheaper than parallel). There is also **synchronous transmission** which is the transmission of data from one device to another, where both devices are controlled by the same clock, and the transmitted data is synchronized with the clock signal.

transmission channel A physical connection between two points that allows data to be transmitted (such as a link between a CPU and a peripheral).

transmission errors Errors due to noise on the line.

transmission media Any means by which data can be transmitted, such as radio, light, etc.

transmission rate The measure of the amount of data transmitted in a certain time.

transmission window A narrow range of wavelengths to which a fibre optic cable is most transparent.

transmissive disk An optical data storage disk in which the reading laser beam shines through the disk to a detector below. Compare with **reflective disk.**

transmitter (TX) A device that will take an input signal, process it (modulate it or convert it to sound, etc.) then transmit it by some medium (radio, light, etc.).

transparent device A device or network that allows signals to pass through it without being altered in any way.

transparent interrupts A mode in which, if an interrupt occurs, all program and machine states are saved, the interrupt is serviced and then the system is restored to its previous states.

transparent paging Software that allows the user to access any memory location in a paged memory system as if it were not paged.

transparent program A computer program which is not obvious to the user or which cannot be seen by the user when it is running.

transphasor An optical transistor, constructed from a crystal, which is able to switch a main beam of light according to a smaller input signal. This is used in the latest research for an optical computer which could run at very high speeds, i.e., at the speed of light.

transponder Communications device that receives and retransmits signals.

transport layer The layer in the ISO/OSI standard that checks and controls the quality of the connection. See also **layer.**

transportable computer A computer which can be carried, but is not as small as a portable or a laptop.

transputer A single large very powerful chip containing a 32-bit microprocessor running at around 10 MIPS, that can be connected together to form a parallel processing system (running OCCAM).

transverse mode noise Interference which is apparent between power supply lines.

transverse scan A method of reading data from a video tape in which the playback head is at right angles to the tape.

trap A device, software or hardware that will catch something, such as a variable, fault or value. A **trace trap** is a breakpoint where a tracing program stops, allowing registers to be examined.

trapdoor A way of getting into a system to change data or browse or hack.

tree (structure) Data structure system where each item of data is linked to several others by branches (as opposed to a line system where each item leads on to the next). If each item of data or node has only two branches, the tree is a **binary tree.**

tree and branch network system A system of networking where data is transmitted along a single output line, from which other lines branch out, forming a tree structure that feeds individual stations.

tree selection sort A rapid form of selection where the information from the first sort pass is used in the second pass to speed up selection.

tremendously high frequency (THF) A radio frequency between 300GHz and 3000GHz.

triad 1 Three elements or characters or bits. **2** A triangular shaped grouping of the red, green and blue colour phosphor spots at each pixel location on the screen of a colour RGB monitor.

tributary station Any station on a multilink network other than the main control station.

TRL see **transistor-resistor logic**

Trojan Horse A program inserted into a system by a hacker that will perform a harmless function while copying information in a classified file into a file with a low priority, which the hacker can then access without the authorized user knowing.

TRUE The logical condition representing binary one. Compare **false.**

truncate To give an approximate value to a number by reducing it to a certain number of digits, so 3.5678 can be truncated to 3.56. This process is called **truncation.**

truncation error An error caused when a number is truncated.

trunk A bus or communication link consisting of wires or leads, which connect different parts of a hardware system.

truth table A method of defining a logic function as the output state for all possible inputs.

truth value Two values (true or false, T or F, 1 or 0) used in Boolean algebra.

TSW see **telesoftware**

TTL (transistor-transistor logic) The most common family of logic gates and high-speed transistor circuit design in which the bipolar transistors are directly connected (usually collector to base). MOS or other electronic circuits or components that can directly connect to and drive TTL circuits are **TTL compatible.**

TTL logic The use of TTL design and components to implement logic circuits and gates.

Turing machine A mathematical model of a device that could read and write data to a controllable tape storage while altering its internal states.

Turing test Test to decide if a computer is "intelligent".

turnaround document A document which is printed out from a computer, sent to a user and returned by the user with new notes or information written on it, which can be read by a document reader.

turnaround time (TAT) 1 The length of time it takes to switch data flow direction in a half duplex system. **2** The time taken for a product to be constructed and delivered **e3 an order has been received.** (In American English) the time taken to activate a program and produce the result which the user has asked for.

turnkey system A complete system which is designed to a customer's needs and is ready to use (to operate it, the user only has to switch it on or turn a key).

turtle A device whose movement and position are controllable, which is used to draw graphics (with instructions in the computer language LOGO). The device either works on a flat surface **(floor turtle)** or draws on a VDU screen **(screen turtle)**; both are used as teaching aids.

turtle graphics graphic images created using a turtle and a series of commands.

twisted pair cable Cheap cable for telephones, with two wires twisted round each other to provide some protection against interference and minimize inductive and capacitative effects of the wires. Compare **coaxial cable.**

two-address instruction An instruction format containing the location of two operands, the result being stored in one of the operand locations.

two-dimensional array An array which locates items both vertically and horizontally.

two input adder see **half adder**

two-level subroutine A subroutine containing another subroutine.

two-part stationery Paper for computers or typewriters with a top sheet for the original and a second sheet for a copy.

two-pass assembler An assembler that converts an assembly language program into machine code in two passes — the first pass stores symbolic addresses, the second converts them to absolute addresses.

two-plus-one instruction An instruction containing the locations of two operands and an address for the result.

two's complement A complement formed by adding one to the one's complement of a binary number, often used to represent negative binary numbers.

TX see **transmitter**

type The definition of the processes or sorts of data which a variable in a computer can contain (this can be numbers, text only, etc.). **Variable data type** is a variable that can contain any sort of data, such as numerical, text, etc. A **string type** can contain alphanumeric characters only.

typographer A person who designs a typeface or text to be printed.

U

UART (universal asynchronous receiver/transmitter) A chip which converts asynchronous serial bit streams to a parallel form or parallel data to a serial bit stream. A **UART controller** uses a UART to convert serial data from a terminal into a parallel form, and then transmits it over a network. See also **USART.**

UBC see **universal block channel**

UHF see **ultra high frequency**

ULA (uncommitted logic array) A chip containing a number of unconnected logic circuits and gates which can then be connected by a customer to provide a required function.

ultra high frequency (UHF) Very high frequency range between 300MHz and 3GHz.

ultrafiche A microfiche with images that have been reduced by more than ninety times.

ultrasonic Sound pressure waves at a frequency above the audio band, above 20KHz.

ultrasound Sound emitted at a frequency above the audio band.

ultraviolet (UV) light Electromagnetic radiation with a wavelength just greater than the visible spectrum, from 200 to 4000 angstroms.

ultraviolet erasable PROM EPROM whose contents are erased by exposing to UV light.

umlaut A printed accent consisting of two dots over a German a, o or u.

unallowable digit An illegal combination of bits in a word, according to predefined rules.

unauthorized access Access to data which has not been authorized.

unary operation A computing operation on only one operand, such as the logical NOT operation.

unattended operation A system that can operate without the need for a person to supervise it.

unbundled software Software which is not included in the price of the equipment.

unclocked circuit An electronic circuit or flip-flop that changes state as soon as an input changes, not with a clock signal.

uncommitted logic array (ULA) A chip containing a number of unconnected logic circuits and gates which can then be connected by a customer to provide a required function.

uncommitted storage list A table of the areas of memory in a system that are free or have not been allocated.

unconditional branch or **jump** or **transfer** An instruction which transfers control from one point in the program to another, without depending on any condition being met. The opposite is **conditional jump.**

underflow The result of a numerical operation that is too small to be represented with the given accuracy of a computer.

underlining A word-processing command which underlines text. The line drawn or printed under a piece of text is an **underline** or **underscore.**

unformatted Disk which has not been formatted. It is impossible to copy to an unformatted disk.

union A logical function that produces a true output if any input is true.

unipolar 1 A transistor that can act as a variable current flow control (an external signal varies the resistance of the device). See also **FET**, **transistor. 2** A transmission system in which a positive voltage pulse and zero volts represents the binary bits 1 and 0. A **unipolar signal** uses only positive voltage levels. Compare with **polar.**

uninterruptable power supply (UPS) A power supply that can continue to provide a regulated supply to equipment even after a mains power failure (using a battery).

unit A single machine (possibly with many different parts). A **desk top unit** is a computer or machine that will fit onto a desk. The **central processing unit (CPU)** is a group of circuits which perform the basic functions of a computer, made up of three main parts: the **control unit** that selects and executes instructions, the **arithmetic and logic unit (ALU)** that performs all the mathematical and logical functions, and the **input/output unit** which is a peripheral (such as a terminal in a workstation) which can be used both for inputting and outputting data to a processor.

unit buffer A buffer that is one character long, usually used to mean that there are no buffering facilities.

universal asynchronous receiver/transmitter (UART) A chip which converts an asynchronous serial bit stream to a parallel form or parallel data to a serial bit stream.

universal block channel (UBC) A communications channel allowing high speed transfer of blocks of data to and from high speed peripherals.

universal device see **UART, USRT, USART**

universal product code (UPC) A standard printed bar coding system used to identify products in a shop (using a bar code reader or at a EPOS). See also **EAN.**

universal programming Writing a program that is not specific to one machine, so that it can run on several machines.

universal set A complete set of elements that conform to a set of rules. The universal set of prime numbers less than ten and greater than two is 3,5, and 7.

universal synchronous asynchronous receiver-transmitter (USART) A chip that can be instructed by a CPU to communicate with asynchronous or synchronous bit streams or data lines.

universal synchronous receiver/transmitter (USRT) A single integrated circuit that can carry out all the serial to parallel and interfacing operations required between a computer and transmission line.

Unix A popular operating system for small micros and large mainframes.

unjustified text Text which has not been justified.

unjustified tape or **idiot tape** Tape containing unformatted text, which cannot be printed until formatting data (such as justification, line width and page size) has been added by a computer.

unmodified instruction A program instruction which is directly processed without modification to obtain the operation to be performed.

unmodulated signal A signal which has not been modulated. See also **base band.**

unpack To remove packed data from storage and expand it to its former state.

unprotected data Data that can be modified and is not protected by a security measure. The section of a computer display that a user can modify is an **unprotected field.**

unrecoverable error A computer hardware or software error that causes a program to crash.

unsigned A number system that does not represent negative numbers.

up (of a computer or program) working or running. **Uptime** is the time during which a device is operational and error free.

up and down propagation time The total length of time that a transmission takes to travel from earth to a satellite and back to an earth station.

UPC see **universal product code**

update 1 A master file which has been made up-to-date by adding new material. An **update file** or **transaction file** is a file containing recent changes or transactions to records which is used to update the master file. **2** Printed information which is an up-to-date revision of earlier information. **3** A new version of a system which is sent to users of the existing system.

up/down counter An electronic counter that can increment or decrement a counter with each input pulse.

upgrade To make (a system) more powerful or more up-to-date by adding new equipment.

upload To transfer data files or programs from a small computer to a main CPU. The opposite is **download.**

UPS (uninterruptable power supply) A power supply that can continue to provide a regulated supply to equipment even after a mains power failure (using a battery).

upper case Capital letters and other symbols on a typewriter or keyboard, which are accessed by pressing the shift key.

uptime The time when a computer is functioning correctly (as opposed to downtime).

upwards compatible or **upward compatible** Hardware or software designed to be compatible either with earlier models or with future models which have not yet been invented.

USART (universal synchronous asynchronous receiver-transmitter) A chip that can be instructed by a CPU to communicate with asynchronous or synchronous bit streams or parallel data lines.

USASCII (USA standard code for information interchange) See **ASCII.**

user A person who uses a computer or machine or software, especially, a keyboard operator.

user area The part of the memory which is available for the user, and does not contain the operating system.

user-definable A feature or section of a program that a user can customize as required.

user-defined characters Characters which are created by the user and added to the standard character set.

user documentation Documentation provided with a program which helps the user run it.

user-friendly A language or system or program that is easy to use and interact with.

user group A club of users of a particular system or computer.

user guide The manual describing how to use a software package or system.

user ID A unique identification code that allows a computer to recognize a user.

user interface Hardware or software designed to make it easier for a user to communicate with the machine.

user-operated language A high-level programming language that allows certain problems or procedures to be easily expressed.

user port A socket which allows peripherals to be connected to a computer.

user's program Computer software written by a user rather than a manufacturer.

USRT see **universal synchronous receiver/transmitter**

utility (program) A useful program that is concerned with such routine activities as file searching, copying files, file directories, sorting and debugging and various mathematical functions.

UV light see **ultraviolet light**

V

V see **voltage**

vacuum tube An electronic current flow control device consisting of a heated cathode and an anode in a sealed glass tube with a vacuum inside it, used in the first generation of computers, now replaced by solid state current control devices such as the transistor.

V & V see **verification and validation**

valid memory address A signal on control bus indicating that an address is available on the address bus.

validate To check that an input or data is correct according to a set of rules.

validity The correctness of an instruction or password.

validity check A check that data or results are realistic.

value see **absolute value, initial value**

value added network (VAN) A network where the transmission lines are leased from a public utility such as the telephone service, but where the user can add on private equipment.

value added reseller (VAR) A retailer who sells equipment and systems which are specially tailored to certain types of operation.

valve An electronic current flow control device consisting of a heated cathode and an anode in a sealed glass vacuum tube, used in the first generation of computers, now replaced by solid state current control devices such as transistors.

VAN see **value added network**

vapourware Products which exist in name only.

VAR see **value added reseller**

variable A computer program identifier for a register or storage location which can contain any number or characters and which may vary during the program run. There are two sorts: **global variable** which is a number that can be accessed by any routine or structure in a program and **local variable,** a number which can only be accessed by certain routines in a certain section of a computer program.

variable data Data which can be modified, and is not write-protected.

variable length record A record which can be of any length.

variable word length computer A computer in which the number of bits which make up a word is variable, and varies according to the type of data.

VCR see **video cassette recorder**

VDT or **VDU** (**visual display terminal, visual display unit**) A terminal with a screen and a keyboard, on which text or graphics can be viewed and information entered.

vector 1 An address which directs a computer to a new memory location. **2** A coordinate that consists of a magnitude and direction.

vector graphics or **vector image** or **vector scan** A drawing system on computers that uses line length and direction from an origin to plot lines.

vector processor A coprocessor that operates on one row or column of an array at a time.

vectored interrupt An interrupt signal which directs the processor to a routine at a particular address.

Veitch diagram The graphical representation of a truth table.

Venn diagram The graphical representation of the relationships between the states in a system or circuit.

verification Checking that data has been keyboarded correctly or that data transferred from one medium to another has been transferred correctly. In **keystroke verification** the check is made on each key pressed to make sure it is valid for a particular application.

verification and validation (V & V) Testing a system to check that it is functioning correctly and that it is suitable for the tasks intended.

verifier A special device for verifying input data.

vertical blanking interval see **raster**

vertical format unit (VFU) The part of the control system of a printer which governs the vertical format of the document to be printed (such as vertical spacing and page length).

vertical justification The adjustment of the spacing between lines of text to fit a section of text into a page.

vertical parity check An error detection test in which the bits of a word are added and compared with a correct total.

vertical redundancy check (VRC) An odd parity check on each character of a block received, to detect any errors.

vertical scrolling Displaying text that moves up or down the computer screen one line at a time.

vertical tab The number of lines that should be skipped before printing starts again.

vertically polarized signal A signal whose waveforms are all aligned in one vertical plane.

very high frequency (VHF) The range of radio frequencies between 30-300 MHz.

very large scale integration (VLSI) An integrated circuit with 10,000 to 100,000 components.

very low frequency (VLF) The range of radio frequencies between 3-30 KHz.

vestigial sideband A single sideband transmission with a small part of the other sideband kept to provide synchronization data, often used in TV transmissions.

vf band see **voice frequency band**

V format Data organization, in which variable length records are stored with a header which contains their length.

VFU see **vertical format unit**

VHD (very high density) A video disk able to store very large quantities of data.

VHF (very high frequency) A radio frequency between 30MHz and 300MHZ (used for broadcasting radio and TV programmes).

video bandwidth The frequency range required to carry TV images.

video camera A camera with optical lenses in front of an electronic device that can convert images into electronic signals in a form that can be displayed on a TV.

video cassette A cassette with video tape in it (either blank for recording, or with a prerecorded film).

video cassette recorder (VCR) A device attached to a TV set, which can be programmed to record TV programmes on videotape and play them back at another time.

video compressor A device that reduces the bandwidth of a TV signal allowing it to be transmitted over a (telephone), using a video expander at the receiving end.

videodisk A read-only optical disk able to store TV pictures and sound in binary form, also capable of storing large amounts of computer data.

video display A device which can display text or graphical information, such as a CRT.

video expander A device that stores one frame of a video image as it is slowly received over a voice grade communications link, with a video compressor used at the transmitting end.

video game A game played on a computer, with action shown on a video display.

video interface chip A chip that controls a video display allowing information stored in a computer (text, graphics) to be displayed.

video memory or **video RAM (VRAM)** High speed random access memory used to store computer-generated or digitized images.

video monitor A device able to display signals from a computer.

video port A connection on a video recorder allowing the data read from the tape to be used in other ways, such as being stored in a computer.

video scanner A device which allows images of objects or pictures to be entered into a computer; new video scanners are designed to scan three-dimensional objects.

video standards Protocols defining video signal formats (there are three main international video standards: NTSC, PAL and SECAM).

video terminal A keyboard with a monitor.

videotext or **videotex** A system for transmitting text and displaying it on a screen, covering information transmitted either by TV signals (teletext) * by signals sent down telephone lines (viewdata).

viewdata An interactive system for transmitting text or graphics from a database to a user's terminal by telephone lines, providing facilities for information retrieval, transactions, education, games and recreation. The user calls up the page of information required, using the telephone and a modem, as opposed to teletext, where the pages of information are repeated one after the other automatically.

virgin tape Tape that has not been recorded on before.

virtual A feature or device which does not actually exist but which is simulated by a computer and can be used by a user as if it did exist.

virtual address An address referring to virtual storage.

virtual circuit A link established between a source and sink in a packet-switching network for the duration of the call.

virtual disk A section of RAM used with a short controlling program as if it were a fast disk storage system.

virtual machine A simulated machine and its operations.

virtual memory or **virtual storage (VS)** Large imaginary main memory made available by loading smaller pages from a backing store into the available main memory only as and when they are required.

virtual terminal Ideal terminal specifications used as a model by a real terminal.

virus A short hidden routine that corrupts all data and files, and which spreads from computer to computer when disks are exchanged.

visual display terminal (VDT) or **visual display unit (VDU)** A terminal with a screen and a keyboard, on which text or graphics can be viewed and information entered.

visual programming A method of programming a computer by showing it or taking it through the processes of what it has to do rather than writing a series of instructions.

visuals Graphics or photographs or illustrations, used as part of a printed output.

VLF (very low frequency) Radio frequencies between 30Hz and 30KHz.

VLSI (very large scale integration) A system with between 10,000 and 100,000 components on a single IC.

voice answer back A computerized response service using a synthesized voice to answer enquiries.

voice band The minimum bandwidth required for recognizable transmission of speech (usually 300 - 3400Hz).

voice data entry or **input** The input of information into a computer using a speech recognition system and the user's voice.

voice grade channel A communications channel (bandwidth usually equal to voice band), which is able to carry speech and some data (such as facsimile).

voice output The production of sounds which sound like human speech, made as a result of voice synthesis.

voice print The identification of a person by registering tones and signals in that person's speech.

voice recognition The ability of a computer to recognize certain words in a human voice and provide a suitable response.

voice response see **voice output**

voice synthesis The reproduction of sounds similar to those of the human voice.

voice synthesizer A device which generates sounds which are similar to the human voice.

voice unit A unit of signal measurement equal to a one millivolt signal across a 600 ohm resistance.

volatile memory or **volatile store** or **volatile dynamic storage** Memory or storage medium which loses data stored in it when the power supply is switched off. The opposite is **non-volatile memory.**

volatility The number of records that are added or deleted from a computer system compared to the total number in store.

volt The SI unit of electrical potential, defined as voltage across a one ohm resistance when one amp is flowing.

voltage dip or **dip in voltage** Sudden fall in voltage which may last only a very short while, but which can affect the operation of a computer system. Another problem may be a **voltage transient** where a spike of voltage is caused by a time delay in two devices switching or by noise on the line. Electricity supply can have peaks and troughs of current, depending on the users in the area. Fluctuations in voltage can affect computers. These problems can be overcome by the use of a **voltage regulator** which provides a steady output voltage even if the input supply varies.

VRAM (video random access memory) High speed random access memory used to store computer-generated or digitized images.

VRC (vertical redundancy check) An odd parity check on each character of a block received, to detect any errors.

VS see **virtual storage**

V series CCITT (UK-European) standards for data transmission using a modem. The following are to be noted: **V.21** = 300 baud transmit and receive, full duplex; **V.22** = 1200 baud transmit and receive, half duplex; **V.22 BIS** = 1200 baud transmit and receive full duplex; **V.23** = 75 baud transmit, 1200 baud receive, half duplex.

VTR see **video tape recorder**

VU see **voice unit**

W

wafer A thin round slice of a large single crystal of silicon onto which hundreds of individual integrated circuits are constructed, before being cut into individual chips.

wafer scale integration One large chip, the size of a wafer, made up of smaller integrated circuits connected together (these are still in the research stage).

wait condition or **state** The state where a processor is not active, but waiting for input from peripherals.

wait loop A processor that repeats one loop of program until some action occurs.

wait time The time delay between the moment when an instruction is given and the execution of the instruction or return of a result (such as the delay between a request for data and the data being transferred from memory).

waiting list see **queue**

waiting state The state of a computer, in which a program requires an input * signal before continuing execution.

wake up a system The code entered at a remote terminal to indicate to the central computer that someone is trying to log-on at that location.

walk through To examine each step of a piece of software.

WAN see **wide area network**

wand A bar code reader or optical device which is held in the hand to read bar codes on products in a shop or warehouse.

warm standby A secondary backup device that can be switched into action a short time after the main system fails. Compare with **cold standby, hot standby.**

warm start The restarting of a programme which has stopped, but without losing any data. Compare **cold start.**

warm up To allow a machine to stand idle for a time after switching on, to reach optimum operating conditions.

wash PROM To erase the data from a PROM.

waste instruction An instruction that does not carry out any action (except increasing the program counter to the location of next instruction).

waveform digitization conversion and storing a waveform in numerical form using an A/D converter.

weighted average An average calculated taking several factors into account, giving some more value than others.

weighted bit A bit having a different value depending on its position in a word. Thegsorting of users, programs or data by their importance or priority.

well-behaved program A program that does not make any non-standard system calls, using only the standard BIOS input/output calls rather than directly addressing peripherals or memory. If it is well-behaved, software should work on all machines using the same operating system.

wetware The human brain or intelligence which writes software to be used with hardware.

What-You-See-Is-All-You-Get (WYSIAYG) A program where the output on screen cannot be printed out in any other form (that is, it cannot contain hidden print or formatting commands).

What-You-See-Is-What-You-Get (WYSIWYG) A program where the output on the screen is exactly the same as the output on printout, including graphics and special fonts.

while-loop A conditional program instruction that carries out a loop while a condition is true.

white writer A laser printer which directs its laser beam on the points that are not printed. With a white writer, the black areas are printed evenly but edges and borders are not so sharp. The opposite is **black writer.**

wide area network (WAN) A network where the various terminals are far apart and linked by radio, satellite and cable. WANs use modems, radio and other long distance transmission methods; LANs use cables or optical fibre links. See also **LAN.**

widow The first line of a paragraph which is printed by itself at the bottom of a column. Compare **orphan.**

wild card A symbol that represents all files or names used when searching for data. It can be an asterisk or a question mark.

WIMP (Window, Icon, Mouse, Pointer) A description of an integrated software system that is entirely operated using windows, icons and a mouse controlled pointer. See also **environment.**

Winchester disk or **drive** A compact high-capacity hard disk which is usually built into a computer system and cannot be removed. A **removable Winchester** is in a sealed unit, which can be detached from a computer when full or when not required.

window 1 A reserved section of screen used to display special information, that can be selected and looked at at any time and which overwrites information already on the screen. An **active window** is the area of the display screen where the operator is currently working; a **command window** is the area of the screen that always displays the range of commands available, often as a single line at the bottom of the screen; an **edit window** is the area of the screen in which the user can display and edit text or graphics; a **text window** in a graphics system, is the small space where the text is held before being allocated to a final area. **2** part of a document which is currently displayed on a screen. **3** An area of memory or access to a storage device. **4** To set up a section of screen by defining the coordinates of its corners, allowing information to be temporarily displayed, overwriting previous information but without altering information in the workspace.

window, icon, mouse, pointer (WIMP) A description of an integrated software system that is entirely operated using windows, icons and a mouse controlled pointer.

windowing 1 The action of setting up a window to show information on the screen. **2** Displaying or accessing information via a window

wipe To clean data from a disk.

wired or **hardwired program computer** A computer with a program built into the hardware which cannot be changed. See also **hardwired program.**

wire printer see **dot-matrix printer**

wire wrap A simple method of connecting component terminals together using thin insulated wire wrapped around each terminal which is then soldered into place, usually used for prototype systems.

WISC (writable instruction set computer) A CPU design that allows a programmer to add extra machine code instructions using microcode, to customize the instruction set.

word 1 A separate item of language, which is used with others to form speech or writing which can be understood. **2** A separate item of data on a computer, formed of a group of bits, stored in a single location in a memory.

word break The division of a word at the end of a line, where part of the word is left on one line with a hyphen, and the rest of the word is taken over to begin the next line.

word count The number of words in a file or text.

word length The length of a computer word, counted as the number of bits.

word mark A symbol indicating the start of a word in a variable word length machine.

word-processing (WP) Using a computer to keyboard, edit, and output text, in the form of letters, labels, address lists, etc.

word-processor 1 A small computer or typewriter with a computer in it, used for word-processing text and documents. **2** A word-processing package or program for a computer which allows the editing and manipulation and output of text, such as letters, labels, address lists, etc.

word serial Data words transmitted along a parallel bus one after the other.

words per minute (wpm or **WPM)** A method of measuring the speed of a printer.

word time The time taken to transfer a word from one memory area or device to another.

word wrap or **wraparound** A system in word processing where the operator does not have to indicate the line endings, but can keyboard continuously, leaving the program to insert word breaks and to continue the text on the next line.

work area The memory space which is being used by an operator.

work disk The disk on which current work is stored.

work file or **scratch file** A temporary work area which is being used for current work.

working store or **scratch pad** An area of high-speed memory used for temporary storage of data in current use.

workspace Space in memory, which is available for use or is being used currently by an operator.

workstation A place where a computer user works, with a terminal, printer, modem, etc.

WORM see **Write Once Read Many times memory**

WP see **word-processing**

WPM or **wpm** see **words per minute**

wraparound or **word wrap** A system in word-processing where the operator does not have to indicate the line endings, but can keyboard continuously, leaving the program to insert word breaks and to continue the text on the next line. In **horizontal wraparound** the cursor moves automatically from the end of one line to the beginning of the next.

writable instruction set computer (WISC) A CPU design that allows a programmer to add extra machine code instructions using microcode, to customize the instruction set.

write head A transducer that can write data onto a magnetic medium.

write once, read many times memory (WORM) An optical disk storage system that allows one writing action but many reading actions in its life.

write-permit ring A ring on a reel of magnetic tape which allows the tape to be overwritten or erased.

write protect To make it impossible to write to a floppy disk or tape by moving a special write-protect tab.

write-protect tab The tab on a floppy disk which if moved, prevents any writing to or erasing from the disk.

writer see **black writer, white writer**

write time The time between requesting data transfer to a storage location and it being written.

writing pad A special device which allows a computer to read in handwritten characters which have been written onto a special pad. See also **OCR**.

WYSIAYG see **what you see is all you get**

WYSIWYG see **what you see is what you get**

X

X see **extension**

X-axis The horizontal axis of a graph.

X-coordinate The horizontal axis position coordinate.

X direction Horizontal movement.

X distance The distance along an X-axis from an origin.

x punch A card punch for column 11, often used to represent a negative number.

X-series Recommendations for data communications over public data networks. X25 is a standard for long-distance dialling and WAN services.

X-Y The coordinates for drawing a graph, where X is the horizontal and Y the vertical value. A device for drawing lines on paper between given coordinates is an **X-Y plotter.**

Y

Y-axis The vertical axis of a graph.

Y-coordinate The vertical axis position coordinate.

Y-direction Vertical movement.

Y-distance The distance along an Y-axis from an origin.

y punch A card punch for column 12 (often used to indicate a positive number).

Z

Z see **impedance**

zap To wipe off all data currently in the workspace; normally pressing CONTROL Z will zap all the text.

Z-axis The axis for depth in a three-dimensional graph or plot.

zero 1 the digit 0; the equivalent of logical off or false state. A **jump on zero** is a conditional jump executed if a flag or register is zero. **2** To erase or clear a file. If the operator **zeros a device,** the contents of the device are erased.

zero compression or **zero suppression** The shortening of a file by the removal of unnecessary zeros.

zero fill To fill a section of memory with zero values.

zero flag An indicator that the contents of a register or result is zero.

zero-level address or **immediate address** An instruction in which the address is the operand.

zero insertion force (ZIF) Chip socket that has movable connection terminals, allowing the chip to be inserted with no force, then a small lever is turned to grip the legs of the chip.

zone A region or part of a screen defined for specialized printing. The **hot zone** is the text area to the left of the right margin in a word-processed document, where, if a word does not fit completely into the line, a hyphen is automatically inserted.

zoom To enlarge an area of text (to make it easier to work on).